CW00825866

MAXSTOKE PARK GOLF CLUB 1898–1998

1898
1998
Maxstoke Park
Golf Club

MAXSTOKE PARK GOLF CLUB
1898–1998

Graham E Crawford

A Square One Publication

First published in 1998 by
Square One Publications
The Tudor House
16 Church Street
Upton on Severn, Worcs WR8 0HT

British Library Cataloguing in Publication Data
is available for this title

ISBN 1 899955 30 5

Printed in England by Biddles Ltd, Guildford, Surrey

This commemorative book is dedicated to the members
of Castle Bromwich / Maxstoke Park Golf Club,
past and present,
without whom this historical record
would not have been possible.

Contents

Editorial

When I first joined the Committee of Maxstoke Park Golf Club, and as I was to be the Club Captain who would be involved in the run up to the Centenary Year, I was invited to serve on the Centenary Committee. Chris Birch at that time was talking to older members gathering information and getting their recollections for inclusion in a commemorative book that would be compiled covering the hundred years lifetime of the Club.

My first input to that was to submit a write up covering the 'Maxies' – a section of the membership comprising some 60 senior members of the Club. I also undertook to obtain information relating to the old Prisoner of War Camp which was located off Castle Lane.

Shortly after this, Chris received a promotion in his employment activities and realised that he would be unable to meet the challenge of producing this book owing to the greater responsibilities involved. Chris wrote to me and asked whether I would consider doing the compiling of the book, I said that I would think about it, and at the next meeting I found myself in the position of being 'volunteered' to take over.

To tackle one hundred years of history is a difficult task. Fifty years of that history related to a golf course that no longer existed. The only aid to those early years was a short document written by the then Secretary of the Club, Dr.W.H.Pooler, entitled 'Looking Backward – Reminiscences of the Ward End Club', and a much later publication 'History of Maxstoke Park Golf Club' written by Bert Jolley in 1982.

But I had to start somewhere, and taking a few names and dates from Dr Pooler's publication, I visited the Birmingham Central Reference Library and the smaller libraries at Castle Bromwich and Ward End. It was really quite astonishing how much information was forthcoming by perusal of old editions of the 'Golfers Handbook' and delving into archive material at these libraries.

I collected all the old Minute Books covering General Meetings, Greens Committee Meetings, House Committee Meetings and Annual Reports from AGMs and spent several weeks reading them and extracting information that I thought was interesting enough for inclusion in the book.

But then to put the information into print. What should be included and what to leave out. How to present competition statistics for interest and yet still retain a readable compilation for the majority. What style should be adopted? What photographs should be included and how to present them? Chapters should always start on a right hand page, and of course the biggest problem of all – time; The nightmare of getting the final copy to the printers on time.

As Club Captain at the same time, it has not been easy to find the time to do the research that has been necessary to confirm items that have been briefly mentioned in earlier records. Nevertheless, it has been interesting and at times very rewarding, especially when an item is found, or someone recalled an incident which most probably has not been known by most members.

To present the history, I have broken the lifetime of the Club into three separate periods, Castle Bromwich days, Maxstoke Castle days and Clubhouse days. I have tried to set out the history into chronological order as best as can be determined from information available. I have talked to long time members to elaborate on particular events that they were involved in, I have added press cuttings, extracts from reference books and photographs whenever available to give as much interest as possible.

Given more time I could well have carried out more research, but at the end of the day, I have been ruled by the time table requested by the publishers. From time to time I have been given a name of a former member who it has been suggested that I should contact. I have not always been able to do this. I have written many letters to sources that I know could have provided information, but for whatever reason I did not always receive replies. That has been disappointing.

However I must give thanks to many members, and indeed past members who have been very helpful with providing photographs, score cards and miscellaneous memorabilia. Frank Blakey, now at Westward Ho, George Dowse, Bill Dudley-Evans, Harry Field, Dennis Shaw, Trafford Stonebridge, Norman Taylor, Ken Williams and many many others, have all at some time helped me with details of events over the years, particularly those days at Castle Bromwich and at the Castle.

In the section on Castle Bromwich I have written about the 'Glory Days' a period in time when the reference books of the day indicated that the golfers from Castle Bromwich where without doubt as good as, and almost certainly better than most golfers from other clubs.

It is therefore, particularly satisfying to be able to say that the Maxstoke Park golfers of 1997 bear comparison. The records that have been broken during the year, the performances of our members, the awards and trophies that have been won, make the closing pages of our Centenary Book as good as any in the Club's history.

I do sincerely hope therefore, that you enjoy my interpretatation of the first hundred years of the Club's history. I do not confess to being any sort of historian; I have included items which I have felt are relevant and hopefully interesting. Almost certainly I have missed out events that could have been included, and this I regret.

One last thank you must go to my wife Joan. She has had to contend with prolonged absences when I have been carrying out Captain's duties, but also when I have been shut away in the spare bedroom which I have used as an office, at times strewn with minute books, photographs, old score cards, Centenary Books from other clubs and much miscellaneous memorabilia.

The success of the Club has been due to the efforts of many past members, the responsibility for the future rests with us and those that follow. I am sure that we can launch the Club into the second hundred years with high hopes and much confidence for that future.

Graham Crawford

Graham Crawford
Club Captain – 1997.

Foreword

From the Chairman of General Committee and Centenary Year Committee

As Chairman of the above committees at Maxstoke Park Golf Club, I am honoured to write the foreword to our Centenary Book.

The book bringing together many stories of the Club's hundred years existence is the work of Chris Birch and our Club Captain of 1997, Graham Crawford. The book is written and compiled by Graham Crawford after some months of research with interviews of many members, past and present, and I am sure you will enjoy reading it.

On behalf of the committee and members I extend grateful thanks to Graham.

I would also like to thank the Centenary Year Committee, and members too numerous to mention for their efforts over the three year life of the Centenary Committee. The members of the Committee are Chris Birch, Graham Crawford, Chris Glynn, Doug Haywood, John Hannon, Neil McEwan, Tom Sutcliffe, Dennis Walker, Frank Williams and Kay Williams.

On a personal note I have had the pleasure of being Committee Chairman for the past five years, and I am pleased to report that the Club is in a very healthy position approaching the end of our first century.

I wish the Club a year of very memorable and successful Centenary celebrations, and another hundred years to follow.

NEIL MUTTER

The Club Captain's Centenary Year Message

I was proud and extremely honoured to be asked to be Club Captain of Maxstoke Park Golf Club, and accepted with a considerable amount of trepidation.

Knowing that my wife Kay will be serving as Lady Captain would have made 1998 a memorable year in any case. But 1998 being the Club's Centenary Year is a special bonus which will make it an extra special year for us both.

I am particularly looking forward to the extra competitions, the PRO/AM, the special exhibition match and the Tripartite matches against Church Stretton and Market Harborough who will be celebrating their Centenary at the same time as Maxstoke Park.

It is my wish that all members have a very enjoyable Centenary Year, and one which will be remembered for many years to come.

Frank Williams
Club Captain – 1998

Centenary Year Message From The Lady Captain

When I was asked to be Lady Captain, my immediate reaction was to say no. But after some reflection I realised what an honour it would be to be Centenary Year Captain. I therefore decided that I had to accept.

I must report that I had many sleepless nights after, wondering what on earth could I do to justify the honour being entrusted to me. Having being on the Centenary Committee since it was formed, I knew that it was going to be a wonderful and exciting year.

For myself and the Ladies Section, I felt I should try and add something extra to a normal year, (not all of them to do with golf). A number of our ladies who have been members for many, many years, now only play 9 holes. So on our 'special days' I will introduce 9 hole competitions so all of our ladies can join in.

Most of all I hope it will be remembered as a happy year, and one on which I can look back on with pride.

K Williams.

Kay Williams
Lady Captain – 1998

An aerial view of the course looking from Coleshill End towards Castle Lane

Chapter One

The Early Days

Information regarding the early days of a golf course which was located at Ward End on land owned by Dr E. Luke Freer, came from an article entitled 'Looking Backward – Reminiscences of the Ward End Club' which was written by another doctor Dr W. H. Pooler.

Dr Freer had the course laid out for his own recreation in 1895 with the assistance of Lindsay Ross, who was at that time the Professional at Sutton Coldfield. A professional was actually installed at this original course, and it was in reality a 'Pay as you Play' concept as the course was open to anyone on payment of a 'green fee'.

In 1896 a competition for professionals was held at the course with a local periodical called 'City Chimes' sponsoring the event. It is stated that Dr Freer was involved with this publication as 'one of his ventures'. The first prize given, by 'City Chimes' was £5 which was a considerable amount in those days, and was won by C. H. Wingate. Charles Wingate was the Professional at Handsworth, having been earlier at Olton, but he ultimately became Professional at Castle Bromwich. Dr Freer gave £2 to the runner up.

In the same competition it is reported that 'Jack Burns playing the 5th hole, drove six balls out of bounds, each shot of course incurring a penalty shot'. It does not stipulate what the ex Champion's score was on that hole but he finished with a score of 90, which considering he was playing 13 off the tee, was probably quite reasonable.

Dr Pooley indicated that 'during the winter of 1897 we played regularly over the Course, but in February 1898, we were informed by Dr Freer that the Course was not paying, and unless a Club was formed to take over, then it would be abandoned'. Accordingly, after a preliminary meeting on February 19th 1898, a further meeting was held on March 5th when it is recorded that 'Mr Hobbiss read out a list of certain members amounting to a a subscription list of 43 guineas'.

At this point, Dr Pooler proposed, and Dr Clark seconded, a motion which was carried that a Golf Club be formed, to be called the 'Ward End Golf Club'.

The first Officers of the Club were:

President	Colonel Ash
Vice President	Dr E. L. Freer
Hon. Secretary	Dr H. W. Pooler
Hon. Treasurer	Dr Clark
Club Captain	Dr Campbell

and

Committee Members:
Messrs. H. I. Hobbiss, T. Homer and W. Pearson.

Reference is made in later 'Histories of the Club' both to the earlier document, and to the Birmingham Reference Library. Unfortunately, despite extensive enquiries at the Library and much delving by their staff, this earlier document has not been found. The Library staff believe that it was probably an article hidden away in a magazine such as 'Tatler' or 'Country Life'.

Dr Pooley stated that "the rent of the ground was fixed at the 'reckless' figure of £20 per annum, which, however, did not include grazing and other rights".

He wrote that "the Course was a very short and narrow one, cut up in all directions by hedges, the turf was not of the old park land or seaside quality, and how Ross (the Greenkeeper) managed to 'tell the usual tale', I cannot imagine. Probably he never attempted it. But most of the members were great sportsmen and keen golfers, and the pleasure extracted from those funny old Links was immense".

A group of club memebers: (left to right) C. H. Wingate (Professional), A. J. Parkes, Dr J. Sangster, Dr A Pierce, A. Fleet (Hon. Secretary), George Maisey (Assistant Professional) and G. J. Withington (Vice President).

Whilst delving into archive material at Ward End Library I came across an entry from the Log Book of Ward End School for 1899 which read:

> November 24th - The employment of boys on the Golf Links seriously interferes with the attendance on some afternoons. The Clerk of the Board has now taken the matter in hand.

WARD END GOLF CLUB.
BALANCE SHEET 1899/1900

EXPENDITURE:	*£*	*s*	*d*
Balance due to Treasurer	2	7	4½
Mower	14	13	1
Printing		18	0
Rolling		16	6
Rent	18	10	0
Groundsman	42	13	2
Postages		11	2
Sub: Mid Golf Club		10	6
Balls	14	3	6
Refreshments	14	16	1½
Extra labour	3	9	10
Oil Harness Tools	1	15	4½
Wire Fencing	5	0	9
Dressing for greens		19	3
Sand boxes		9	9
Blacksmith for repairs	1	14	6
Donkey and fodder	2	16	3
Flags		13	5
Painting Pavilion	1	15	0
Water	2	10	0
Tool Shed	3	10	6
Notice Board		7	6
Keys and Badges		16	9
Prizes and Medals	4	2	0
	£139	0	5½

INCOME:	*£*	*s*	*d*
To Subscriptions	52	10	0
Hire of Mower	14	3	6
Tennis Rent	3	0	0
Refreshments	25	16	8½
Balls	15	18	9
Entries (Medal)	4	18	0
Entries (Competition)	8	10	6
Visitors Fees		8	0
Keys, Badges etc.		3	9
Balance to Treasurer	13	11	3
	£139	0	5½

Audited and found correct:
Horace A. Titmuss
S. H. Wighams

The Club slowly grew and the members increased in numbers, and it became apparent that the course at Ward End was inadequate, and the

Committee looked around for a more suitable location. At a Committee meeting held on March 28th 1901, the Hon. Secretary Dr Pooler reported that “he had received an offer of land suitable for Links at the back of the ‘Bradford Arms’, Castle Bromwich”. On April 6th 1901, a Special General Meeting was held, and it was resolved that “the land at Castle Bromwich be taken over from May 1st at an Annual rent of £20”.

At the Annual General Meeting of the Club held a month later, it was resolved “that the name of the Club be changed to the Castle Bromwich Golf Club”. The new club began with a membership of 28 in total, and by May 6th six holes were more or less ready for play. An opening Medal Competition was held and Dr Campbell the Club Captain had the honour of driving off for the first competition on the new course.

The Club remained on the site only until 1906, by which time three further holes had been added, The membership had increased in numbers and standards had risen accordingly. By this time there had been a desire amongst the members to go for an eighteen hole course in the area, and once again enquiries were made for a suitable site. These enquiries resulted in an area of Hodge Hill Common of some 90 acres, which was part of the Earl of Bradford’s Estate being offered. It lay on the north side of Hodge Hill Common and adjoined the old Bromford Bridge Race Course. It was an undulating area with a sandy subsoil, and therefore extremely dry even after heavy rainfall. It was the ideal choice and it was agreed that the move should be made without delay.

More or less in the centre of the area was a fine old Tudor Mansion which was known as ‘Haye House’, which had been the Dower House for Castle Bromwich Hall, or Bradford Hall as it was sometimes called, and which lies in the old village of Castle Bromwich. Haye House was an obvious choice as the Club House for the new Castle Bromwich Golf Club.

The new course was designed and laid out by one of Golf’s ‘greats’ Harry Vardon, but tribute must be made to Dr H. W. Pooler who submitted a number of ideas which were incorporated into the plan.

The old course remained in use until March 31st 1906, whilst the new course was being developed, and the members moved out on that date. The new eighteen hole course was formally opened by the President, Viscount Newport, (later Lord Bradford) on October 24th 1906.

THE FIRST EIGHTEEN HOLE COURSE

The members of the Club became increasingly proud of that first eighteen hole course at Castle Bromwich. The fairways and greens were good, but more significantly, as a winter course it was without a rival in the Birmingham area. There was not a single soft wet part anywhere on the entire course. The members were loyal and enthusiastic and their numbers grew steadily until the membership list equalled those of the most prosperous clubs in the area.

The quality of golf by the members also improved and in 1911 the Club won not only the the Midland Championship, but also the Warwickshire Union Cup. The Championship team comprised Rev. E. S. Ulyat, C. E. Black and J. Ernest Hill. Ulyat later on finished in a high position in the 1919 Amateur Championship.

He was a tower of strength to the Club, but unfortunately his connections with the Club were not long. Black was also of tremendous value to the Club, not only as Captain of the first team, but in the role of House Secretary, and in this capacity it is recorded that 'the Club has never been better served'.

The Warwickshire Union Cup winner was H. W. Weedon. 1911 was a famous year in the Club's history and to commemorate the achievements, the members celebrated by means of an extremely enjoyable dinner.

DISSATISFACTION WITH THE LAYOUT OF THE COURSE

It does appear remarkable, that despite the enthusiasm of the members and how proud they were of that first eighteen holes, the rapidity with which it became accepted that the course was out of date. It was opened in 1906 – in less than a decade (1913 to be exact) many members were dissatisfied with it. Nonetheless, the standard of golf had improved, and so had the quality of the balls and equipment used. The experience gained by the members at other courses had also widened. The course retained all the admirable qualities of good fairways and greens to which earlier reference has been made, but the course had now become too short.

Criticism was made of the greens, they were not always laid out as they should have been. Too many of them were blind, many sloped away as you approached, and often a reasonable approach found an unmerited resting place in a trench bunker at the back of the green. Too many of the bunkers were circular, straight sided 'pot' variety situated in close proximity to the greens. A comparatively trivial misjudgement in the execution of an approach shot was often unduly penalised.

From being satisfied and congratulatory, the members' thoughts passed in seven years to dissatisfaction and much criticism. Whilst not all were of this frame of mind, the majority were, and as the Club had acquired additional land, it was decided to ask a Mr H. S. Colt (a Golf Course Architect) to look at the course and to suggest improvements.

THE RE-DESIGN OF THE COURSE

Mr Colt arrived and even members most dissatisfied with the existing layout, were not quite prepared for what he suggested, whilst the doubters were staggered by his proposals. He virtually recommended the scrapping of the old course and the creation of an entirely new layout. This led to much argument and a war of differing opinions amongst the members, which was won eventually by those advocating change. It was apparently quite remarkable what faith the members had in Mr Colt's ability and reputation. Some had knowledge of his work on other courses in the Birmingham area, but most members had not. He had only provided a pen and ink drawing of his plan to guide them, but his main ideas appealed to the majority, and the work of reconstruction was authorised. Fortunately. the finished arrangement converted the remaining sceptics which restored the old pride and enthusiasm to the members.

Shortly after the course opened in 1906, a professional by the name of Reid was appointed in 1908. In 1913 he was followed by Charles Wingate, who remained until 1947, when he retired at the age of 70. During his long term as Professional, George Maisey and John Sutton were his assistants. George Maisey eventually went to Robin Hood Golf Club and John Sutton went to Great Barr Golf Club.

THE WAR YEARS 1914–1918

Shortly after the opening of the re-designed layout of the course, came the First World War, which arrested the progress of the Club, as it did that of so many other things. Many members responded to the 'call to arms' and many others had to give up their golf. Alas, some of them never returned to drive a golf ball on the links where they had spent so many happy hours. The commemorative plaque inside the entrance to our present Club House at Maxstoke Park gives the names of those forty three members who went to the war from Castle Bromwich Golf Club and also the names of Frank Dudley Evans, William H. Silvester and Charles H. Wasbourne, the unfortunate ones, who gave their lives for their country.

Fortunately, those members who had to remain behind kept things going, and by careful management, steered the Club through the changes and difficulties, and brought it prosperity beyond the expectations of those who had looked anxiously forward in the dark days of Autumn 1914.

THE GOLDEN YEARS

After the 1914/1918 war, the next two decades brought the name of Castle Bromwich Golf Club into prominence. For many years it was accepted as being second only to Little Aston as an outstanding golf course for its excellence. The course was used on many occasions for important competitions, both at professional and amateur levels.

The Club won many Championships over this period of time and there were many exceptional golfers at the Club.

HORACE J. SHAW

One of the 'characters' associated with the Club was Horace Shaw. His introduction to the Club was as a caddie when he was a boy. Later in 1913 he joined the ground staff and in 1926 he became assistant to the Head Greenkeeper, Mr R. Marks (father of Tom Marks). He took over as Head Greenkeeper during the second world war, following which he became the Steward of the Club at Haye House. When the Club eventually moved from Castle Bromwich in 1947, he stayed on at Haye House as the manager when it was taken over by 'Ansell's' and then became the 'Comet' public house as it is known today.

Other things apart Horace Shaw was also a fine golfer. As a young lad he used to practice golf at the rear of the Club House in what used to be the paddock in earlier days, with another youngster T. P. Perkins. It was practice which stood them both in good stead, as 'Ollie' Shaw as he was better known, became an excellent golfer, whilst Philip Perkins achieved the highest pinnacle of fame by winning the Amateur Open Championship in 1928 at Prestwick.

Horace Shaw (far right) and three visitors about to play at Castle Bromwich

Horace Shaw invariably drove prodigious distance off the tee with a wood and without a tee peg. Greenkeepers were not members of golf clubs in those days but he had the distinction of becoming British Green keeper's Champion playing off scratch.

His son John Shaw recalled that his father had been invited to play at Copt Heath, and during his round he made ten birdies. As a caddie 'Ollie' remembered carrying for many well known people at Castle Bromwich amongst them were Sir George Robey the 'Prime Minister of Mirth' and Fred Emney another comedian of the day. He recalls "they were both better comedians than golfers". Other well known celebrities were Mr Bill Camkin, whose company manufactured snooker tables, and who was a Director of Birmingham City Football Club, and he played with snooker stars of the day, Joe Davis, Tom Newman and Willie Smith.

Many famous football players played regularly at the course, amongst them being Howard Spencer, the Aston Villa player who many old stagers swear was the finest full back ever to play for the Club. George Duncan and James White, both British Open Champions also played the course from time to time.

One particular incident which occurred in the early 1920's that Horace Shaw never forgot. Carrying for Captain Peter Leslie on the 180 yard eighth hole where the green was not visible from the tee, the ball finished on the lip of the hole, so close that it could have blown in. Captain Leslie, vastly relieved that he had been spared the customary honour of buying a bottle of whisky for his colleagues to celebrate 'a hole in one', then teed up his ball on the 150 yard ninth hole. He and his opponents stood astonished as the shot went straight to the green, rolled gently towards the pin and into the hole.

Horace Shaw with his wife Nellie, remained at the 'Comet' for twenty six years before moving to the 'Duke' at Sutton Coldfield from where he retired two years later. He died twelve months after retiring.

THOMAS PHILIP PERKINS

During these memorable years there were many fine golfers at the Club, and most of them achieved some degree of success from time to time. One player, however, reached the very pinnacle of success whilst with the Club, Thomas Philip Perkins. According to the various accounts written about him, Philip was a remarkable young man who fought the problems of ill health at an early age, and yet achieved the highest honours in amateur golf both for himself and for the Club.

Philip was born on September 3rd 1904 at West Bromwich, and whilst very young his family moved to 950, Alum Rock Road, Washwood Heath. the family home which still stands today. At 12 years of age, Philip was diagnosed as having a weak heart, and he was advised 'to take gentle exercise and to get plenty of fresh air'. His uncle, a Mr Sam Lane, took him to Castle Bromwich and enrolled him as a Junior Member at the Club. In the next twelve months he made such progress that he entered and won the 'Ward End Cup'. This apparently caused consternation amongst the older members, and attempts were made to challenge his winning the award, but it was allowed to stand.

Philip practised for hour after hour on the course and was utterly dedicated in this respect, and he reached a very high standard. In 1921 at the age of 16 he won the Warwickshire Amateur Championship and then continued to win it for the next eight years.

WARWICKSHIRE AMATEUR CHAMPIONSHIP.

Year.	Winner.	Club.	Venue.	Score.
1906	B. Norbury	Stratford-on-Avon	Olton	162
1907	T. S. Fishwick	Harborne	Harborne	153
1908	F. W. Clive	North Warwickshire	Sutton Coldfield	160
1909	F. W. Clive	North Warwickshire	Coventry	156
1910	W. F. Hutchings	Stratford-on-Avon	Castle Bromwich	150
1911	H. B. Barker	Olton	Whitnash	162
1912	H. B. Barker	Olton	Olton	154
1913	H. B. Barker	Olton	Harborne	151
1914–1919	No Championship.			
1920	W. Archdale	Edgbaston	Castle Bromwich	169
1921	T. P. Perkins	Castle Bromwich	Copt Heath	154
1922	T. P. Perkins	Castle Bromwich	Coventry	159
1923	T. P. Perkins	Castle Bromwich	Robin Hood	156
1924	T. P. Perkins	Castle Bromwich	Olton	152
1925	T. P. Perkins	Castle Bromwich	Whitnash	146
1926	T. P. Perkins	Castle Bromwich	Harborne	164
1927	T. P. Perkins	Castle Bromwich	Sutton Coldfield	153
1928	T. P. Perkins	Castle Bromwich	Ladbrook Park	158
1929	T. P. Perkins	Castle Bromwich	Walmley	149
1930	W. A. Stockwin	Walmley	Handsworth	153
1931	H. Hall	Castle Bromwich	Castle Bromwich	149

In 1927 he won the English Amateur Championship at Little Aston and in the same year he tied with W. R. Torrance as leading amateur in the Open Championship at St. Andrews. The following year he was the leading amateur in the 'Open' played at Sandwich finishing in 14th position.

ENGLISH AMATEUR CHAMPIONSHIP.

For conditions governing the Championship see page 56.

Year	Winner.	Runner-up.	Venue.	By.
1925	T. F. Ellison	S. Robinson	Hoylake	1 hole
1926	T. F. Ellison	Sq. Lead. C. H. Hayward	Walton Heath	6 and 4
1927	T. P. Perkins	J. B. Beddard	Little Aston	2 and 1
1928	J. A. Stout	T. P. Perkins	Royal Lytham	3 and 2

Prior to the eventful tournaments which highlighted his year, Philip Perkins represented England in the international match against Scotland at Troon. Partnering another excellent golfer from the Midlands Dr William Tweddell of Stourbridge in the 'Foursomes' they won three and two, and in the singles he recorded a halved match.

ENGLAND v. SCOTLAND

At Troon, 19th May 1928.

FOURSOMES

ENGLAND.	Matches.	SCOTLAND.	Matches.
R. H. Wethered, Worplesdon, C. J. H. Tolley, Royal Liverpool (4 and 3)	1	A. Jamieson, jun., Pollock, W. J. Guild, Murrayfield	0
Dr Wm. Tweddell, Stourbridge, T. P. Perkins, Castle Bromwich (3 and 2)	1	J. L. C. Jenkins, Troon, R. Scott, jun., Glasgow	0
Sir E. W. E. Holderness, Bart., Walton Heath, J. A. Stout, Bridlington (3 and 2)	1	W. B. Torrance, Edinburgh Burgess, W. L. Hope, St George's Hill	0
E. F. Storey, Royal Worlington, R. W. Hartley, Sunningdale	0	R. Harris, Royal and Ancient, Major K. Thorburn, Sunningdale (1 hole)	1
R. H. Hardman, Birkdale, J. B. Beddard South Staffs.	½	W. Campbell, Kirkhill, T. A. Torrance, Sandy Lodge	½
	3½		1½

SINGLES.

ENGLAND.	Matches.	SCOTLAND.	Matches.
Dr Wm. Tweddelll (4 and 3)	1	A. Jamieson, jun.	0
R. H. Wethered (3 and 2)	1	J. L. C. Jenkins	0
C. J. H. Tolley (2 and 1)	1	R. Scott, jun.	0
Sir E. W. E. Holderness, Bart. (6 and 4)	1	W. B. Torrance	0
J. A. Stout (3 and 2)	1	R. Harris	0
T. P. Perkins	½	W. L. Hope	½
E. F. Storey (2 and 1)	1	W. J. Guild	0
R. H. Hardman (2 and 1)	1	T. A. Torrance	0
R. W. Hartley (2 and 1)	1	W. Campbell	0
J. B. Beddard (2 and 1)	1	Major K. Thorburn	0
	9½		0½

Later that year he finished as runner up in the English Amateur Championship at Royal Lytham and in the same month travelled to Prestwick to play in the Amateur Championship. His two 'Open' Championship placings are shown in 1927, with Bobby Jones as winner for the second time, and in 1928 with Walter Hagen, another famous American, as winner. Interesting to note that in 1927 Philip finished two shots adrift of Henry Cotton, an Englishman who went on to win the 'Open' and in 1928 he finished three shots better than Cotton.

In the 1928 'Open' event, a link with Castle Bromwich can be seen where the name of Harry Vardon, the designer of the course finished just five places from last.

The report from the Amateur Championship at the semi final stage at Prestwick suggested that 'Philip Perkins, a 23 year old salesman from Castle Bromwich, had come through a relatively soft half of the draw without scares, and his play had improved as the week went on'.

The semi final was an 'Anglo–Scottish' affair, and Philip Perkin's

THE 'OPEN' CHAMPIONSHIP

1927—*At St Andrews.* Entries 207. Qualified 108 (Professionals 92, Amateurs 16). Finally qualified to play in the last 36 holes, 54 (Professionals 46, Amateurs 8).

Name.	Score..
Mr. R. T. Jones, Atlanta, U.S.A. . . .	68, 72, 73, 72—285
Aubrey Boomer, St Cloud	76, 70, 73, 72—291
Fred Robson, Cooden Beach . . .	76, 72, 69, 74—291
Joe Kirkwood, U.S.A. .	72, 72, 75, 74—293
E. R. Whitcombe, Bournemouth . .	74, 73, 73. 73—293
C. A. Whitcombe, Crews Hill . . .	74, 76, 71, 75—296
B. Hodson, Newport, Mon. . . .	72, 70, 81, 74—297
A. G. Havers, Coombe Hill . . .	80, 74, 73, 70—297
T. H. Cotton, Langley Park . . .	73, 72, 77, 76—298
P. H. Rodgers, St Anne's Old	76, 73, 74, 77—300
R. Vickers, Heswall .	75, 75, 77, 73—300
Mr T. P. Perkins, Castle Bromwich . .	76, 78, 70, 76—300
Tom Williamson, Notts.	75, 76, 78, 71—300

Name.	Score.
Percy Alliss, Berlin .	73, 74, 73, 80—300
Alex. Herd, Moor Park .	76, 75, 78, 71—300
Mr W. B. Torrance, Edinburgh Burgess .	72, 80, 74, 74—300
G. R. Buckle, Edgbaston	77, 69, 77, 78—301
C. Johns, Purley Downs	74, 78, 73, 76—301
J. Barnes, U.S.A. .	76, 76, 72, 77—301
D. A. Curtis, Bournemouth . . .	73, 76, 79, 74—302
J. Gassiat, France .	76, 77, 73, 76—302
E. Stevens, U.S.A. .	76, 73, 74, 79—302
A. Compston, unattached	74, 78, 79, 72—303
J. Smith, Wentworth .	81, 73, 73, 76—303
H. C. Kinch, Woodcote Park	80, 73, 73, 77—303
Len Holland, Gerrard's Cross . . .	75, 75, 71, 82—303
D. M'Culloch, Troon .	74, 77, 78, 75—304
C. H. Gadd, Brancepeth	74, 74, 78, 79—305
T. King, jun., R. W. Norfolk . . .	73, 74, 74, 84—305
W. Kennett, U.S.A. .	78, 75, 75, 78—306

opponent was William Tulloch from Glasgow, a Scottish International. Philip's golf was immaculate and he won by a margin of 6 and 5. His opponent in the final was Roger Wethered, who although being another well known International player, had not been consistent during the early rounds, and Philip Perkins was looked upon as being the favourite. A correct analysis as it transpired, as he was always ahead and went three up at the twelfth. Wethered won his first hole at the next and went to lunch two down.

After lunch Philip went three up again by the ninth, and went further ahead at the eleventh, when Wethered seeing his ball move in the rough, sportingly penalised himself. Three holes later it was all over as Wethered chipped past the hole from light rough at the back of the green, missed the return and conceded.

Having won the Amateur Championship, Philip Perkin's excellence was rewarded when he was selected to visit America as a member of the 'Walker Cup' Team. Unfortunately, despite his reputation he lost both the matches that he played in, the foursomes match, partnered again by Dr William Tweddell by 7 and 6, and his singles against Bobby Jones, rather heavily to the margin of 13 and 12.

1928—*At Sandwich.* Entries 271. Qualified 113 (Professionals 100, Amateurs, 13). Finall qualified to play in last 36 holes, 52. (Professionals 46. Amateurs 6).

Name.	Score.
Walter Hagen, U.S.A.	75, 73, 72, 72—292
Gene Sarazen, U.S.A.	72, 76, 73, 73—294
A. Compston, unattached	75, 74, 73, 73—295
Percy Alliss, Berlin	75, 76, 75, 72—298
Fred Robson, Cooden Beach	79, 73, 73, 73—298
Jose Jurado, Argentine	74, 71, 76, 80—301
Aubrey Boomer, St Cloud	79, 73, 77, 72—301
Jim Barnes, U.S.A.	81, 73, 76, 71—301
W. Melhorn, U.S.A.	71, 78, 76, 77—302
W. H. Davies, Prenton	78, 74, 79, 73—304
F. Taggart, Wilmslow	76, 74, 77, 78—305
A. Whiting, Ry. St George's	78, 76, 76, 75—305
Jack Smith, Middlesex	79, 77, 76, 74—306
Mr T. P. Perkins, Castle Bromwich	80, 79, 76, 72—307
W. T. Twine, Bromley	75, 79, 77, 76—307
Stewart Burns, Cruden Bay	76, 74, 75 83—308
Maj. C. O. Hezlet. R. Portrush	79 76, 78, 76—309
Mr A. J. Evans, Rye	80, 79, 82, 78—309
T. H. Cotton, Langley Park	77, 75, 83, 75—310
Geo. Duncan, Wentworth	75, 77, 78, 80—310
D. M'Culloch, Troon	78, 78, 78, 76—310
Abe Mitchell, private	78, 75, 82, 76—311
T. Williamson, Notts	77, 73, 77, 84—311
J. Ockenden, Hanger Hill	80, 78, 79, 75—312
S. Wingate, Templenewsam	75, 82, 79, 76—312
Mr W. L. Hope, St George's Hill	84, 75, 75, 78—312
G. Gadd, Roehampton	83, 73, 78, 78—31[illegible]
R. Whitcombe, Parkstone	79, 77, 81, 75—31[illegible]
Jean Gassiat, France	76, 77, 81, 78—31[illegible]
R. G. Wilson, Croham H'rst	82, 73, 77, 80—31[illegible]
A. R. Bradbeer, Burnham	83, 76, 78, 75—31[illegible]
A. J. Young, Sonning	77, 77, 78, 81—31[illegible]
A. J. Lacey, Leighton Buzzard	8[illegible], 77, 79, 77—31[illegible]
E. Ray, Oxhey	77, 78, 80, 79—314
J. Holley, Castle	80, 78, 79, 77—314
H. C. Jolly, Foxgrove	84, 73, 75, 82—314
G. Faulkner, Bramley	80, 75, 81, 78—314
W. M. Watt, R.A.C.	79, 76, 78, 82—315
T. Barber, Cavendish	77, 78, 81, 79—315
J. M'Dowall, Turnberry	82, 75, 80, 78—315
R. Stewart, Australia	79, 75, 82, 79—315
Mr T. A. Torrance, Sandy Lodge	79, 74, 81, 81—315
B. Hodson, Newport	80, 79, 79, 78—316
J. Braid, Walton Heath	80, 79, 81, 76—316
Mr R. Hartley, Cooden Beach	79, 77, 76, 82—316
A. Massey, France	79, 79, 79, 79—316
L. Wallace, Royal Belfast	79, 80, 75, 83—316
H. Vardon, South Herts	78, 79, 80, 80—317
F. W. H. Kenyon, Creigiau	79, 79, 81, 78—317
P. Hirigoyan, France	81, 74, 78, 83—318
A. Tingey, Frinton	81, 78, 81, 85—325
E. Barker, Boyce Hill	81, 78, 77, 89—325

AMATEUR CHAMPIONSHIP.

Entrance fee, £2, 2s. For rules governing the Championship, see pages 37-39.

Year.	Winner.	Runner-up.	Venue.	By.	No. of Ents.
1920	Cyril J. H. Tolley	R. A. Gardner	Muirfield	37th hole	165
1921	W. I. Hunter	A. J. Graham	Hoylake	12 and11	223
1922	E. W. E. Holderness	J. Caven	Prestwick	1 hole	252
1923	R. H. Wethered	R. Harris	Deal	7 and 6	209
1924	E. W. E. Holderness	E. F. Storey	St Andrews	3 and 2	201
1925	Robert Harris	K. F. Fradgley	Westward Ho!	13 and 12	151
1926	Jesse Sweetser	A. F. Simpson	Muirfield	6 and 5	216
1927	Dr Tweddell	D. E. Landale	Hoylake	7 and 6	197
1928	T. P. Perkins	R. H. Wethered	Prestwick	6 and 4	220

It must surely be exceptional, that in the team was the name of Dr A. R. MacCallum, another fine golfer from Castle Bromwich – how many clubs can boast of the achievement of two members in the same team. Dr MacCallum played County golf for Staffordshire for many years.

WALKER CUP USA v GREAT BRITAIN

At Chicago Golf Club, Wheaton, U.S.A., 30th and 31st August 1928.

FOURSOMES.

U.S.A.		GREAT BRITAIN.	
George Von Elm and Jesse Sweetser (7 and 6)	1	T. P. Perkins and Dr Wm. Tweeddell ..	0
"Chick" Evans and R. T. Jones (5 and 3)	1	Major C. O. Hezlet and W. L. Hope ..	0
H. R. Johnston and Francis Ouimet (4 and 2)	1	E. F. Storey and T. A. Torrance ..	0
Watts Gunn and R. Mackenzie (7 and 5)	1	J. B. Beck and Dr A. R. MacCallum ..	0
	4		0

SINGLES.

U.S.A.		GREAT BRITAIN.	
R. T. Jones (13 and 12)	1	T. P. Perkins	0
Watts Gunn (11 and 10)	1	R. H. Hardman	0
F. Ouimet (8 and 7)	1	Major C. O. Hezlet	0
Jesse Sweetser (5 and 4)	1	W. L. Hope	0
G. Von Elm (3 and 2)	1	Dr W. Tweeddell	0
H. R. Johnston (4 and 2)	1	E. F. Storey	0
R. Mackenzie (2 and 1)	1	G. N. C. Martin	0
Chick Evans	0	T. A. Torrance (1 hole)	1
	7		1

Grand Aggregates—U.S.A. 11 matches; Great Britain, one match.

Whilst in America, Philip Perkins was runner up in the USA Amateur Championship, losing in the final once again to Bobby Jones, by the margin of 13 and 11 which is still the biggest winning margin ever achieved.

AMERICAN AMATEUR CHAMPIONSHIP.

(Prior to Organisation of the U.S.G.A.)

Year.	Winner.	Club.	Runner-up.	Venue.	By.
1907	Jerome D. Travers	Montclair . .	Arch. Graham .	. Cleveland	6 & 5
1908	Jerome D. Travers	Montclair . .	Max H. Behr .	. Midlothian, Ill.	8 & 7
1909	R. Gardner .	Hinsdale . .	H. C. Egan .	. Wheaton, Ill.	4 & 3
1910	W. C. Fownes, jr.	Oakmont . .	W. K. Wood .	. Brooklyn	4 & 3
1911	H. H. Hilton .	Royal Liv'pool .	F. Herreshoff .	. Apawamis	at 37th hole
1912	Jerome D. Travers	Montclair . .	Charles Evans .	. Wheaton, Ill.	7 & 6
1913	Jerome D. Travers	Do. .	J. G. Anderson .	. Garden City .	5 & 4
1914	F. Ouimet . .	Woodlands .	J. D. Travers .	. Vermont .	6 & 5
1915	R. A. Gardner .	Hinsdale .	J. G. Anderson .	. Detroit .	5 & 4
1916	Chas. Evans .	Edgewater . .	R. A. Gardner .	. Hinsdale Merion	4 & 3
1917-18	No Championship owing to the Great War.				
1919	D. Herron . .	Pittsburg . .	R. T. Jones .	. Oakmont .	5 & 4
1920	C. Evans . .	Edgewater . .	F. Ouimet . .	. Engineers Club Roslyn, L.I.	5 & 4
1921	J. Guildford .	Woodland . .	Robert Gardner	. St. Louis, Clayton	7 & 6
1922	J. Sweetser .	Siwanoy . .	Chas. Evans .	. Brookline .	3 & 2
1923	Max Marston .	Pine Valley .	Jesse Sweetser .	. Flossmoor	at 38th hole
1924	R. T. Jones, Jr. .	Atlanta . .	G. von Elm .	. Merion Cricket Club, Philadelphia	9 & 8
1925	R. T. Jones, Jr. .	Atlanta . .	W. Gunn . .	. Oakmont .	8 & 7
1926	Geo. Von Elm .	Rancho . .	R. T. Jones .	. Baltustrol .	2 & 1
1927	R. T. Jones, Jr. .	Atlanta . .	C. Evans . .	. Edgewater Minikahda	8 & 7
1928	R. T. Jones, Jr. .	Atlanta , .	T. P. Perkins .	. Brae Burn .	10 and 9

Philip Perkins, winner of the Amateur Chapionship – 1928, and Bobby Jones, winner of the American Amateur Championship – 1928.
This was the first time that the United States champion had met British champion in the final.

It should be noted that Bobby Jones has been cited as the best ever amateur golfer, and it is interesting to note that his playing in the 1928 final was his sixth appearance and four of those were as winner.

Philip Perkins won many other events during his amateur days but they are not all recorded in the Club records and there are probably too numerous to mention. It is apparent from those quoted that he was an extraordinary golfer.

He held the Amateur record at Castle Bromwich with 69 for a number of years, and also at Walmley Golf Club with 71. The Club, has over the years, and even today, had some fine golfers, but none so far has had such a wonderful and brilliant record, or an international reputation such as his.

Shortly after the American Amateur Championship, Philip Perkins returned to America as he had established business connections there. Unfortunately, problems with the American financial markets about that time affected his interests considerably, and he turned professional at the Willoughby Country Club in Ohio to provide himself with an income.

Today, we still retain a connection with Thomas Philip Perkins. We hold the 'Perkin's Putter' Competition which is an eighteen hole stroke play competition held in conjunction with the October medal every year, and is 'awarded' to the member returning the best nett score of the three divisions.

The putter is the actual putter that Philip used in his 1928 Amateur Championship, but in reality, rather than awarding the putter to the winner, after presentation it is returned to safe keeping in the trophy cabinet in the Lounge of the Clubhouse.

A photograph of Thomas Philip Perkins is also positioned at the entrance to the lounge of the Clubhouse adjacent to the door from the Gent's Locker Room.

Philip Perkins and his *Walker Cup* partner of 1928, Dr William Tweddell of Stourbridge playing together in an exhibition match at Stratford upon Avon in 1931.

Tweddell was Captain of the British Walker Cup Team of 1928 at Chicago Golf Club and again in 1936 at Pine Valley. Both players were members at Stratford upon Avon when the picture was taken. In the 'Golfer's Handbook' of 1929, amongst the 'Who's Who in Golf' Philip Perkins has a lengthy inclusion, which in itself is an honour not readily given to many amateur golfers.

Perkins, Thomas Philip, *b.* West Bromwich, 3rd September, 1904. Clubs—Castle Bromwich, Stratford-on-Avon, Brandwood House, Fox Hills, Staten Island, N. Y. City, Lido Country Club, Lido Beach, Long Island, U.S.A. In 1927 won English Amateur Close Championship, Midland Amateur Championship, and tied with W. B. Torrance as first British Amateur in Open Championship with a score of 300. In 1928 won British Amateur Championship, was runner-up in English Close Championship, and was first British Amateur in the Open. Won Warwickshire County Gold Medal for eight years in succession. Runner-up in American Amateur Championship, Royal St Georges Vase, and Fox Hills Invitation Tournament. Played for England *v.* Scotland, 1927, 1928, and Britain *v.* America in Walker Cup, 1928. Holds Amateur record, Castle Bromwich, 69; Walmley, 71. Has done eighth hole, Castle Bromwich and eighth Fox Hills, each in one stroke. Favourite links: Little Aston. Favourite shots: Iron and mashie. Address—950 Alum Rock Road, Washwood Heath, Birmingham.

A memorable photograph for Midland golf clubs. Philip Perkins and William Tweddell where both winners of the British Amateur Open Championship. Tweddell at Hoylake in 1927, and Perkins at Prestwick in 1928.

No. 950 Alum Rock Road where he was brought up as a young man, the house is about a mile from the old course and clubhouse.

Philip Perkins settled in America as a Professional and in 1932 came close to achieving even greater fame, finishing as runner up to Gene Sarazen in the United States 'Open'.

1932—*At Flushing, Long Island.*

G. Sarazen, Lakeville	74, 76, 70, 66—286
T. P. Perkins, New York City	76, 69, 74, 70—289
R. Cruickshank, Pt. Richmond	78, 74, 69, 68—289
L. Diegel, Agua Caliente	73, 74, 73, 74—294
W. Cox, Brooklyn	80, 73, 70, 72—295
J. Jurado, Argentine	74, 71, 75, 76—296

It is known that Philip Perkins returned to England in the late '50s when his mother died. He visited Maxstoke Park and actually played a few games there at that time. On his return to the States the Club lost touch with him, and were unsuccessful in trying to contact him to come over and open the new Clubhouse in 1969.

AMERICAN OPEN CHAMPIONSHIP.

After 1894 decided by Medal Play. 72 holes being played from 1898.

Year.	Winner.	Club.	Venue.	Score
1894	Willie Dunn	Shinnecock Hills St Andrews, New York, defeated Willie Campbell 2 holes		
1895	H. J. Rawlins	Newport	Newport	173
1896	J. Foulis	Chicago	Southampton	152
1897	J. Lloyd	Essex	Wheaton, Ill.	162
1898	Fred Herd	Chicago	Shinnecock Hills	328
1899	W. Smith	Do.	Baltimore	315
1900	Harry Vardon	Ganton	Wheaton, Ill.	313
1901	W. Anderson	Pittsfield	Myopia, Mass.	315
1902	L. Auchterlonie	Glenview	Garden City	305
1903	W. Anderson	Apawamis	Baltusrol	307
1904	W. Anderson	Apawamis	Glenview	303
1905	W. Anderson	Apawamis	Myopia	314
1906	Alex. Smith	Nassau	Onwentsia	295
1907	Alex. Ross	Brae Burn	Chestnut Hill, Pa.	302
1908	Fred M'Leod	Midlothian	Myopia, Mass.	322
1909	Geo. Sargent	Hyde Manor	Englewood, N.J.	290
1910	Alex. Smith	Wykagyl	Philadelphia	289
1911	J. J. M'Dermott	Philadelphia	Wheaton, Ill.	307
1912	J. J. M'Dermott	Atlantic City	Buffalo, N.Y.	294
1913	Mr F. Ouimet	Woodland	Brookline, Mass.	304
1914	Walter Hagen	Rochester	Blue Island	297
1915	Mr J. D. Travers	Montclair	Baltusrol	290
1916	Mr Charles Evans	Edgewater	Minneapolis	286
1917-18	No Championship owing to the Great War.			
1919	Walter Hagen	Rochester	Braeburn	301
1920	E. Ray	Oxhey	Inverness	295
1921	Jim Barnes	Pelham	Washington	289
1922	G. Sarazen	Titusville	Glencoe	288
1923	Mr R. T. Jones	Atlanta	Inwood, L. I.	296
1924	Cyril Walker	Englewood	Oakland Hills	297
1925	Wm. MacFarlane	Oak Ridge	Worcester	291
1926	Mr R. T. Jones	Atlanta	Scioto	293
1927	T. D. Armour	Congressional	Oakmont	301
1928	J. Farrell	Quaker Ridge	Olympia Fields	294
1929	Mr R. T. Jones	Atlanta	Winged Foot, New York	294
1930	Mr R. T. Jones	Atlanta	Interlachen	287
1931	B. Burke	Round Hill	Toledo	292
1932	G. Sarazen	Lakeville	Flushing, L.I.	287
1933	Mr J. Goodman	Omaha	Glenview, Ill.	283
1934	O. Dutra	Brentwood Heights	Merion	299
1935	S. Parks	South Hills	Oakmont	292
1936	T. Manero	Greensboro	Springfield	282

It is interesting to note that Harry Vardon, designer of the Castle Bromwich course, won the American 'Open' in 1900 at Wheaton Illinois, and Philip Perkins' 'tormentor', Bobby Jones, won the event four times in 1923, 1926, 1929 and 1930.

The British 'Amateur Open' Cup taken at Kenilworth Golf Club following Warren Bladon's win in 1996.

A section of the large photograph displayed in the lounge showing Philip Perkins with the 'Amateur Cup' and many of the Club members who attended the commemorative garden party.

DR. A. R. MacCALLUM

Dr MacCallum was a very fine golfer who was actually a member of two clubs. He was of Scottish descent and to his golfing colleagues he was simply 'Archie'. He lived in Wolverhampton and according to Bill Dudley-Evans who knew him, he played at South Staffs Golf Club during the week, but played at Castle Bromwich at week ends and during the winter. This apparently was quite common and many other good golfers joined Castle Bromwich so that they could play regularly in the winter, the course being so well drained.

According to the old honours boards he only won one competition at Castle Bromwich, the Challenge Cup, which he won in 1924. However he played fairly regularly for Staffordshire, making his debut in 1928 against Warwickshire, when he lost. He made 8 appearances for his county, the final appearance being in 1938 against Worcestershire when he won both his foursomes and the singles.

As pointed out earlier, Dr MacCallum played in the same 'Walker Cup' Team as Philip Perkins against the United States at Chicago in August 1928. He only played in the Foursomes which he lost, as did the rest of the team who were 'whitewashed' 4 games to 0.

Twice he reached the final of the Midlands Counties Amateur Championship, losing to H. Arnold in 1929 but winning against his 'Walker Cup' Captain, Bill Tweddell, in 1933. Duncan Sutherland another two club man, Robin Hood and Castle Bromwich, won the event in 1936 also against Bill Tweddell.

MIDLAND COUNTIES AMATEUR COMPETITION.

Year.	Winner.	Runner-up.
1895	C. S. Hayward	E. P. Wright
1896	C. S. Hayward	Dr Robertson
1897	A. M. Chance	E. F. Chance
1898	E. F. Chance	H. Bainbridge
1899	T. Fitzherbert	T. W. Piggott
1900	F. W. Clive	Dr Robertson
1901	C. A. Palmer	Dr Robertson
1902	S. C. Healing	F. C. Carr
1903	F. M. Lindner	F. W. Clive
1904	C. A. Palmer	F. Woolley
1905	E. Blackwell	T. K. Ashton
1906	E. Blackwell	F. C. Carr
1907	C. A. Palmer	F. M. Lindner
1908	F. A. Woolley	F. C. Carr
1909	F. A. Woolley	B. Norbury
1910	J Humphries	F. C. Carr
1911	F. A. Woolley	F. C. Carr
1912	E Blackwell	J. Humphries
1913	F. A. Woolley	F. C. Carr
1914	F. A. Woolley	H B. Barker
1915-18	No Competition owing to the Great War.	
1919	J. B. Beddard	F. Scarf.
1920	C. Bretherton	F. Scarf.
1921	C. Bretherton	F. S. Withers
1922	J. B. Beddard	G. N. P Humphries
1923	I. S. Sidebottom	J. L. Holmes
1924	W. H. Priest	J. B. Beddard
1925	R. P. Humphries	Stanley Lunt
1926	R. P. Humphries	W. A. Bennett
1927	T. P. Perkins	C. S. Buckley
1928	D. S. Bruce	Dr G. J. Moore
1929	H. Arnold	Dr A. R. M'Callum
1930	D. A. Fiddian	C. S. Buckley
1931	E. W. Fiddian	L. Smith
1932	S. T. Matthews	S. Lunt.
1933	Dr A. R. M'Callum	E. W. Fiddian
1934	S. Lunt	A. R. Allen
1935	C.Stowe	E. W. Fiddian
1936	D. M. Sutherland	E. W. Fiddian

Enquiries at South Staffs Golf Club with regard to any achievements that Dr MacCallum may have had at that Club drew a blank. For some reason not explained, they have no details of pre war performances I was told however that he had played for Scotland.

I have confirmed this with the Scottish Union of Golf Clubs, but apparently he only played once, against England in 1929.

However, the Staffordshire Union of Golf Clubs put me in touch with a long time member of the Bloxwich Golf Club, Peter Squire, now a very sprightly gentleman, some 93 years young. I visited him at the Golf Club where he still plays and is obviously their oldest inhabitant. He stated that he only plays 9 holes these days, but 18 holes occasionaly if it is a nice day.

Peter Squire played golf with Archie MacCallum on many occasions and recalled that he made his own Staffordshire debut when 'Archie' cried off. He also mentioned that he was a good friend of Bill Dudley-Evans and had much to do with him when he was involved with Staffordshire Golf, and Bill with Warwickshire. Like Bill his membership of his Club goes back a long time – he joined Bloxwich in 1924.

The main purpose of my visit was to get a copy of a photograph which hangs on the wall in the Lounge at Bloxwich. This photo' shows a group of Club members who supported a Golf Exhibition Match in aid of a Walsall Children's Holiday Camp. The four 'celebrities' in the match were Dr G. J. Moore, Dr Archie' R. MacCallum, Philip Perkins and Dr William Tweddell. All four of them were amateur internationals, and MacCallum, Perkins and Tweddell members of the 1928 'Walker Cup Team'.

On the photograph they are the four in the centre of the second row. Moore in front of the left hand pillar, 'Archie MacCallum in the light jumper, Phil Perkins with the tie and 'Bill' Tweddell to his left.

Golf exhibition match, 1928. Proceeds went to Walsall schoolchildren's holiday camp. Among the players are, second row: Dr G. J. Moore (Irish International), Dr A. R. MacCallum (Scottish International & member Walker Cup Team, 1928), T. P. Perkins (English International & member Walker Cup Team, 1928, English Champion, 1927, Amateur Champion, 1928), Dr W. Tweddell (English International & member Walker Cup Team, 1928, Amateur Champion, 1927).

HONOURS AND ACHIEVEMENTS

As mentioned earlier, the Club soon became one of the leading clubs in the Midlands and in 1920 they won the Warwickshire Club Championship an achievement that they then repeated on eight other occasions in the nineteen years period up to the Second World War.

WARWICKSHIRE CLUB CHAMPIONSHIP.

Year.	Winners.	Venue.	Scores
1906	Olton	Olton	506
1907	Arden	Harborne	494
1908	Olton	Sutton Coldfield	496
1909	Olton	Coventry	497
1910	Olton	Castle Bromwich	479
1911	Olton	Whitnash	495
1912	Olton	Olton	492
1913	Olton	Harborne	478
1914–1919	No Championship.		
1920	Castle Bromwich	Castle Bromwich	524
1921	Castle Bromwich	Copt Heath	502
1922	Coventry	Coventry	490
1923	Coventry	Robin Hood	497
1924	Castle Bromwich	Olton	497
1925	Coventry	Whitnash	473
1926	Harborne	Harborne	515
1927	Castle Bromwich	Sutton Coldfield	483
1928	Castle Bromwich	Ladbrook Park	488
1929	Castle Bromwich	Walmley	482
1930	Walmley	Handsworth	476
1931	Castle Bromwich	Castle Bromwich	464
1932	Walmley	Copt Heath	464
1933	Harborne	Coventry	476
1934	Castle Bromwich	Robin Hood	477
1935	Harborne	Olton	454
1936	Ladbrook Park	Moor Hall	481
1937	Harborne	Harborne	456
1938	Castle Bromwich	Whitnash	449
1939	Coventry	Sutton Coldfield	478

OFFICERS OF THE CLUB

During the period of time when the Club enjoyed such success, tribute must be made to the enthusiasm and ability of certain members of the Committee who contributed in no small way to that success.

Mr Arthur Fleet, the Hon Secretary was a man who had held office continuously since 1909. Length of service is a measure of success. All clubs, no matter of what activity are glad to get honorary officers, and having got them, they do not retain them unless they are carrying out their duties satifactorily. In Arthur Fleet's case the members expressed their appreciation in 1931 by awarding him a 'Life Membership' of the Club. He did however remain in office until 1941 when he moved to Wolverhampton after thirty two years service as Hon. Secretary.

Other members whose work on behalf of the Club was worthy of mention were Mr H. T. Perry who for many years was Secretary of the Greens Committee, and in later years was Chairman of that same Committee. In this latter capacity, he achieved remarkable success for the improvement of the course.

Mr William Abbot, who was Hon. Treasurer of the Club for ten difficult years during the First World War and afterwards, and Mr John Hall, who had been Treasurer since 1921, and who was the guiding influence in establishing the consolidation of the Club's financial position. He continued in office until his death in 1942.

Dr P. Campbell
1898–1904

Dr H. W. Pooler
1905–1906

Dr J. Cochrane
1907–1908

H. J. Hobbiss
1909

H. T. Perry
1910

W. Bentley
1911

C. K. Black
1912

W. G. Oxley
1913

J. R. Woodward
1914–1915

A. Fleet
1916

W. H. Abbott
1917

H. T. Perry
1918–1919

F. Parkes
1920

A. Armishaw
1921

G. H. Tyler
1922

A. A. Bott
1923

H. C. Wright
1924

John Hall
1925

E. H. Maddocks
1926

F. Fletcher-Mills
1927

A. S. Langley
1928

W. J. Maryan
1929

R. Roden
1930

G. J. Withington
1931

G. Allman
1932

J. Sangster
1933

M. MacDonagh
1934

J. Broughton
1935

Harry Hall
1936

A. Dudley-Evans
1937

C. H. Alger
1938

E. G. Lawrence
1939

L. Greenwood
1940

G. Stabbings
1941

T. A. Neale
1942

H. Crump
1943

H. T. Perry
1944
For his 4th term as Club Captain having held office earlier in 1909, 1918 and 1919.

W. N. Dudley-Evans
1945
Bill went on to become the longest serving member and held office in a number of administrative positions both within the Club and Warwickshire County Golf.

CASTLE BROMWICH GOLF CLUB LTD

HAYE HOUSE, CASTLE BROMWICH

TELEPHONE No. 0389 EAST.

OFFICIALS.

President :
THE RIGHT HON. THE EARL OF BRADFORD.

Vice-Presidents :
W. H. ABBOTT, A. ARMISHAW, J. COCHRANE, A. DUDLEY EVANS, A. FLEET, F. JONES, F. FLETCHER MILLS, H. T. PERRY, F. PARKES, H. W. POOLER, G. H. TYLER, C. F. WALKLEY, G. J. WITHINGTON, J. R. WOODWARD.

Captain :
J. BROUGHTON.

Hon. Secretary :
ARTHUR FLEET, "Lyndhurst," Castle Bromwich.

Hon. Treasurer :
JOHN HALL, "Coombe," Beech Hill Road, Wylde Green.

Chairman of Committee :
E. J. HALLMARK.

Chairman of Green Committee :
H. T. PERRY.

Hon. Sec. of Green Committee :
J. P. NICHOLSON.

Chairman of House Committee :
G. ALLMAN.

Committee :
L. W. GREEN, E. J. HALLMARK, A. S. LANGLEY, M. MACDONAGH, E. H. MADDOCKS, W. H. MARYAN, W. PROVOST, R. RODEN, F. WILLIAMSON.

Hon. Auditors :
MESSRS. TYLER AND WHEATCROFT.

Professional :
C. H. WINGATE.

Front page of Member's Handbook, 1935

1997 photograph at Hodge Hill Girl's School looking across the terrain of the old 16th and 17th fairways.

THE COURSE

As time passed and the Club gained experience, two significant matters were recorded. Reference was made earlier to the difference which the introduction of new equipment, clubs and balls made to the course in pre war days. This improvement was ongoing, and the Green's Committee had hard work in trying to counteract the advantages gained in this respect by lengthening many holes, and tightening up in certain areas. It became necessary to reduce the par to 73 and the Standard Scratch to 71.

Descriptive information of the course indicated that 'the course is situated on the Birmingham side of Castle Bromwich village, and covers about 90 acres. It is laid out on the upland slopes bordering the Birmingham (Bromford Bridge) Race Course and the right bank of the River Tame.

The land has a fine sporting undulation throughout, and the turf for an inland course is very good. The sub soil being sand, the course recovers from rain with remarkable rapidity, and water in bunkers is a very rare occurrence'.

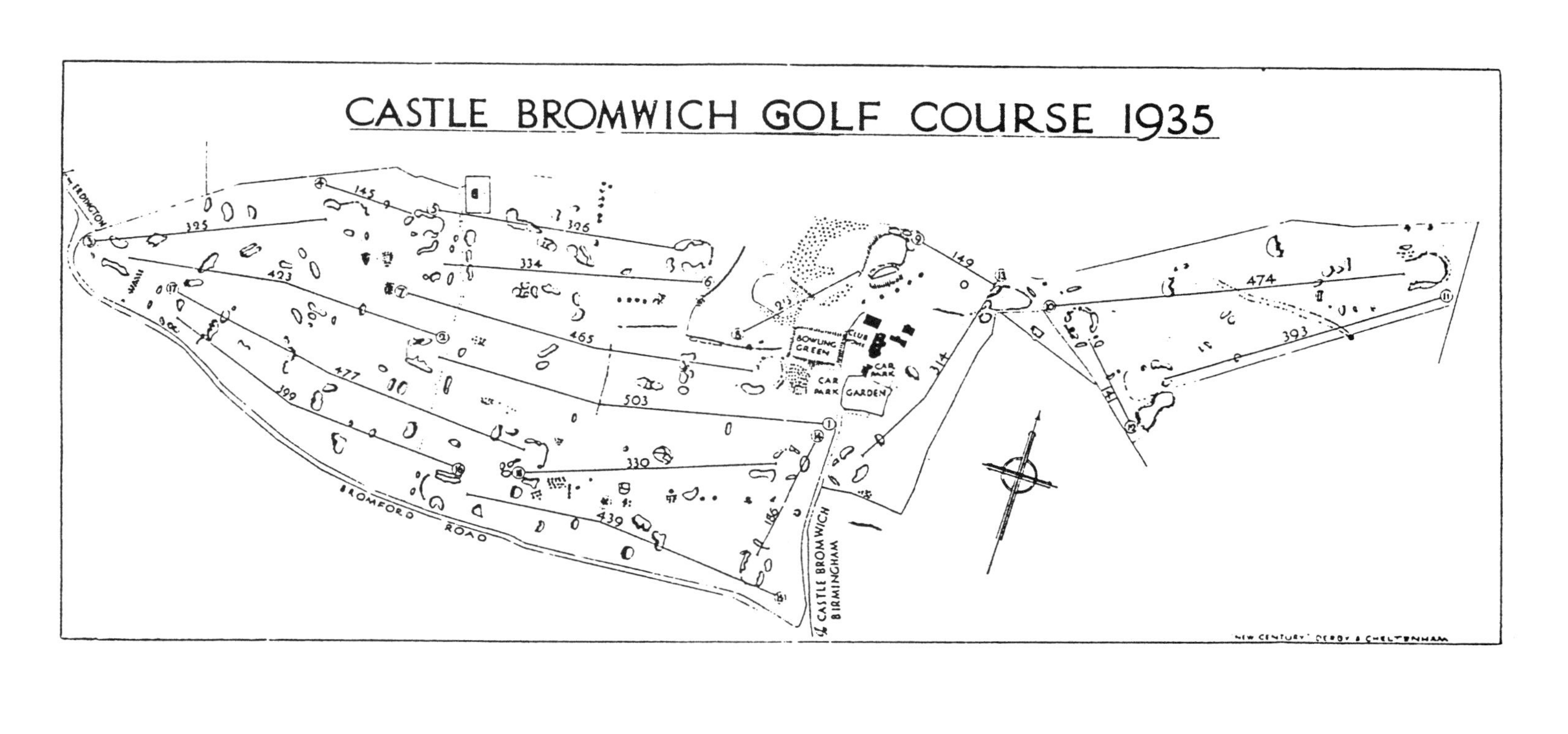
CASTLE BROMWICH GOLF COURSE 1935
ERDINGTON
325
145
326
334
423
465
477
399
503
330
439
186
215
149
314
474
393
BOWLING GREEN
CLUB
CAR PARK
CAR PARK
GARDEN
BROMFORD ROAD
To CASTLE BROMWICH BIRMINGHAM
NEW CENTURY, DERBY & CHELTENHAM

Maxstoke Park Golf Club

LENGTH AND PAR OF HOLES

Hole	*Length*	*Par*	*Stroke Index*	*Hole*	*Length*	*Par*	*Stroke Index*
1	503	5	2	10	474	5	1
2	423	4	6	11	393	5	9
3	325	4	10	12	141	3	17
4	145	3	18	13	314	4	5
5	326	4	12	14	186	3	15
6	334	4	4	15	439	5	11
7	465	5	8	16	399	4	3
8	213	3	14	17	477	5	7
9	149	3	16	18	330	4	13
	2883	35			3153	38	

TOTAL 6036 YARDS

MATCH PLAY ODDS

SINGLES: Three quarters of the difference between the two players.

FOURSOMES: Three eighths of the difference between the combined handicaps.

A fraction of a half or more to count as a stroke.

DESCRIPTION OF THE HOLES

No. 1. A fine long hole, 503 yards, the longest on the course with bunkers on the right and left from the tee. An old road has to be carried in the approach to the green.

No. 2. An interesting hole, not too long at 423 yards and the green can be reached with two good wood shots. The tee shot must be placed accurately, or a difficult second will result, since the green is well guarded on both sides.

No. 3. 325 yards, a ‘dog leg’ to the left with bunkers on the right and left from the tee, and again a well guarded green for the second shot.

No. 4. The shortest hole on the outward nine, just 145 yards, but there are large bunkers waiting to trap the wayward shot, and the player needs a perfect pitch to ensure a 'safe' three.

No. 5. 396 yards, probably two woods for most golfers. The tee shot must be placed with considerable care to avoid a very difficult approach.

No. 6. 334 yards, similar clubs needed as the previous hole, the old road has to be carried just before the green.

No. 7. Another interesting hole at 465 yards. It can be reached with two fine shots, but the handicap man will probably need three if he places each shot well. The low handicappers will require a good second to reach the green since there is a fine range of bunkers to be negotiated. The green is a good one – built into the side of a hill.

No. 8. An excellent one shot hole at 149 yards. The only thing to aim for is to be on the green with your tee shot. The green is built up with bunkers behind and awaiting slices on the right, Over running the green is heavily penalised.

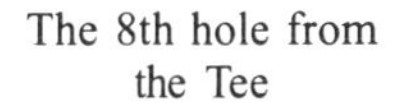

The 8th hole from the Tee

The 9th Green

No. 9. Another short hole of 149 yards. The green is narrow and consequently the tee shot requires considerable care.

No. 10. 474 yards. A long hole running downhill with out of bounds on the left, and a bunker to carry off the tee, about 150 yards away. The second shot must be straight as there is plenty of trouble on either side of the green.

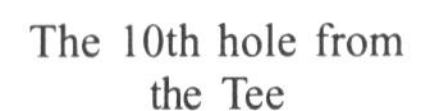
The 10th hole from the Tee

No. 11. A very good two shot hole with plenty of trouble awaiting a poor tee shot. At 393 yards it is not too long, but the green is well guarded with out of bound and a pond on the left, and grass mounds, bunkers and trees on the right.

No. 12. 141 yards, the shortest on hole on the course, the green is well bunkered on both sides and in front.

The 13th Green

No. 13. A drive and mid iron to this 314 yard 'dog leg'. There is a large bunker on the right requiring a very long carry, and out of bounds on the left. The tee shot must be well placed to ensure an open approach to the green, which is well guarded in front and at each side.

No. 14. 186 yards a firm iron shot. The player has to keep very straight to be on the green, which is bunkered right and left and protected in front.

No. 15. An excellent two shot hole. 439 yards and a good carry required from the tee. The second needs to be played accurately since the green is well protected on both sides.

No. 16. 399 yards. A long straight drive required followed by a good second to the green.

No. 17. Another long hole 477 yards, but with favourable conditions, (following wind and plenty of run), it is possible to reach the green in two, but both shots must be straight, as there are bunkers on either side from the tee. To get an open second to the green, the player must carry a bunker about 150 yards from the tee.

No. 18. 330 yards – a good drive and long iron. The green is well protected, and to obtain a good line of approach, the tee shot must be carefully placed. The green is large and undulating.

The 18th hole from the Tee

At this point of the course the fairway was probably at the lowest point and from the sloping ground at each side it does appear that there were significant undulations on the course.

A wintry scene looking from the club house towards the eighth green.

This photograph taken in March 1997 from roughly the same spot does give a clear indication of the slopes on the course, and the fall in ground level is probably close to thirty metres. Outlines of old bunkers and areas where turf were removed are also apparent.

SUBSCRIPTIONS AND VISITOR'S FEES

GENTLEMEN:	Entrance fee six guineas, and Annual Subscription six guineas.	
LADIES:	Entrance fee three guineas, and Annual Subscription three guineas.	
VISITORS:	Playing with member	2 shillings per day
	Not playing with member	3 shillings per day
	Saturdays, Sundays and Bank Holidays with member	3 shillings and 6 pence
	Not playing with member	5 shillings
	Per week	10 shillings and 6 pence

The entry for the Castle Bromwich Golf Course in the 1929 Edition of the 'Golfer's Handbook' lists the numbers of members, gives the names of the Hon. Secretary, Professional and Greenkeeper, and the charges made for playing at the course, and is included for interest:

Castle Bromwich G. C., Ltd., Haye House, Castle Bromwich. Tele. No. 389, East. Membership, 350. Hon. Sec., A. Fleet, Lyndhurst, Castle Bromwich. (p), C. H. Wingate. Greenkeeper, R. H. Marks. Records (a) 69, T. P. Perkins; (p) 70, C. H. Wingate. 18 holes. Station—Castle Bromwich (10 minutes). Visitors, playing with a member, 2s per day; 3s 6d Saturdays, Sundays and public holidays; 10s 6d per week.

THE CLUB HOUSE

The Club House was an old 16th Century Tudor Mansion, in earlier days being the Dower house for Castle Bromwich Hall, and it went by the name of 'Haye House'. It comprised 19 rooms and stood on high ground and was visible from every part of the course.

In 1945 the Club began their move to Maxstoke Park, but the members retained the use of the Club House until 1948 when the lease of the land at Castle Bromwich expired. The Club Steward, Horace Shaw, remained and the Club House was taken over by 'Ansells' and was turned into a public house and given the name of the 'Comet'.

The 'Comet' nowadays stands in Collingbourne Avenue, amidst an estate of bright red bricked post war housing. For some time the only 'green' remaining at the 'Comet' was the bowling green, but this seems to have long disappeared, whilst the practice putting area is now an open

The club house as seen from the course.

The club house from the front in winter time.

patio area with tables and chairs for summer time drinking. It is believed that the two upper storeys of the old 'Haye House' had to be removed because of deterioration in the condition of the timbers above the ground floor.

FIXTURE LIST 1939–40

Perusal of the immediate pre war Fixture List indicates that many of the early competitios have survived and are still played for today, albeit not always with the same format.

There were not so many inter club fixtures, and it is interesting to note that they were played as 1st and 2nd matches, on a home and away basis, on the same day, but always on a Saturday. This presumably was for two reasons; Firstly, in pre war days, the working day probably finished at five thirty or even six o'clock, which did not give time for evening matches, and secondly, not many people had cars in those days, and they would almost certainly have to rely on public transport to get to away matches.

There were also a number of 'B' Team matches, always played on a Wednesday, which in those days was a traditional 'half day' especially for shop workers.

CASTLE BROMWICH GOLF CLUB LIMITED.

FIXTURES, 1939-40.

DATE			
S	Mar.	4	Medal.
S	„	11	
W	„	15	Wednesday Cup.
S	„	18	
S	„	25	Challenge Cup (32 to qualify).
S	April	1	Medal. Daily Telegragh and Morning Post Competition.
S	„	8	
M	„	10	Easter Monday.
S	„	15	Harborne, 1st Home, 2nd Away (Four-ball).
W	„	19	Wednesday Cup.
S	„	22	Newport Cup, 1st Round and Final, 36 Holes.
W	„	26	Olton "B" Home.
S	„	29	Sutton Coldfield, 1st Away, 2nd Home (Four-ball).
W	May	3	Walmley "B" Home.
S	„	6	Medal and Final, 36 holes.
Tu	„	9	Warwickshire County Championship at Sutton Coldfield.
W	„	10	Robin Hood "B" Away.
S	„	13	Captain's Day.
W	„	17	Wednesday Cup and Final, 36 Holes
S	„	20	Handsworth, 1st Away, 2nd Home (Singles).
M	„	22	Ladies' County Match, Warwickshire v. Staffordshire at Castle Bromwich.
W	„	24	North Worcester, "B" Home.
S	„	27	
M	„	29	Whit Monday.
S	June	3	Medal and Captains' Cup.
W	„	7	Robin Hood "B" Home.
S	„	10	Ward End Cup, 36 Holes.
S	June	17	Newport Cup, 2nd Round.
W	„	21	Wednesday Cup.
S	„	24	Ladbrook Park, 1st Away, 2nd Home (Four-ball).
W	„	28	Ladies' Day.
S	July	1	Medal and Phil Perkins Putter.
M	„	3 }	Midland Counties Meeting at Castle Bromwich.
Tu	„	4 }	
S	„	8	Veterans' Cup, 18 Holes Medal
W	„	12	Walmley "B" Away.
S	„	15	Newport Cup, 3rd Round.
W	„	19	Wednesday Cup.
S	„	22	North Worcester, 1st Away, 2nd Home (Singles).
S	Aug.	5	Medal.
M	„	7	Bank Holiday.
S	„	12	
W	„	16	Wednesday Cup.
S	„	19	Newport Cup, 4th Round.
S	„	26	
W	„	30	"News of the World," Midland Section Qualifying Round, at Castle Bromwich.
S	Sept.	2	Medal and Championship, 36 Holes
S	„	9	Walmley, 1st Away, 2nd Home (Singles).
W	„	13	Olton "B" Away.
S	„	16	Match, Captain v. Secretary.
W	„	20	Wednesday Cup.
W	„	20	North Worcester "B" Away.
S	„	23	Newport Cup, 5th Round.
S	„	30	
S	Oct.	7	Medal.
S	„	14	Newport Cup, 6th Round.
W	„	18	Wednesday Cup.
W	„	18	Whist Drive and Dance.
S	Oct.	21	
S	„	28	
S	Nov.	4	Medal.
W	„	15	Wednesday Cup.
Th	„	23	Whist Drive and Dance.
S	Dec.	2	Medal.
W	„	20	Wednesday Cup.
Tu	„	26	Boxing Day.
	1940		
S	Jan.	6	Medal.
W	„	17	Wednesday Cup.
F	„	19	Whist Drive and Dance.
S	Feb.	3	Medal.
W	„	21	Wednesday Cup.

CASTLE BROMWICH GOLF CLUB

LIST OF CLUB MEMBERS – 1939

NAME	ADDRESS	TELEPHONE
Abbott, A. H.	65, Stanmore Road, Edgbaston	EDG. 2492 EDG. 3337
Abbott, W. H.	Longdon Croft, Copt Heath	KNOWLE 260 MID. 2003
Abelson, L. A.	138, Swanshurst Lane, Moseley	SPR. 2585
Adie, E. J.	141, Sandford Road, Moseley	SOU. 2042
Alger, C. H.	213, Bromford Rd., Birmingham 8	EAS. 1580
Alger, J. K.	213, Bromford Rd., Birmingham 8	
Allaway, T.	45, Goldieslie Road, Wylde Green	SUT. 1264 EAS. 1242
Alldridge, A. E.	86, Beaufort Avenue, Ward End, 8.	AST. 3149
Alldridge, C. F.	313, Bromford Road, B'ham, 8	STE. 2324
Allman, G.	"Chetwynd," Bradford Road, Castle Bromwich.	CAS. 2083
Allso, B. H.	10, Stonor Park Road, Solihull	SOL. 2015 EAS. 0637
Anderson, D. McNeil	Montrose, Blythe Way, Solihull	SOL. 0640
Argent, J. T.	Glenlyon, Hampton-in-Arden	Hampton 180
Armishaw, A.	67, Ventnor Avenue, Ward End, Birmingham, 8	STE. 2802
Armishaw, A., Jnr.	142, Moor End Lane, Erdington	
Avery, E. W.	49, Southam Road, Hall Green	SPR. 1472
Bain, M. S.	Heath House, Highfield Road, Washwood Heath, B'ham.	
Baines, W.	49, Blenheim Road, Moseley	
Baker, M. R.	"The Sycamores," Albert Road, Stechford	STE. 2411
Ball, W. H.	43, Mansfield Road, South Yardley	ACO. 2262
Ballard, R. N.	4, Melplash Avenue, Solihull	SOL. 0822
Basford, H.	643, Church Road, Yardley.	STE. 2361
Beauchamp, Dr. A.	"Hendra," Wash Lane, Yardley	STE. 2603
Beddows, J.	"Milton," Sherbourne Drive, Acocks Green	CEN. 1916
Birch, F. A.	92, Coleshill Road, Ward End, Birmingham, 8	STE. 2545
Bird, H. W.	"Wylde Green," Sutherland Avenue, Petts Wood, Orpington, Kent.	
Black, R. A.	17, Rollason Road, Erdington	ERD. 1935
Blakey, F. T.	96, Elmdon Lane, Marston Green	EAS. 1171
Blewitt, A. H.	Sherbourne Cottage, Coleshill	Col. 36 CEN. 3601
Bollins, A. V.	355, Warwick Road, Solihull	SOL. 0275
Bowen, E. C.	"Fairview," Portway, near Alvechurch	
Bradford, Rt. Hon. The Earl of	Weston Park, Shifnal	
Braham, J. E.	Milton House, Mary Road, Stechford	STE. 2137
Brailsford, A. J.	22, Maxstoke Road, Wylde Green	
Bridge, H. N.	291, Stoney Lane, Yardley	STE. 2169 MID. 5071.
Bridgwater, J. P.	366, Church Road, Yardley	CEN. 7860 STE. 2023
Brockington, W. A.	Birstall, Leicestershire	Birstall 2
Brodie, J. D.	279, Slade Road, Erdington.	ERD. 1838.
Broughton, J.	16, Reddings Road, Moseley	SOU. 0030 MID. 5901-2
Brown, A. D.	527, Church Road, Yardley	STE. 2071
Brown, G. W.	48, Chester Road, Castle Bromwich	CAS. 2195
Brown, J. L.	Rose Lodge, Yardley Fields Road, Stechford	STE. 2632
Brown, L. A.	"Rose Lodge," Yardley Fields Road, Stechford.	STE. 2632
Bryant, S.	Hartopp, Mirfield Road, Solihull	SOL. 1536
Buchan, Dr. D.	132, Heathfield Road, Handsworth	NOR. 0070
Buchan, Dr. D. R.	130, Heathfield Road, Handsworth	
Bunch, J. S.	22, Victoria Rd., Acocks Green	ACO. 1029
Bunch, W. H.	34, Oakfield Rd., Selly Park	SEL. 0397
Bunting, A. H.	14, Morden Road, Stechford	STE. 2588
Bushill, H.	24, Arthur Road, Erdington	ERD. 0266
Butler, E. H.	167, Yardley Fields Road, Yardley	STE. 2187
Camelinat, N.	Streetly Lane, Four Oaks	
Camelinat, N. A.	530, Church Road, Yardley, Birmingham, 9	STE. 2056
Capewell, G.	Elsecar, Water Orton	CAS. 2172
Casey, H. G.	27, Frederick Road, Stechford	STE. 2017 MID. 3761
Cash, E. Percy	31, Boden Road, Hall Green	MID. 5153
Cashmore, F. C.	"Stoneleigh," 102, Kingston Green Road, Olton	ACO. 0379
Cashmore, G. A.	Ditto ditto ditto	ditto
Challis, C. W.	Burcombe, 42, Mirfield Road, Solihull	SOL. 0666
Chamberlain, R. H.	239, Boldmere Road, Wylde Green	ERD. 0761
Chambers, H. C.	"Kerri," Blakesley Road, Yardley	STE. 2174
Chambers, G. R.	Ditto ditto ditto	ditto
Chick, J. J.	25, Rollason Road, Erdington	
Chick, J. N.	25, Rollason Road, Erdington	
Clayton, A. H.	Brierlea, Knighton Drive, Four Oaks	F.O. 458 BRO. 1065
Clayton, D.	"Withen's," Barker Road, Sutton Coldfield	SUT. 2188
Clements, W. S.	13, Gravelly Hill North	EAS. 1242 & ERD. 1358
Cochrane, Dr. R.	Sutton Street, Birmingham	AST. 0132
Cochrane, Dr. J.	391, Station Road, Yardley	STE. 2605
Cooke, G. T.	157, Coleshill Road, Ward End.	STE. 2519
Cooke, H. K.	88, Brockhurst Road, Ward End	
Copley, E.	5, Pakenham Road, Edgbaston	MID. 4676
Cox, Harry E.	16, Lozells Road, B'ham, 19	NOR. 2101
Crump, F. E.	107, Bustleholme Lane, West Bromwich	STO. 2057
Crump, H.	26, Brockhurst Road, Ward End	
Darrah, J. H.	"Westholm," Old Chester Rd., Castle Bromwich	CAS. 2180
Davies, E. J.	42, Vicarage Road, Yardley	STE. 2179 AST. 0926
Dolphin, J.	"The Ness," Old Station Road, Hampton-in-Arden	Hampton 67 NOR. 0264
Dorr, J. A.	80, Kingsbury Road, Erdington	ERD. 0554
Edwards, G. J.	"Lyndhurst," Gravelly Hill North	ERD. 0564
Edwards, D. A. C.	Selwyn House, Pilkington Avenue, Sutton Coldfield	SUT. 2422
Edwards, H.	"Girgenti," Elmdon Lane, Marston Green, B'ham.	STE. 2486
Elliott, T. L.	12, Farquhar Road, Edgbaston	CEN. 1296 EDG. 1953
Emmott Stanley	35, Salisbury Road, Birchfield, Birmingham, 19	
Evans, A. Dudley	"Fairlea," Castle Bromwich	
Evans, W. N. Dudley	Ditto ditto ditto	COL. 4609
Evans, L.	311, Orphanage Road, Erdington	ERD. 0922 „ 0365
Evans, R.	"The Hawthorns," Rollason Road, Erdington	ERD. 1022 CAL. 0814
Evans, R. B.	Dovey Villa, 10, Westbourne Avenue, Ward End, B'ham, 8	CEN. 6210
Fieldsend, C. F.	54, Haunch Lane, King's Heath	HIG. 1289
Fleet, Arthur	"Lyndhurst," Castle Bromwich	CAS. 2061 EAS. 0389
Fletcher, J. W.	111, Russell Road, Moseley, Birmingham, 11	SOU. 1953

Name	Address	Telephone
Gardner, T. S.	109, Wood End Lane, Erdington.	ERD. 1503 ERD. 2121
Glassey, W. H.	"Overley," Station Rd., Yardley	STE. 2647
Glissan, R. J.	Malins Lee, Monmouth Drive, Sutton Coldfield	SUT. 2830
Gray, J.	300, Washwood Heath Road, Birmingham	EAS. 1005
Green, A.	75, College Road, Moseley	SPR. 2097
Green, F. J.	208, Mansell Road, Small Heath	VIC. 1456 VIC. 2261
Green, J. R.	Whateley Green, Castle Bromwich.	CAS. 2070 CEN. 8211
Green, L. W.	36, Reddings Road, Moseley	CEN. 7294 SOU. 1982
Greenwood, L. E.	"Seville House," Tyburn, B'ham.	CAS. 2204
Griffin, T. W.	137, Stoney Lane, Yardley	STE. 2798
Hall, J.	"Coombe," Beech Hill Road, Wylde Green	ERD. 0078
Hall, H.	19, Emmanuel Rd., Wylde Green	ERD. 1482
Hall, P. J.	"Merville," Beeches Drive, Erdington	
Harman, C.	815, Chester Road, Erdington	ERD. 0840
Harpur, F. C.	89, Antrobus Road, Sutton Coldfield	SUT. 2877 ERD. 2121
Hathaway, H. R.	32, Beaudesert Rd., Handsworth	CEN. 5920 NOR. 2386
Hawker, G. W.	120, Church Lane, Handsworth Wood	NOR. 0358
Hawkes, T. B.	97, Wake Green Road, Moseley	SOU. 2202
Hawkins, E. A.	Bracken, Dovehouse Lane, Solihull	ACO 0388 VIC. 0690
Haynes, F. H.	632, Washwood Heath Road	EAS. 1124
Haynes, S.	2, Cambridge Avenue, Wylde Green	EAS. 1415 ERD. 1758
Helliwell, P.	164, Albert Road, Stechford	STE. 2303
Hepworth, F.	194, Waterloo Road, South Yardley	ACO. 1443
Hewett, J. E. O.	"Fern House," Washwood Heath Road, Birmingham	EAS. 0510
Higgs, Roland	Lloyds Bank Ltd., Coleshill	Col. 47
Hill, H.	226, Stechford Road, Ward End	
Hill, J. E.	"Farcroft," Aberdovey, Merioneth	ABD 38
Honigs-Berger, Dr. Max.	143, Flaxley Road, Stechford.	STE. 2083
Howard, S. G.	"Westbourne," Beech Hill Rd., Wylde Green	ERD. 0243
Huband, G. T.	"Southfield," Blakesley Road, Yardley	STE. 2140 MID. 1179
Hunt, H.	159, Russell Road, Moseley	SOU. 1771 VIC. 0418
Illston, A. S.	384, Station Road, Yardley.	STE. 2101
Jarrom, T.	248, Mansel Road, Small Heath	
Jenks, T.	30, Treaford Lane, Alum Rock	
Johnson, H.	"Cresswell," 55, Sutton Road, Erdington	ERD. 1724
Jones, A. F.	8, Newhall Street, Birmingham	CEN. 4040
Jones, F.	16, Livingstone Rd., Handsworth	BIR. 4355
Jones, O.	Ditto ditto ditto	ditto
Jones, J. H.	51, Emmanuel Rd., Wylde Green	CEN. 2541
Jordan, A. G.	294, Stechford Road, Washwood Heath, Birmingham	
Kendrick, F. J.	Barclays Bank Ltd., 2, Alum Rock Road, Saltley	EAS. 0547
Kennedy, A. S.	194, Kingsbury Road, Erdington	
King, Basil	The Willows, 65, Trafalgar Rd. Moseley	SOU. 3101
Kirk, Dr. A.	667, Washwood Heath Road.	EAS. 0356
Kirk, W.	"Glenhurst," Blakesley Road, Yardley	STE. 2537
Knowles, C.	263, Stoney Lane, Yardley	STE. 2353
Lane, S. J. A.	"Brantwood," Driffold, Sutton Coldfield	SUT. 2174
Langley, A. S.	"The Laurels," Castle Bromwich	CAS. 2049
Lawrence, E. G.	49, Havelock Road, Birchfields	BIR. 4167 AST. 1555
Lawrence, J. E.	Ditto ditto ditto	BIR. 4167
Lillie, Dr. J. P.	796, Washwood Heath Road, Birmingham	EAS. 1049
Lloyd, Arthur	St. Keverne, Church Road, Yardley	STE. 2658
MacCallum, Dr. A. R.	243, Tettenhall Road, Wolverhampton	Tettenhall 51420
MacDonagh, M.	4, Orchard Road, Erdington	ERD. 0618
MacDonagh, K. C.	4, Orchard Road, Erdington	ERD. 0618
Mackey, D. E.	31, Tenbury Road, Kings Heath	
Mackie, Dr. A. H.	304, Washwood Heath Rd., B'ham	EAS. 0892
Mackie, Dr. A. D. B.	Edzell House, Whateley Green, Castle Bromwich	CAS. 2242
McDowall, J.	"Ennerdale," Monmouth Drive, Sutton Coldfield.	SUT. 1126. MID. 5071
McDowall, J., Junr.	Eastfield, Darnick Road, Sutton Coldfield	SUT. 3405
Maddocks, E. H.	The Shrubbery, Four Oaks	F.O. 168 EAS. 1371
McGovern, Dr. J.	818, Alum Rock Road, Birmingham	EAS. 1196
McMahon, R. P.	11, Wake Green Road, Moseley	SOU. 1087
Malley, J. H.	Abingdon Lodge, The Crescent, Solihull	SOL. 0688 NOR. 1256
Mancus, E.	23, Rosafield Avenue, Quinton	
Marks, J.	"Norfolk House," Brueton Avenue, Solihull	SOL. 0840
Marshall, P. W.	50, Grove Avenue, Moseley	SOU. 0548
Marriott, H.	"Tabor," Streetsbrook Road, Solihull	SOL. 1526
Marston, A.	83, Earlsbury Gardens, Handsworth	CEN. 1775
Marston, A. D.	Ditto ditto ditto	
Maryan, W. H.	58, Hodge Hill Common, Birmingham, 8	CAS. 2039
Matthews, J. E.	106, Coleshill Road, Ward End Birmingham, 8	STE. 2122
Matthews, J. S.	40, Dover Road, Birkdale, Southport	
Metcalfe, Rev. H. E.		
Menzies, E. A.	14, Hodge Hill Road, B'ham, 8	
Milburn, G. B.	52, Emmanuel Road, Wylde Green	ERD 2121
Millington, A.	Police Station, Victoria Road, Aston	EAS. 1111
Mills, F. Fletcher	15, Winsley Avenue, Bournemouth, E.	Southbourne 2170
Mills, W. W.	"Monterey," Blakesley Road, Yardley	STE. 2020
Milner, A. E.	89, Brockhurst Road, Washwood Heath, B'ham.	STE. 2285/6 STE. 2670
Mitchell, J.	7, Eastbourne Avenue, Ward End	STE. 2706
Moore, C. H.	893, Chester Road, Erdington	AST. 0167 ERD. 1865
Morrison, G. E.	"Cassillis," Land Lane, Marston Green, Birmingham	MAR. 2228 MID. 4583
Morgan, T. W.	168, Somerville Road, Small Heath	VIC. 3082
Myatt, P. E.	"Kingston," Blakesley Road, Yardley	CEN. 2078 STE. 2414
Neale, G. R.	18, Sharmans Cross Road, Solihull.	CEN. 6634 SOL. 1395
Neale, T. A.	1, Newhall St., Birmingham	CEN. 1928 CAS. 2091
Newport, Viscount	Weston Park, Shifnal	
Nicholas, E. F.	195, Coleshill Road, B'ham, 8	STE. 2168 VIC. 1071

Nicholson, J. P.	90, Lyttelton Road, Stechford.	CEN. 1146-7 STE. 2429
O'Keefe, Dr. D.	92, Brockhurst Road, B'ham, 8	
Oxley, W. G.		
Park, H. E. M.	268, Robin Hood Lane, Hall Green	
Parker, W. H.	6, Grantham Road, Bearwood	
Parkes, A. J.	17, Wake Green Road, Moseley	SOU. 0487
Parkes, F.	"Grassendale," Warwick Road, Solihull	AST. 3251
Parkes, F. C.	"Sillwood," Monkseaton Road, Sutton Coldfield	SUT. 2057 AST. 3251
Parkes, H. D.	Mirfield Road, Solihull	ERD. 0026
Parsons, H. R.	620, Church Road, Yardley	STE. 2150 CEN. 6811
Payne, W. G.	"May Blossom," Stechford Rd., Birmingham, 8	CAS. 2216 EAS. 1501
Payne, G. Junr.	Ditto ditto ditto	CAS. 2216
Pearse, G. Junr.	Royston, Blackroot Road, Four Oaks	SUT. 1750
Peek, H. R.	32, Coleshill Road, Ward End	STE. 2617,2558
Perkins, T. P.	Kirtland Country Club, Willoughby, Ohio, U.S.A.	
Perring, A. G.	36, Goldieslie Road, Wylde Green	CEN. 2159 SUT. 2372
Perry, H. E.	34, Fir Tree Road, Erdington	CEN. 2786
Perry, H. T.	24, Southbourne Avenue, Ward End	STE. 2391
Phillips, F. H.	"Woodford," Cremorne Road, Four Oaks	F.O. 743
Phipps, H. C.	"Stoneleigh," 102, Kineton Green Road, Olton	ACO. 0379
Pierce, Dr. A.	43, Washwood Heath Road, Birmingham	EAS. 0630
Pierce, S.	43, Washwood Heath Road, Birmingham	EAS. 0630
Pinkerton, B. D.	44, Radstock Avenue, Ward End, Birmingham, 8	STE. 2808
Platts, P. S.	22, Orchard Road, Erdington	ERD. 1010
Pooler, Dr. H. W.	"The Hollies," Ashover, Derbyshire	ASH. 219
Potter, Nelson	67, Newhall Street, Birmingham	ERD. 1434 CEN. 1831/3
Powell, F.	17, Warwick Place, Leamington Spa	
Price, F. T.	635, Church Road, Yardley	STE. 2777 CEN. 7518
Provost, W.	75, Wylde Green Road, Sutton Coldfield	SUT. 1234 AST. 1728/9
Purcell, Dr. J.	267, Birchfield Road, B'ham, 20	BIR. 4444
Radnall, E. A.	Holly Lodge, Castle Bromwich	CAS. 2087
Radnall, E. E. A.	470, Brook Lane, Moseley	SPR. 2139
Radnall, E. W.	"Southfield," Castle Bromwich	CAS. 2013
Ralston, J.	98, Coleshill Rd., Birmingham, 8	STE. 2395
Rawlins, G. B.	Rose Neath, Middleton Road, Streetly	STR. 7193
Rayer, F. H.	Chester Road, Castle Bromwich	CAS. 2196
Richmond, Bernard	Bracken, Maney Hill Road, Sutton Coldfield	EAS. 1015
Roberts, H. C. W.	"Highcroft," Old Chester Road, Castle Bromwich	CAS. 2052
Roden, R.	15, Wretham Road, Handsworth	AST. 2312
Rogers, H.	30, Frederick Rd., Birmingham, 15	EDG. 2414
Salt, E. W., M.P.	"Avon Hurst," Tiddington, Stratford-on-Avon	S. Avon 514 MID. 5455
Sangster, Dr. J.	"Parkfield," Gravelly Hill, Erdington	EAS. 0952
Sangster, Dr. J. H.	Ditto ditto ditto	ditto
Sangster, S. M.	"Parkfield," 101, Gravelly Hill, Birmingham	EAS. 0952
Sapcote, R.	2, Carisbrooke Rd., Edgbaston	BEA. 2255
Scrivener, A.	875, Tyburn Road, Birmingham	ERD. 2274
Shakespeare, S. H.	174, Edmund St., Birmingham	EDG. 0878 COL. 4406
Shaw, A. E.	Ashfield Villa, 218, Stoney Lane, Birmingham, 25	STE. 2771
Shaw, A. G.	212, Alum Rock Road, Saltley	EAS. 0874
Shaw, E. R.	"Parkfield," 368, Church Road, Yardley	STE. 2033 MID. 5437
Sheasby, J. W.	13, Coleshill Road, Ward End	STE. 2561
Skipper, C. T.	"Swallowdene," 34, Belvedere Road, Coventry	
Smart, W. P.	4, St. Augustines Rd., Edgbaston	MID. 1927/8 EDG. 1879
Smith, A. Parton	204, Station Road, Wylde Green	SUT. 2596 CEN. 1021
Smith, R.	281, Yardley Green Road, Small Heath	STE. 2028
Smith, W. P.	7, Coleshill Road, Birmingham, 8	STE. 2392
Sornet, L. A.	44, Chester Road, Castle Bromwich	CAS. 2158
Sutherland, D. M. G.	Ivy House, Avenue Road, Dorridge	KNOWLE 2606
Sutherland, I. G.	Ivy House, Avenue Road, Dorridge	" "
Stubbings, G.	"Homeleigh," Blakesley Road, Yardley	STE. 2649
Stubbings, G. Junr.	"Glenavon," Boultbee Road, Wylde Green	ERD. 0355
Swain, G. W.	60, Golden Hillock Road, Birmingham, 10	VIC. 1180
Thompson, W.	75, Chester Road, Castle Bromwich	CAS. 2089
Titt, W. G. J.	Bank House, Coleshill	Col. 47
Tobin, Dr. P.	690, Alum Rock Road, B'ham, 8	EAS. 1706
Tomlinson, J. O.	Grimstock, Coleshill	CEN. 2811 Coleshill 71
Trentham, H. F.	35, Coleshill Road, Ward End.	STE. 2756
Tyler, G. H.	75, New Street, Birmingham	MID. 5707 SOU. 2725
Upton, B. J.	"Iserlon," Castle Bromwich	ERD. 1698-9
Utting, L. J.	"Ryecroft," 138, Penns Lane, Erdington	CEN. 5755 ERD. 1075
Vaughan, W. D.	"Westmount," Bradford Road, Castle Bromwich.	CAS. 2057
Wagner, M. R.	Whateley Green, Castle Bromwich	CAS. 2189
Walford, R.	Peewit Cottage, Barnt Green	EAS. 1371
Walker, Francis A.	4, Jaffray Road, Gravelly Hill, Birmingham	ERD. 1576 MID. 1846
Walker, Fred	78, Holly Lane, Erdington	
Walker, H.	Castle Bromwich	
Watson, J. D.	South Road, Northfield	PRI. 1002
Watton, L. C.	193, Belchers Lane, Bordesley Green	
Welburn, T.	"Hemplow," School Rd., Castle Bromwich	MID. 5117
Whatmough, J. W.	"The Woodlands," Vicarage Road, Yardley.	STE. 2650 MID. 5071
Wichman, F. C. W.	45, Woolmore Rd., Marsh Hill, Erdington.	
Wilder, V. W.	869, Chester Road, Erdington	ERD. 1860
Wiley, C. H.	"Penrhyn," Hollyfield Road, Sutton Coldfield	SUT. 1095
Wiley, P. A.	Hotel Bonair, Esplanade, Paignton, Devon	
Wilkinson, J.	"Ivernia," 191, Flaxley Road, Stechford	
Wingate, C. H.	42, Lyttelton Road, Stechford	
Winnall, G. E.	"Luccombe," Vesey Road, Wylde Green	SUT. 2261 CEN. 1711
Withington, G. J.	"The Gables," Francis Road, Stechford	STE. 2833
Wood, A. J.	"Branscombe," Station Road, Wylde Green	SUT. 3055
Wood, Frank	"Glayfran," Monmouth Drive, Sutton Coldfield	SUT. 1990
Woodward, J. R.	40, Meadow Hill Road, Kings Norton	KIN. 1235
Wright, E.	48, Alum Rock Road, Saltley	EAS. 0085
Wright, N. E.	Ditto ditto ditto	ditto
Youngson, A.	554, Washwood Heath Road Ward End	CEN. 1665 EAS. 0578

COMPETITIONS AND TROPHIES

GOLD MEDAL:

Monthly qualifying rounds are to be held in two divisions, and a minimum of four cards must be returned. The best twelve aggregates of four cards in each division will qualify for final. Gold Medals are awarded to the Winners of each Division and Bronze Medals to the runners up.

WINNERS OF THE GOLD MEDAL

1899	J. E. Burgum
1900	J. Westwood
	A. W. Robson
1901	T. S. Fishwick
	A. W. Robson
1902	A. J. H. Boyton
	A. W. Robson
1903	H. I. Hobbiss
	H. W. Pooler
1904	J. Foster
	Rev. H. E. Metcalfe
1905	H. T. Perry
1906	W. G. Oxley
1907	J. G. Riddell
1908	W. G. Oxley
1909	J. G. Riddell
1910	W. Bennett
1911	C. K. Black
1912	F. Parkes
1913	A. Armishaw
1914	M. S. Bain
1915	W. H. Abbott
1916	R. Walford
1917	A. Armishaw
1918	G. Henderson
1919	J. R. Green
1920	G. C. Pearson
1921	F. Parkes
1922	E. H. Maddocks
1923	G. Allman
1924	A. Black
1925	A. E. Allen
1926	A. Armishaw
1927	A. Armishaw
1928	S. Wilson
1929	W. N. Dudley-Evans
1930	P. E. Myatt
1931	M. MacDonagh
1932	M. Macdonagh
1933	G. R. Chambers
1934	M. MacDonagh
1935	A. D. Marston
1936	C. H. Alger
1937	G. R. Chambers
1938	W. N. Dudley-Evans
1939	M. MacDonagh

VETERAN'S CUP:

Restricted to members aged 50 years and over. Winner to hold Cup for twelve months and to receive a replica.

1927	A. Armishaw	1933	G. Stubbings
1928	G. H. Tyler	1934	T. A. Neale
1929	H. E. M. Park	1935	T. A. Neale
1930	T. W. Griffin	1936	G. Stubbings
1931	J. T. Argent	1937	H. E. M. Park
1932	T. A. Neale	1938	A. Dudley-Evans

WEDNESDAY CUP:

Played under same concept as Gold Medal but with one division only. Winner awarded a Silver Bowl.

1915	A. T. Bryant	1928	S. H. Shakespeare
1916	J. Watson	1929	S. H. Shakespeare
1917	F. Parkes	1930	R. Sapcote
1918	A. Armishaw	1931	C. Harman
1919	A. Armishaw	1932	E. P. Cash
1920	J. Lawrence	1933	D. R. Buchan
1921	J. Lawrence	1934	J. W. Whatmough
1922	A. E. Allen	1935	Bernard Richmond
1923	W. J. Gibson	1936	H. Johnson
1924	F. B. Prike	1937	H. Edwards
1925	C. Lindall	1938	C. H. Alger
1926	J. Broughton	1939	S. M. Sangster
1927	S. H. Shakespeare		

NEWPORT CUP:

Bogey Competition. Six qualifying rounds are held, and a minimum of three cards must be returned to qualify. Only one Division. The best twelve aggregates of three cards qualify for final. Winner to hold Cup for one year and to receive a replica.

1907	J. Foster	1914	W. B. Williams
1908	H. T. Perry	1915	R. Walford
1909	J. R. Woodward	1916	R. Walford
1910	W. G. Oxley	1917	D. Macadie
1911	H. T. Perry	1918	A. Armishaw
1912	C. K. Black	1919	G. C. Pearson
1913	E. J. Adie	1920	F. Parkes

1921	T. P. Perkins	1931	Harry Hall
1922	T. P. Perkins	1932	G. R. Chambers
1923	A. E. Allen	1933	M. MacDonagh
1924	J. R. Green	1934	A. J. Parkes
1925	A. J. Parker	1935	A. J. Parkes
1926	T. P. Perkins	1936	A. J. Parkes
1927	J. H. Darrah	1937	C. H. Alger
1928	W. H. Parks	1938	G. R. Chambers
1929	F. R. Carr	1939	A. D. Marston
1930	C. H. Alger		

WARD END CUP:

Medal Play over 36 holes. Handicap limit 18. Winner to hold Cup for twelve months and to receive a replica.

1918	M. S. Bain	1929	J. McDowell
1919	F. Powell	1930	A. J. Ward
1920	T. P. Perkins	1931	T. Holmes
1921	R. Evans	1932	L. W. Green
1922	A. S. Lucas	1933	T. Holmes
1923	S. L. Elliott	1934	G. Stubbings
1924	J. D. Cochrane	1935	J. O. Tomlinson
1925	Walter Henman	1936	A. J. Parkes
1926	F. Parkes	1937	L. C. Watton
1927	A. S. Lucas	1938	E. E. A. Radnall
1928	F. E. Ford	1939	K. C. MacDonagh

CASTLE BROMWICH CHALLENGE CUP:

A qualifying Medal round (handicap limit 18) is played and the first thirty two qualify to go forward to a match play knock out format competition. Winning finalist to hold trophy for twelve months and to receive replica.

1904	H. E. Metcalfe	1911	H. W. Weedon
1905	G. K. Black	1912	W. Parkes
	P. Campbell	1913	T. Parkes
1906	H. E. Metcalfe	1914	W. H. Abbott
	J. Foster	1915	A. S. Langley
1907	W. Bentley	1916	A. H. Blewitt
1908	H. T. Perry	1917	F. Parkes
1909	H. C. Wright	1918	E. C. Smith
1910	A. E. DeVall	1919	F. Dowell

1920	R. Walford	1930	A. J. Parkes
1921	P. A. Wiley	1931	C. H. Alger
1922	J. R. Green	1932	E. P. Cash
1923	F. Parkes	1933	T. Holmes
1924	A. R. MacCallum	1934	G. Stubbings – Junior
1925	A. H. Abbott	1935	G. Stubbings – Junior
1926	J. Herbert Shaw	1936	J. P. Nicholson
1927	G. Allman	1937	G. R. Chambers
1928	Harry Hall	1938	J. A. Dorr
1929	R. W. Davies	1939	J. H. Sangster

CHAMPIONSHIP CUP:

Stroke play Competition. 36 holes to be played off scratch.

1914	A. S. Langley	1928	Harry Hall
1915	M. S. Bain	1929	Harry Hall
1916	John Jones	1930	Harry Hall
1917	M. S. Bain	1931	C. H. Alger
1918	R. Walford	1932	Harry Hall
1919	W. E. Woodward	1933	Harry Hall
1920	W. E. Woodward	1934	Harry Hall
1921	T. P. Perkins	1935	Harry Hall
1922	T. P. Perkins	1936	G. R. Chambers
1923	T. P. Perkins	1937	Harry Hall
1924	T. P. Perkins	1938	Harry Hall
1925	T. P. Perkins	1939	
1926	T. P. Perkins		
1927	T. P. Perkins		

RESULTS OF COMPETITIONS AND MATCHES

A selection of press reports in the mid '30s clearly indicated that there were many fine golfers at Castle Bromwich Golf Club. Harry Hall was plus 1, C. H. Alger, E. C. Bowen, G. R. Chambers played off scratch. The highest handicap from F. T. Blakey, H. Crump, W. N. Dudley-Evans, M. Macdonagh, A. D. Marston, T. A. Neale, A. J. Parkes and F. Williamson was 4.

There were at least fifteen other single figure handicaps. Many of the Club members were doctors, and a considerable number were businessmen with their own companies that were household names.

Duncan M. G. Sutherland was a member who became a leading amateur of considerable repute in the immediate post war years. Presumably because of the impending closure of the course he left and joined Robin Hood Golf Club after the war, and his name is prominent on their Championship boards with many victories to his name. In the early '50s when Marston Green Municipal Golf Course opened as an 18 hole course I was present when an exhibition challenge match was played between Bill Adwick the Marston Green Professional, partnered by Jack Cawsey of Pype Hayes, against Duncan Sutherland and Carl Bretherton, another famous amateur of the day.

CASTLE BROMWICH

CHALLENGE CUP

F. T. Blakey....	73— 2..71	J. A. Dorr......	86— 6..80
L. Evans	85—14..71	J. Ralston......	90—10..80
W. Dudley Evans	79— 6..73	Nelson Potter...	93—12..81
J. P. Nicholson..	83— 9..74	A. G. Jordan ...	95—14..81
J. MacDowall ...	83— 8..75	P. S. Platts.....	99—13..81
H. Casey	87—11..76	W. H. Ball	91— 9..82
C. H. Alger	77 sc. 77	F. C. Harpur ...	100—18..82
Dr. J. H. Sangster	80— 3..77	E. P. Cash	88— 5..83
A. D. Marston...	81— 4..77	C. B. Pooley....	93—10..83
H. D. Parkes....	95—18..77	H. E. Perry	97—14..83
G. R. Chambers .	77+ 1..78	D. E. Mackey...	102—18..84
G. Stubbings. jun.	87— 9..78	H. R. Hathaway.	102—18..84
W. Thompson...	92—14..78	H. Crump	93— 8..85
B. H. Allso	93—15..78	G. W. Brown ...	100—15..85
E. C. Bowen	79 sc. 79	R. Smith.......	104—18..86
R. B. Evans	88— 9..79	L. E. Greenwood	96— 8..88

CASTLE BROMWICH

DIVISION I

C. H. Alger	69 sc. 69	K. C. MacDonagh	83—10..73
A. D. Marston...	74— 4..70	G. Stubbings. jun.	81— 7..74
F. T. Blakey	73— 1..72	J. Sangster	85—10..75
H. Edwards.....	79— 7..72	S. M. Sangster ..	80— 3..77
B. H. Allso	86—14..72	H. Casey.	88—11..77
W. H. Ball......	82— 9..73	J. McDowall. jun.	86— 8..78

DIVISION II

A. Marston	87—18..69	R. Ballard......	98—23..75
F. C. Harpur	94—25..69	E. E. A. Radnall.	93—16..77
R. Roden.......	91—20..71	A. H. Clayton...	95—18..77
V. W. Wilder....	87—15..72		
S. G. Howard ...	98—24..74		
E. J. Davies	93—18..75		

CASTLE BROMWICH

DIVISION I

W. N. D. Evans .	77— 6..71	R. B. Evans....	85— 9..76
F. T. Blakey....	74— 2..72	G. B. Milburn...	90—14..76
J. T. Argent	87—14..73	J. A. Dorr......	83— 6..77
T. A. Neale	80— 6..74	C. H. Alger.....	78 sc. 78
H. Edwards.....	81— 7..74	J. Whatmough..	87— 9..78
H. Casey	85—11..74	E. C. Bowen....	79 sc. 79
A. G. Jordan....	88—14 74	H. Crump	87— 8..79
G. Stubbings. jun.	84— 9..75	Nelson Potter ..	91—12..79
G. R. Chambers .	75+ 1..76	P. E. Myatt	90—10..80
Dr. J. Sangster..	79— 3..76	C. B. Pooley....	90—10..80
		H. Basford	93—13..80

DIVISION II

E. E. Radnall ...	88—18..70	A. Green	96—18..78
J. Dolphin......	89—16..73	H. C. Chambers.	100—22..78
F. Hepworth....	91—18..73	G. W. Brown ...	94—15..79
E. F. Nicholas...	97—23..74	W. S. Clements..	95—16..79
B. H. Allso	90—15..75	E. J. Davies ...	97..18..79
G. E. Winnall...	93—16..77	E. H. Butler....	99—20..79
S. J. A. Lane....	95—18..77	E. A. Hawkins..	98—18..80
W. Heuman.....	98—21..77	R. Roden	100—20..80

CASTLE BROMWICH.

DIVISION I.

W. Dudley Evans	75— 4..71	G. Stubbings ...	86—12..74
T. A. Neale	79— 8..71	J. P. Lillie	87—13..74
F. T. Blakey ...	75— 3..72	A. D. Marston. .	77— 3..74
F. Williamson...	76— 4..72	H. Hall	74+ 1..75
H. Casey	86—14..72	J. Whatmough..	82— 7..75
H. Crump	82— 8..74	J. McDowell....	83— 8..75
E. Lawrence	87—13..74		

DIVISION II.

H. E. Perry.....	87—15..72	E. A. Radnall...	94—15..79
B. Richmond ...	91—17..74	C. E. Neale.....	95—16..79
A. E. Milner	90—15..75	A. Marston	94—15..79
E. J. Adie	98—23..75	W. D. Vaughan.	99—20..79
A. Jordan	92—16..76	H. E. M. Park..	96—16..80
W. H. Kirkby...	97—21..76	F. H. Rickards..	100—20..80

PHIL. PERKINS PUTTER, 1935.

W. Dudley Evans	75— 4..71	T. A. Neale	79— 8..71

To play off November 2, 1935.

Harry Hall's score of 67 broke the Amateur Course Record set by Philip Perkins some ten years earlier.

CASTLE BROMWICH

WARD END CUP

G. R. Chambers	138 sc. 138	A. D. Marston	150— 6..153
L. C. Watton	174—36..138	A. E. Milner	177—24..153
E. E. Radnall	175—36..139	J. T. Argent	181—28..153
V. W. Wilder	174—34..140	H. Hathaway	191—36..155
F. T. Blakey	146— 4..142	A. G. Jordan	181—28..153
C. H. Alger	145 sc. 145	G. W. Brown	184—30..154
J. Marks	173—24..149	J. Tomlinson	179—24..155
M. MacDonagh	168— 8..150	E. A. Hawkins	191—36..155
W. N. D. Evans	160—10..150	E. C. Bowen	156 sc. 156
W. Thompson	178—28..150	H. Crump	174—16..158
A. E. Penfold	171—20..151		

CASTLE BROMWICH.

P. PERKINS PUTTER AND MEDAL.

DIVISION I.

A. D. B. Mackie	86—14..72	F. Williamson	83— 4..79
W. Thompson	87—14..73	F. Blakey	81— 2..79
H. Hall	72+ 1..73	P. E. Myatt	87— 8..79
C. H. Alger	74 sc. 74	M. MacDonagh	81— 2..79
W. Dudley Evans	79— 4..75	T. A. Neale	86— 6..80
H. Edwards	84— 9..75	H. Basford	94—14..80
C. B. Pooley	85—10..75	H. N. Bridge	90— 9..81
H. E. Perry	89—14..75	A. D. Marston	85— 3..82
G. R. Chambers	78 sc. 78	H. Crump	91— 8..83
A. Armishaw, jun	92—14..78	Dr. Sangster	91— 7..84
G. Allman	85— 6..79		

DIVISION II.

B. H. Allso	88—15..73	E. W. Ingall	94—16..78
G. W. Brown	95—20..75	P. Helliwell	99—20..79
H. E. M. Park	94—18..76	A. E. Milner	95—15..80
W. Henman	97—21..76	H. C. Chambers	105—22..83
J. Mare	93—16..77	J. Beddows	105—22..83
A. G. Jordan	94—16..73	A. Marston	104—18..86

CASTLE BROMWICH.

DIVISION I.

*Harry Hall	67+ 1..68	P. E. Myatt	82— 8..74
H. Edwards	79—11..68	A. J. Parkes	78— 3..75
H. Casey	83—12..71	J. H. Darrah	80— 5..75
E. G. Lawrence	85—14..71	C. B. Pooley	85—10..75
F. T. Blakey	75— 3..72	C. H. Alger	76 sc. 76
G. Stubbings	84—11..73	W. Dudley Evans	80— 4..76
A. D. Marston	77— 3..74		

* Mr. Hall's score of 67 gross constitutes a record for the course at its present length.

DIVISION II.

H. Basford	85—16..69	W. D. Vaughan	95—20..75
B. H. Allso	88—15..73	G. B. Milburn	91—15..76
W. Thompson	89—15..74	K. MacDonagh	92—16..76
G. D. Johnson	94—20..74	A. S. Illston	96—20..76
L. C. Watton	93—18..75	E. E. A. Radnall	97—21..76
H. E. M. Park	93—18..75	T. Allaway	98—22..76

The Amateur Course Record again broken with the gross 66 score of G. R. Chambers.

CASTLE BROMWICH

DIVISION I

G. R. Chambers	66 sc. 66	J. Sangster	83— 7..76
S. M. Sangster	73— 5..68	J. A. Dorr	83— 6..77
C. H. Alger	70 sc. 70	P. E. Myatt	87—10..77
H. Hall	70+ 1..71	H. Crump	86— 9..78
A. J. Parkes	75— 2..73	J. P. Nicholson	87— 9..78
M. MacDonagh	77— 4..73	H. Casey	89—11..78
A. Pierce	81— 8..73	J. P. Lillie	90—12..78
H. Basford	87—14..73	E. P. Cash	84— 5..79
A. G. Jordan	87—14..73	R. A. Black	90—11..79
W. Thompson	87—14..73	K. C. MacDonagh	90—11..79
F. Blakey	76— 2..74	W. Dudley Evans	85— 5..80
T. A. Neale	80— 6..74	A. Kirk	89— 9..80
C. B. Pooley	84—10..74	G. B. Milburn	94—14..80

G. R. Chambers's score of 66 gross constitutes a new amateur record for the course.

CASTLE BROMWICH v. FINHAM PARK

Played at Castle Bromwich

CASTLE BROMWICH		FINHAM PARK	
H. Hall and C. H. Alger (2 and 1)	1	R. J. Nauen and G. H. Horne	0
G. R. Chambers and E. C. Bowen (5 and 3)	1	H. M. Yardley and R. Booth	0
A. J. Parkes and J. A. Dorr (5 and 4)	1	A. Elson and J. A. Simmons	0
A. D. Marston and W. N. Dudley Evans (5 and 3)	1	S. Harley and W. P. Lousada	0
F. T. Blakey and E. P. Cash (2 and 1)	1	D. Kaye and A. H. Edwards	0
S. M. Sangster and T. A. Neale (5 and 4)	1	A. R. Lane and S. C. Hill	0
	6		0

Maxstoke Park Golf Club

The Castle Bromwich Golf Club Limited

Telephone No. East 0389. *Registered Offices:* "Haye House," Castle Bromwich.

OFFICERS AND COMMITTEE, 1938-39

President:
THE RIGHT HON. THE EARL OF BRADFORD.

Vice-Presidents:

W. H. Abbott.	F. Fletcher Mills.	R. Roden.
A. Armishaw.	F. Parkes.	G. H. Tyler.
A. Dudley Evans.	H. T. Perry.	G. J. Withington.
Arthur Fleet.	H. W. Pooler.	J. R. Woodward.
Frank Jones.	W. Provost.	

Captain	C. H. Alger.
Hon. Treasurer	John Hall.
Hon. Secretary	Arthur Fleet.
Chairman of Green Committee	H. T. Perry.
Hon. Secretary of Green Committee	E. Percy Cash.
Hon. Secretary and Chairman of House Committee	L. E. Greenwood.
Assistant to Hon. Treasurer and Hon. Secretary...	W. N. Dudley Evans, A.C.A.

Committee:

G. Allman.	J. A. Dorr.	A. S. Langley.
J. Broughton.	H. Hall.	M. MacDonagh.
G. W. Brown.	H. Hill.	T. A. Neale.

Hon. Auditors:
Tyler and Wheatcroft, Central House, 75, New Street, Birmingham, 2.

Annual Report and Statement of Accounts

FOR THE YEAR ENDING 25TH MARCH, 1939

TO BE PRESENTED TO THE

THIRTY-FIRST ORDINARY GENERAL MEETING

to be held at the GOLF CLUB HOUSE, Castle Bromwich, Birmingham
on Wednesday, 24th day of May, 1939, at 7-30 p.m.

LIST OF COMMITTEE ATTENDANCES.

	Times Summoned	Times Attended		Times Summoned	Times Attended
C. H. Alger	11	6	H. Hall	11	10
G. Allman ...	11	4	J. Hall	11	9
J. Broughton ...	11	6	H. Hill	11	10
G. W. Brown ...	11	10	A. S. Langley ...	11	10
E. P. Cash	11	5	M. MacDonagh ...	11	9
J. A. Dorr	11	8	T. A. Neale ...	11	9
A. Fleet	11	11	H. T. Perry	11	9
L. E. Greenwood ...	11	8			

VICE-PRESIDENTS' ATTENDANCES.

A. Armishaw	11	8	R. Roden	11	1
A. Dudley Evans ...	11	5	G. H. Tyler	2	2
F. Jones	3	2	G. J. Withington ...	11	11
W. Provost	11	3			

The Castle Bromwich Golf Club Limited.

Dr. Income and Expenditure Account for the Year ended 25th March, 1939. Cr.

1938 £	EXPENDITURE.	£ s. d.
711	To Rent, Rates, Taxes, Insurance, Telephone and Water ...	701 10 1
1,237	,, Wages, Ground Staff, etc., and Salaries	1,213 10 0
131	,, Expenditure on Course, Repairs and Renewals to Plant, etc. ...	160 18 7
53	,, Prize Medals, etc.	38 6 1
26	,, Subscription and Fees	29 3 0
58	,, Printing, Stationery and Stamps	74 3 5
5	,, Bank and Professional Charges ...	5 13 6
—	,, Resurfacing Car Park	50 0 0
20	,, Amount written off Plant and Tools, etc.	20 0 0
—	,, Amount written off Furniture and Lockers	27 11 0
17	,, Sundries	9 5 4
—	,, House Account Deficiency ...	51 19 0
117	,, Balance carried forward ...	—
£2,375		£2,382 0 0
	To Balance brought forward ...	192 8 6
	,, Balance carried forward ...	73 6 1
		£265 14 7

1938 £	INCOME.	£ s. d.
117	By Entrance Fees	105 0 0
1,792	,, Subscriptions	1,757 19 6
65	,, Locker Rents	62 5 0
233	,, Visitors' Fees	207 19 6
69	,, Competition Receipts	56 7 6
99	,, House Account Surplus ...	—
—	,, Balance carried forward ...	192 8 6
£2,375		£2,382 0 0
	By Balance brought forward from last year	265 14 7
		£265 14 7
	By Balance brought forward... ...	73 6 1

BALANCE SHEET, 25th March, 1939.

1938 £	LIABILITIES.	£ s. d.
456	Sundry Creditors	496 12 9
266	Surplus Account	73 6 1
£722		£569 18 10

1938 £	ASSETS.	£ s. d.	£ s. d.
298	CASH IN HAND AND AT BANK		160 0 8
124	Stock on hand, House Account		129 18 2
	PLANT, TOOLS AND IMPLEMENTS, ETC.		
	As at 25th March, 1938	250 0 0	
250	*Less* amount written off ...	20 0 0	
			230 0 0
	FURNITURE AND LOCKERS—		
	As at 25th March, 1938	50 0 0	
	Add Additions during year	27 11 0	
		77 11 0	
50	*Less* Amount written off	27 11 0	
			50 0 0
£722			£569 18 10

EXTRACTS FROM AGM MINUTE BOOK

June 1933

There were only 36 in attendance including Bill Dudley Evans . . . Agreed to move the 'Strawberry Tea' match from Wednesday to Saturday . . . The 'North versus South' match be recognised as a club fixture and that the teams be 'Captained' by the Club Captain and the Hon. Secretary. Recommended that a 'shower be installed in the Club House'.

June 1934

Membership quoted as 390 members . . . Recommendation that 'narrow trenches be dug between adjoining fairways and that any ball which crossed them be deemed out of bounds'.

June 1935

Balance Sheet indicated that House profit margin remained at 24.5% despite increased expenditure on rates, taxes and course maintenance . . . Visitor's Fees dropped by £110 . . . Recommended that 'to relieve congestion on competition days it would be appropriate to start on a Par 3 hole' . . . and that 'flag sticks be coloured in a different manner, in order to make the position of the holes clearer from a distance'.

June 1936

Much criticism of the Accounts presented . . . Decrease in turnover of £200 . . . Profit margin had dropped from 24.5% to 23.19% which was explained in a decrease in food sales profit margin from 12.6% to 6.13% whereas bar profits had risen by 1% . . . After acceptance of the Balance Sheet, members were told that 'they received good value for their £6.6.0. subscription charge and that providing this was kept up they had little cause for complaint'.

June 1937

Balance Sheet indicated that Bar takings had dropped by £49 despite profit margin increasing from 23% to 25% . . . it was pointed out that 'gross profit margins were arrived at after cost of feeding the staff had been charged' . . . the Committee had decided to form a Finance Committee 'in order to more efficiently control the finances of the Club'. Chairman G. J. Withington made reference to the golfing achievements of Harry

Hall, G. R. Chambers, E. C. Bowen and George Massey without actually saying what they were . . . Request made that 'long grass around greens should be cut and that on competition days, the holes on 'one shot' holes should be at the back of the greens and stones should be removed from bunkers.'

A letter from the President, The Earl of Bradford, was read out to the members in which he stated that 'he follows the fortunes of the Club with interest, and will continue to do all he can to promote its welfare, because he fully realises the importance of preserving facilities for sports and exercise in all parts of the country'. He also expressed 'his willingness to continue as President of the Club as long as members wanted it'.

June 1938

Balance Sheet indicated that House Income amounted to £3026 realising a profit of £817 with profit margin of 27% . . . Rent, rates, taxes and general expenditure had risen to £711. Balance of surplus for the year of £265.14.7 carried forward. Age of eligibility for the Veteran's Cup raised from 50 to 60 years . . . recommended that 'only six societies be allowed to play the course each year and that the Club should organise an 'Open' meeting'.

1939

There were several significant happenings during the course of the year which forever changed the ambitions of the members, and signalled the end of golf at Castle Bromwich. The Second World War had much to do with it, but a further letter from the President gave notice that he intended to terminate the Club's lease on the course at the end of the year. The AGM was called early in March to give warning to the members.

March 1939

The Club Membership numbered 360 comprising:

Life and honorary members	23
Ordinary members	232
Junior members	7
Lady members	81
Lady junior members	9
Country / Temporary members	15

Castle Bromwich won the Warwickshire County Championship with a record score and Harry Hall won the Bronze Medal . . . G. R. Chambers won the T. P. Cooke Cup . . . the First Team played 6 matches winning them all . . . the Second Team played 5 with only one win and 4 lossses and the 'B' Team played 7 winning 4 and 3 losses.

Obviously, at the time of printing the year's accounts, being unaware of the threat of losing the course, it was reported to members that the Club had taken over and developed an additional piece of land, and this had involved making a a new green and alteration to an existing one.

Referring to the Balance Sheet it was pointed out that there was a deficit of £192 and special expenditure during the year included the entire decoration of the Smoke Room and Steward's Quarters, paving of the Car Park and the provision of a Cash Register.

The address to the members stated:

'You have already had an intimation from your Committee to the effect that the position with regard to our continued use of the course is very uncertain. It is intended to make a full statement hereon at the Annual Meeting, and it is chiefly for that reason that this year's meeting has been held earlier than usual'.

The statement to the members which was read out after acceptance of the Balance Sheet was as follows:

The lease under which we now rent the Golf Course is due to expire in March 1948, nearly nine years hence. At every suitable opportunity for nearly 40 years since we first rented the course, (then on a yearly tenancy), we tried to have the terms of the lease so modified as to improve our position from the standpoint of security of tenure.

Although we have never regarded the lease as being wholly satisfactory from our point of view, we have, until very recently, held the opinion that we would be able to enjoy the use of the course for a much longer period than may yet prove to be the case. In our judgement we had good reasons for this belief.

In justification:

Our landlord, Lord Bradford, has been President of the Club for many years. Our contacts with him have always been of a distinctly friendly nature, he has been kept aware of our many improvements to the course and the Club House and surroundings. On different occasions he has expressed his attitude towards the Club and its future in a manner and in terms which induced the view that if there were any radical change in the position, it would at least, be preceded by ample notice of intended action.

The letter from Lord Bradford (mentioned earlier) addressed to the Hon. Secretary, Mr Arthur Fleet, dated June 17th 1937 was then read out once again to the members.

That letter at its first reading two years earlier, was the subject of widespread, enthusiastic comment by the Club's members, all the more as it was so much im keeping with his Lordship's repeated expressions of goodwill and interest in the Club's fortunes.

As recently as July 1938, negotiations were opened, primarily at the insistance of Lord Bradford's agent E. G. Potter, which ended in the renting the site of two cottages, now demolished, and the adjoining area, which forms part of the new 12th hole of the course. The letter from Mr Potter accompanying the completed documents, with the supplementary lease endorsed was dated December 9th 1938, just over five months ago.

The transaction described was not indicative of likely disturbance, on the contrary, it helped to encourage the Committee to embark on substantial expenditure on modification of the 11th hole, and the construction of a new 12th, both holes, as they are at present, only having been in play for two months.

On March 7th, an interview took place between Mr Potter and Mr Fleet at which Mr Fleet was told to his utter amazement, that it was intended to take possession of the whole of the course for reasons then indicated.

A meeting was sought with Lord Bradford at which he indicated that assurances that he had made from time to time, were made in good faith, but that circumstances had changed, and in view of death duties, taxation and general upkeep, he had no alternative but to take advantage of an opportunity which had presented itself to dispose of the land. He stated that if he did not take advantage of the offer he had received, it was likely that the Birmingham Corporation would put a compulsory purchase on the land at a considerably lower price.

Despite rigorous arguments and appeals, he insisted that he wanted the Club to vacate the course at the end of the year. It was also learnt that he had sold some 4 acres of land to 'Ansells' adjacent to the 4th green and they intended to build a Public House there. 'Ansells' however were quite happy for the Club to use the land until such time that they needed it. and intimated that this would not before March 1940.

Mr Potter did appear to be determined to get the Club off the site and pointed out that as there was a gun site on the course, it would not be possible to use the course. This was refuted by the Club Committee who had already obtained permission to 'play around' the gun site by the War Office. The gun site comprised a 3.7 inch Anti Aircraft gun with accommodation for the detachment, and as a result of their occupation, the course had to be reduced to 15 holes.

In the event the 1939–1945 intervened, all building plans were scrapped, and the Club obtained a reprieve, albeit through tragic circumstances, and remained at Castle Bromwich until 1946. By December of 1939, alternative sites at Packington Park, Moxhull, Maxstoke and several others were inspected. An option was obtained at Maxstoke Park for about £50, but the move was unavoidably put in abeyance for the duration of the war.

ITEMS OF INTEREST FROM THE WAR YEARS.

1941

Arthur Fleet resigned as Club Secretary, after some 32 years in office, due to moving to Wolverhampton, had been in Office since 1909 . . . Lord Bradford reduced the Club's rent in view of the disruption caused by having a gun battery on the course. Nellie Shaw who was the wife of Horace Shaw, recalled that 'golf continued to be played during the war and that some 50 bombs had fallen on the course due to its close proximity to factories and Castle Bromwich Airfield.' Horace Shaw at the time was Head Greenkeeper following the retirement of R. Marks (father of Tom Marks).

Frank Blakey recalls that on one occasion he played early one morning in a Medal competition, and that towards the end of the round he carefully avoided fresh bomb holes on the fairway, He remembered that he had a good card and was quite annoyed when he reached the Club House to find that the Competition had been cancelled as one or two of the craters contained unexploded bombs.

1942

An attempt was made to obtain compensation from the War Office for the inconvenience caused by the gun battery, and the loss of several holes . . . there was no response as apparently the President had actually sold the

BALANCE SHEET, 25th March, 1942.

LIABILITIES.

1941 £		£ s. d.	£ s. d.
644	Sundry Creditors		597 6 11
250	General Reserve		250 0 0
	Income and Expenditure Account—		
	Balance brought forward from last year	217 0 10	
	Less Excess of Expenditure over Income	17 7 7½	
217			199 13 2½
£1,111			£1,047 0 1½

ASSETS.

1941 £		£ s. d.	£ s. d.
498	CASH IN HAND AND AT BANK		378 18 2½
58	Sundry Debtors		1 10 0
325	Stock on hand, House Account		456 11 11
	PLANT, TOOLS AND IMPLEMENTS, ETC.		
	As at 25th March, 1941	180 0 0	
	Less Amount written off	20 0 0	
180			160 0 0
50	FURNITURE AND LOCKERS— As at 25th March, 1941		50 0 0
£1,111			£1,047 0 1½

The Balance Sheet for the year recorded a loss of £17.7.7.

land to them . . . thanks were extended at the AGM to: G. Stubbings for supplying and erecting an Air Raid Shelter; A. E. Shaw for providing and installing a bath in place of the foot bath; H. T. Perry for providing new flags for the greens; M. MacDonagh for obtaining new tyres for the tractor; Harry Crump for supplying new external notice boards and to R. Evans for providing spare parts for the mowers.

Membership had dropped to 205 members comprising:

Ordinary members	116
Life and Honorary	25
Junior members	1
Lady members	42
Junior Ladies	1
Country members	20

1943

A new member on the Committee, one who was to serve the Club for many years subsequently – Douglas Marston . . . Doug had joined Castle Bromwich as a teenager in 1927 . . . problems for the Bridge Club – playing cards were in short supply and the members experienced difficulties in obtaining replacements . . . a new frying pan was requested for use in the kitchen, permits were needed for such purchases, and on a happier note a sum of £61.10.0. was raised for the Merchant Navy.

1944

A new Secretary – Bill Dudley Evans. Bill had joined the Club as a Junior in 1921, he became Assistant Secretary in 1933, and was to retain an association with the Club for over 70 years, surely an achievement worthy of entry in the Guinness Book of Records; a payment of £1 was paid to sons and daughters of Club Members who were serving in the Armed Forces . . . complaints made regarding visitors who were abusing the Club Rule of only 12 visits per year.

1945

Club Captain – Bill Dudley Evans. Long serving Treasurer John Hall and two past Captains, T. A. Neale and E. G. Lawrence all passed away . . . a lengthy lease at Maxstoke offered and negotiations more or less finalised regarding move.

1946

A Special General Meeting of members was held at the Club House on May 11th to consider the proposals concerning the transfer to Maxstoke Park.

A brief outline of the proposals put to members indicated that:

'Total area of the Park is 130 acres, of which 124 acres could be leased for 50 years as a Golf Course, and 6 acres can be taken on 99 year lease for a Club House and Staff Quarters. The rental would be approximately the same as pre war rental at Castle Bromwich (for 90 acres), and for the first ten years would be set at £175 per annum.

Substantial modern brick buildings are available for use as temporary accommodation until such time as it is possible to obtain a building licence for the proposed new Club House.

It is the recommendation of the Committee that members supporting the Maxstoke proposition will not be called upon to pay an increased subscription for at least 2 years, but that this would not apply to new members'.

It is interesting to note that in a much longer document that gave much more information about the move it stated that:

'The six acres of ground that we can secure for 99 years, will be more than enough for our permanent Club House. It will permit provision of a green, or greens, for bowling, for tennis and similar sports facilities.

When the time comes that we are permitted to build, we suggest the incorporation in the Club House, of a billiard room.

Within the six acres of ground we recommend the erection of two dwelling houses, as Steward's and Greenkeeper's cottages.

The making of a limited number of 'Life Memberships' on payment of a fixed amount might be considered'.

Chapter Two

A Short History of Maxstoke Castle

Maxstoke Castle was built around 1345 by William de Clinton, Earl of Huntington for his nephew John de Clynton, who inherited the Castle on the death of his uncle in 1354. The description quoted for the licence granted by Edward III was for 'a dwelling place' rather than a castle. In reality, it was a 'fortified manor house', and could have withstood attack by marauding gangs which abounded in the 14th Century.

The Castle has a rectangular courtyard, surrounded by a 2 metre thick curtain wall beyond which is a moat. At each corner of the courtyard is an octagonal tower, two of which contained accommodation for retainers. In the centre of the east wall is a projecting gatehouse from which access is gained to the moat walk.

In bygone days the approach to the Castle was by way of the old roadway which nowadays crosses the golf course, from the track which enters the course at the rear of the 15th tee.

During the First World War and for a short period afterwards, the Castle was used as a convalescent home for wounded soldiers. In 1934, Beaumount Fetherston-Dilke and his family moved out of the Castle and went to live at Leamington Spa. The Castle was leased to a syndicate who turned it into a Country Club. They spent a considerable amount of money renovating the Castle, and on the grounds, but went into liquidation with the outbreak of the Second World War in 1939.

The War Office then took over, and requisitioned the Castle and other buildings as accommodation for an army unit. From 1940, the Ministry of Aircraft Production used the Castle for the safe storage of aircraft engine components, and they remained there until January 1946, when Beaumont Fetherston-Dilke and his wife Stella returned to take up residence again at the Castle.

They were met by a scene of dirt, disorder and dilapidation, both inside and outside the Castle. The grounds and gardens had been totally neglected and a prisoner of war camp, now the practice area, was still in use. A compensation amount awarded by the Government for the damage caused was sufficient to redecorate one room.

No major work of modernisation or improvement was undertaken between 1946 and 1964 and the structure and interior of the Castle declined.

In 1946, the parkland at the Castle, which for many years had provided grazing, was leased to Castle Bromwich Golf Club. The Castle stables were used as the Club house. Immediately work commenced on setting out a golf course, initially for just 9 holes, but in stages to 12, then 15 and finally to 18.

In 1947, shortly after the course was opened, Beaumount Fetherston-Dilke was elected as President of what is now Maxstoke Park Golf Club. He was a good friend to the Club and remained as President until his death in 1968 at the wonderful age of 92.

A panoramic view from the southern tower of the castle taken in more tranquil times before golf was introduced to Maxstoke Park

After the death of Beaumount, his son Charles B. Fetherston Dilke inherited Maxstoke. He retired from the Royal Navy with the rank of Captain and settled there with his wife, Pauline. They embarked on a major programme of restoration to the Castle over a period of ten years. Charles Fetherston-Dilke was elected President of the Golf Club in 1968: he often

Entrance to Maxstoke Castle

walked the course with his dog and invariably would pass the time of day and exchange a few friendly words.

In 1989, Charles and his wife moved out of the Castle to Keeper's Cottage adjoining the Park. and shortly after he stood down as Club President after some 20 years. Their son Michael, with his wife Rosemary and family, moved into the Castle in 1989 and undertook a further programme of restoration and alteration to bring the living accommodation in the Castle more to the needs of a young family. Michael and Rosemary thereby continue the pattern of family ownership and occupation of Maxstoke Castle, which will extend to 400 years in 1999.

Michael C. Fetherston-Dilke was elected President of Maxstoke Park Golf Club in 1996, coinciding with the Club's 50 year occupancy at Maxstoke, but more significantly continued the family line of Presidency held by his father, Charles, and grandfather, Beaumount.

EXTRACT FROM 'THE BORDERLAND OF BIRMINGHAM' by J. N. O. HINGELEY in 1906

"There are two pleasant walks from Coleshill which the initiated seldom fail to avail themselves of. One leads across Coleshill Park towards Castle Bromwich. The other and less known, is entered from the churchyard, and leads on, downhill and across streams by pleasant rustic bridges, to Maxstoke Park. The distance is about a mile, and on the way we cross the junction railway a few yards from Coleshill Station – the smallest, most difficult to discover, and least used station within fifty miles of Birmingham. Have no fear of trains – one passes each way daily.

Thence onwards there is plenty to see and hear. The whirr of partridges, the call of pheasants, the scurried flight of rabbits anticipate one's entrance to the Park itself. Keep to the 'public footpath' and eschew all other roads unless 'business' takes you castlewards. Let the velvety turf – hundreds of years agrowing – and sight of timber, fur and feather, satisfy you. Look out for the rabbits in the thin coppice to the left, and keep a sharp eye for the first sign of the fine herd of deer. Usually they may be descried in the vicinity of the lake, which our path divides into two unequal portions. And now let us take our ease under the leafy branches, and as we look towards the massive walls of the Castle itself 'so near and yet so far' we can gossip of its traditions, its history, before resuming our walk to the Priory which its one time owners founded.

Unfortunately its interior is, to the world at large, terra incognito. *Its owner has consistently resisted every inducement to make the*

Castle a show place, only yielding to the soft suasion of the 'Warwickshire Photographic Society' to permit photographs of its wonderfully interesting apartments. And if you would know what like is the building which lies within those four square walls, you must hie you to Birmingham and consult the records of that same survey. Then you may see most excellent 'counterfeit presentments' of the noble banqueting hall, the chapel, the kitchen, and the many other features of this noteworthy Plantagenet building.

It was built – or rebuilt possibly – as the result of a 'licence to crenellate' granted in 1346 to William de Clinton by Edward III. Of history – popularly so called – it has none. No seige, no garrison, no royal visitor, no murder even – nothing of note is connected with the building, unless indeed, most notable of all, it be the record that a strong fortress in the hands of wealthy owners, has passed through six centuries of unbroken peace! It is unquestionably to that fact that it owes its existence as a residence today, since no occasion for 'dismantling' it has ever arisen".

WARTIME AT MAXSTOKE

In 1940 Maxstoke Castle was taken over by the Ministry of Aircraft Production and used for the safe storage of aircraft engine components which had been manufactured in Coventry. The section of the Park adjacent to Castle Lane was taken over in 1942 for the erection of a Prisoner of War Camp. The buildings on the site were wooden huts, and were laid out in a line to the right of our current roadway, where the main practice area is now laid out.

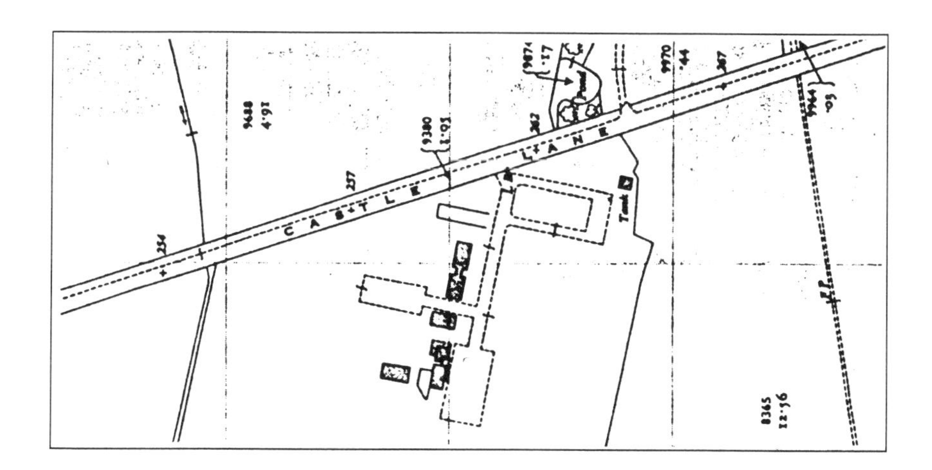

For the most part the prisoners were Italian, but in the later stages of the war, Germans arrived. The Italians had a relatively easy time and most of them worked on local farms, and were quite happy with their lot. At the end of the war the Italians were sent home fairly quickly, but the Germans did not get released until 1948.

A letter in the 'Coventry Evening Telegraph' some years ago from a Mrs Gibson, whose husband ran a nursery and market garden at Meriden, indicated that several Italians were sent to help in the gardens and greenhouses.

A group of Italians taken at Maxstoke

Another letter from a gentleman from Atherstone related that he often stopped by the Camp and threw cigarettes over the fence to the prisoners. Tony Reading recalled as 'naughty schoolboys' taunting the prisoners and getting chased down Castle Lane.

I have made contact with two Germans who were at Maxstoke, Horst Huhn and Walter Roske. Horst went home in 1948, but returned in 1951 and married a local Coleshill girl, who worked in the Coleshill Post Office. He arrived at Maxstoke in September 1945, after being captured by Americans at the Battle of the Bulge, had been in various camps, and arrived at Maxstoke from Moreton in the Marsh.

He recalls that "the entrance to the Camp was more or less where our present driveway is. The first building was where we were searched each day on return from ditch digging or whatever other duties. Opposite was a building which was used as a 'theatre'. The other barracks were positioned gable end on, facing the driveway. At the back of the Camp were large water tanks, and as the Camp was overcrowded, we were housed in a large bell tent, several of which were erected to the left of the Camp driveway".

Present day members may well have noticed that in dry summers, circular patterns of discoloured grass are evident along the 3rd fairway,

The Fountain and Buildings of the old Prisoner of War Camp

which clearly identifies where the tents were erected.

Horst states that "the hierachy was simple; German POWs were 'policed' by other Germans with discipline administered by a German Camp Commandant. He was an extremely unpleasant and autocratic man.

Overall responsibility for the Camp came under the care of an English Camp Commander whom I remember to be a "pleasant, fair man who treated us well". (The person he refers to was Major Atkins, who after the war retired from Army Service, and turned out for the local cricket team at Nether Whitacre).

He goes on to say that "the English 'Tommies' were always fair to us, although on my arrival at the Camp, a pair of fine American gloves that I had 'come by' were 'confiscated'. Luckily, the cigarettes that I had saved and carefully hidden in an old sugar bag were never discovered".

Major Atkins

"Our days were spent ditch digging, and the sorties we made were highlighted by the many scenic routes taken by our friendly English bus driver as we made our way around the Warwickshire countryside. Generally the time at the Camp was uneventful, but I have the memory of a 'run in' with the German Commandant. As breakfast consisted of a watery gruel described as porridge, I decided to stay in bed and miss breakfast. One of the German 'camp police' saw me and threatened to report me if I refused to attend breakfast. I told him to do so if he wished. He did and I was summoned to the German Commandant.

When I arrived at his hut he wasn't there so I waited. After some time he did arrive and walked past me and into the hut – so I decided to keep him waiting as I had waited. After some time he called me into his hut and I walked in and stood before him". "Why didn't you salute me?" he demanded angrily. I replied that "in my opinion, my war was over and so were my saluting days. He was furious and ordered me out of the hut. He then ordered me in again and gave me another chance to salute which I refused to do and so we achieved deadlock."

Later I was informed that for my insubordinate behaviour, I was to be given extra duties in addition to ditch digging, and was told to clean the English Sergeants Mess every evening. In the event this punishment never took place, as I was moved to Henley in Arden (the 'naughty boys' Camp) the very next week".

"Time passed quickly, and the one harvest that we had been told to bring in before being sent home, became two, then three. In June 1948 I was sent home, but in 1951 I returned to the 'green and pleasant land' this time to stay".

Walter Roske was only a teenager when he was called into the Army. He was injured and captured quite early on and sent to the the UK. He describes his experiences of wartime and the time that he spent in hospital and as a POW.

"At the age of 16½ I had to give up my apprenticeship because I had to 'join up'. I trained in Poland and joined the 'Westfront'. On 29th April 1944 I was captured and taken to Brussels. After a short time I was transported to England. The journey was by bus and train to Inverness in Scotland. After 2 months I was taken to Grimsby Prison. Two or three months later I arrived at Maxstoke fit for work. As a 17 year old youth I spent 4 years there, until I was allowed home in March 1948.

It was an experience and a change for me as for many other prisoners, to work on a farm. In the evenings in the camp, I made toys, aeroplanes, chess figures and later rope slippers which I tried to sell outside the camp. That is how I came to know the Hardman family. who had four daughters.

(The Hardmans lived in Marston Green and I have known them for over 50 years)

From then on life in the camp was not so sad and lonely, as I was often invited to join the family at their home and was treated like a son. I made a few repairs. I was allowed to call them Mama and Papa, the daughters were Margaret, Dorothy, Gwen and Barbara. The Christmas that I spent with this family I have never forgotten even to this day.

In 1948 I was repatriated and on 6th March 1948 I rejoined my parents. Happy to be home, but sad to leave the Hardman family to whom I owe so much and taught me how to be a young man".

"A connection remains however. Up until 1989, Christmas cards and photos were always exchanged. Then in 1990 I was invited over to a Pearl wedding anniversary of Barbara, who was 14 years of age when I knew her, and her husband. They celebrated 30 years of marriage with 70 people present, and I was invited along with my wife. I cannot express with words, how I was

Walter Roske at Maxstoke

welcomed into this family. Sadly, Mr and Mrs. Hardman were no longer alive, but the four daughters now all have families, children and grand children. We had five unforgettable days.

They brought me to Maxstoke and I stood at the camp entrance where for four years I lived. After so many years, everything looked so peaceful, no more barracks, everything had gone. At such a view I obviously shed a few tears. A few years later the couple who celebrated their anniversary came to visit and I was able to show them my Berlin. Unfortunately, I only have one picture of the camp which I could let you see. Could you make use of my pass and documents from the camp? I cannot remember the names of any other prisoners. I am 69 years old and a pensioner. I worked for 40 years in the Berlin Gas Works".

At the time of Walter's visit to England in 1991, Margaret the eldest of the Hardman girls, now the wife of George Cuthbertson, contacted Horst Huhn and a meeting was arranged between the two Germans. They spent a few hours together at this reunion, some 50 years after they were together at Maxstoke.

Another letter in the 'Coventry Evening Telegraph' from Frank Rowell who recalls that in 1949 "he and several volunteers went to Maxstoke and dismantled two huts that they had purchased from the Ministry of Works. These were from the POW Camp, one of them was the Chapel and the other sleeping quarters. He recalled that the Chapel was a work of art inside with beautiful paintings and glowing with colour". The huts were transported to the Canley Social Club and were attached to the side of the main entrance to the original club building which only had one room. The Club opened Easter 1950.

The other reminder of the old Prisoner of War Camp, which visitors to

Walter Roske and his wife Herta in 1994

Horst Huhn and his wife with Walter Roske in 1991

Bench fabricated by Italian prisoners in present day position adjacent to the 2nd Tee.

Maxstoke can examine, are the two remaining stone benches which are situated alongside the second and ninth tees. These were made by the Italians in a 'terrazzo' chipping fashion and have inset chess boards in the centre of the seating slabs. Originally there were four, but unfortunately the others were damaged. On the earlier photograph showing the POW Camp they are clearly evident spaced around the central ornamental structure.

No. of enclosure in Form 48
Serial No. in A. & D. Book or in Form 38 — 5006/44

Army Form I 1220.
R.A.F. Form 39.

HOSPITAL OR SICK LIST RECORD CARD.

Army or R.A.F. No. 605214 — Branch or Trade
Surname ROSKE — Christian Names Walter
Rank Axn. — Unit R.A.D. A.B.&.C. 2/391.
Age 17 — Total Service not known — Under instruction as
H ital or Station rendering this form — Raigmore Hospital, Inverness.
Dates of:—
Arrival as direct admission 24/10/44 from Horton E.M.S. Hospital, Epsom.
,, transfer — from
Discharge to duty
,, as an invalid or to unit for invaliding
Transfer 16/1/45 to 16 P.W. Camp, Aberladie.
Death
Number of days under treatment 85 days
CLINICAL NOTES:
Disease or injury S.W. left leg

Section of medical card of Walter Roske after treatment at Haigmore Hospital, Inverness, discharging him to POW camp at Aberladie as an invalid.

Chapter Three

Early Days At Maxstoke

Immediately after VJ day, (the end of the war against Japan) members of the Club revived the plans for an alternative site, and the Committee looked into the option obtained for moving to Maxstoke Park. At that time the Club had a 'princely' sum of £2500, which they had received from the sale of turf taken from the greens at Castle Bromwich.

A rental was agreed with Beaumount Fetherston-Dilke. With virtually no money, the remainimng members, now reduced to about 70, decided to do the work themselves at Maxstoke.

Volunteer work parties went over daily to prepare the new course. J. P. Nicholson was the guiding light at this time and supervised the work requirements, apparently tirelessly and with tremendous energy and enthusiasm.

At first only 9 holes were laid, and the greens and fairways were more or less mown areas of the park. These holes were on the far side of the lake away from our present Club House, and today form the majority of our 'back' 9 holes. Areas of the park were planted with potatoes. The Prisoner of War Camp was still in use at that time, and the Stables at the Castle needed refurbishing before any hope of accommodation was entertained.

Members still retained 'Haye House' at Castle Bromwich as their Club House, and during those early days, members commuted to Maxstoke, usually by coach at weekends. Albert Green who was Assistant Greenkeeper at Castle Bromwich, took over as Head Greenkeeper and travelled daily on his bicycle from the old course.

Tons of ashes were obtained from 'Hams Hall' which Tom Marks remembers were free, but that we had to pay 12 shillings and sixpence (62½ pence) per lorry load, for transporting them. Good quality soil was obtained at 8 shillings and sixpence (42½ pence) per load whilst sand cost a seemingly high price of £10 per load.

As the Club had virtually no equipment, a bulldozer was hired from time to time, to level fairways and to lay out new greens. A local farmer, Mr Tyack, loaned the members a harrowing machine, and many other items of equipment were begged and borrowed to supplement the meagre equipment that the Club did have.

This equipment was originally stored in an old 10 bay Tithe Barn situated close to the Castle, but that building collapsed on a very windy night in the '60s. Originally, each hole had a 'temporary' tee laid when the course was laid out, but some of them did become permanent.

In due course the 9 holes came into play, and a Professional Grenville Lovatt was appointed, his Shop was a wooden hut found at Maxstoke which was moved and positioned in the Castle Courtyard.

THE FIRST 9 HOLE COURSE AT MAXSTOKE

Hole 1 (Now our 11th) A new tee had to be raised adjacent to the moat and loads of soil were needed to achieve this It was originally intended that the Green would be positioned further along our present 11th fairway, but in the event it was situated well back, more or less where our present 150 yard marker is set, by the large oak tree on the right of the present fairway.

Hole 2 (Now our 12th) This hole was intended to be a par 4, but started as a par 3 with the tee position roughly where the fairway bunker is located. There was much rabbit activity in this area and considerable filling in of warrens was carried out.

Hole 3 (Now our 13th) Considerable quantities of soil removed on both sides of the green to make bunkers. Soil spread at rear of new 6th hole towards 7th tee to make up ground.

Hole 4 (Now our 14th) Green originally laid, but not satisfactory due to area being prone to wetness; turf was lifted, 4 inches of ash spread over whole area and turf relaid.

Hole 5 (Now our 8th) Considerable filling in of approaches and front of green. 14 loads of ashes were used on the green. Early criticism of tree on left of green, and recommendations were made that it be lopped to improve line in to green. The tree has survived and still causes problems to wayward approaches.

Hole 6 (Now our 7th) New tee made well back, but reservations that it might compromise players on the 5th green. Presumably they were happy with the position as it has remained to this day. Tons of ashes spread at back of green towards 7th tee.

Hole 7 (Now our 15th) Fencing on left hand side repaired to prevent cattle encroaching on to course. Apparently a rough area of the park as fairway had to be levelled and long grass cut between this hole and the 4th hole.

Hole 8 (Now our 16th) Rough area at right of green excavated to provide a shallow bunker.

Maxstoke Park Golf Club

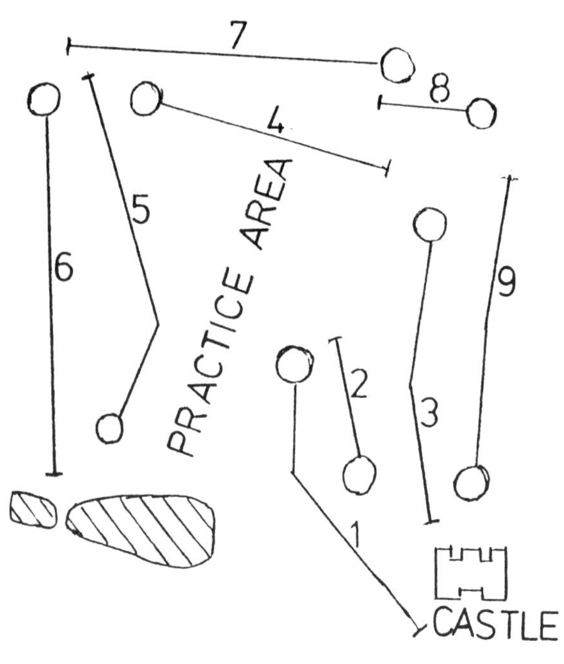

1 | 2 | STYMIE 3 | MEASURE 4 | 5 | 6

Castle Bromwich Golf Club Ltd.

Handicap............................ *Date*..

Name of Player.. *Competition*..

Marker's Score	Hole	Length	Bogey	Stroke Index	Score	Result
	1	375	5	9		
	2	203	3	15		
	3	444	5	7		
	4	335	4	13		
	5	506	5	3		
	6	468	5	5		
	7	318	4	11		
	8	137	3	17		
	9	416	4	1		
		3202	38			

Marker's Score	Hole	Length	Bogey	Stroke Index	Score	Result
	10	375	5	10		
	11	203	3	16		
	12	444	5	8		
	13	335	4	14		
	14	506	5	4		
	15	468	5	6		
	16	318	4	12		
	17	137	3	18		
	18	416	4	2		
		3202	38			
		3202	38			
		6404	76			

Marker's Signature...

BOGEY PLAY.

Holes won..................................

,, lost..................................

Result

In Bogey Competitions Competitors must enter their actual score for all holes won or halved.

If hole is won put +
If hole is halved put O
If hole is lost put —

MEDAL PLAY.

Gross Score..............................

Handicap..............................

Net Score

Course layout in 1950

Hole 9 (Now our 17th) Considerable amounts of sand needed and much rolling to produce an acceptable base for turfing. Fencing along left hand side needed extensive repair in order to prevent sheep entering the course, which happened frequently.

For some time the greens were all guarded with a single strand wire fence to prevent damage from animals and to reduce the amount of unnecessary intrusion on to the approaches.

I played the course when it was 9 hole, with a member Dick Coward, and my recollection was with regard to the density and height of the rough. Apparently the Ministry of Agriculture insisted that it was left each year so that 2 cuttings of hay could be taken from the rough areas.

Hand mowers were used to cut the greens, many of them belonging to members, and the fairways were cut by gang mowers powered by an old 1928 'Fordson' Tractor. The large wheels had tyres with integral metal spikes, and these 'Dunlop' designed prototype tyres were believed to be the first tailored for use on golf courses.

In 1948, the expiration of the lease at 'Haye House' terminated and the members then took over the Stables at Maxstoke for their headquarters. The entrance to the course was by way of the drive leading to the Castle. The mens changing rooms were located in the old Coach House, and the Ladies' changing room and locker room flanked the inner courtyard alongside the small lounge/club house.

The accommodation was dismal, sparse and inadequate. It was cold and yet because of its antiquity it had an air of history and charm. The lounge was a very dark, high ceilinged room, no larger than our present 19th hole bar, and had small windows almost at roof height. The room was heated with an open fireplace. Members had to take care in manoeuvering to the Bar due to an uneven floor, the threadbare Persian carpet, and the problem of avoiding several wooden pillars which extended from floor to ceiling. The small Bar occupied a corner of the room. The walls were bare brick which had been covered with gloss paint.

It was accepted however, that for the time being there was not much chance of making any significant improvement, and that eventually the Club would need to provide alternative and better accommodation if it was to survive.

The Annual Report for the year ending March 1949 reported a loss of £1201 for the year. The Committee stated "that applications for membership is encouraging, and that they had every confidence in the future of the Club, providing sufficient additional finance is forthcoming". It was recommended that 'the Annual Subscription *which had remained unchanged at £6.6.0. for 25 years* should be increased to £8.8.0. for Full Male Members, and to £4.4.0. for Lady Members'.

The membership was quoted as 168 members shown as:

Life and Honorary Members	17
Full Male Members	91
Junior Members	2
Lady Members	20
Lady Junior Members	1
Country Members	10
Temporary Non Playing Members	27

Amongst items of expenditure were £135 paid to the War Office in connection for turf removed from Castle Bromwich, and £200 paid to the Landlord, Lord Bradford, in connection with dilapidations at 'Haye House'. These items were explained away as 'being a final settlement of claims which had originally been considerably in excess of the amounts finally paid'.

It was pointed out to members that 'a sum in the order of £2000 would be required to carry the Club over the next two to three years at Maxstoke'. The following proposals were put to members as a way of achieving this figure:

1. A limited number of Life Memberships be granted at a suggested figure of £100.
2. By way of loans to the Club, free of interest.
3. By a personal guarantee to the Bank
4. By gifts and donations.

Mr John Ralston, the Chairman stated that 'the Committee were prepared to guarantee raising £750 towards the sum, if the general body of the members would undertake to raise the balance of £1250.

Reading from the Minute Book it was apparent that the AGM was a stormy one. Members argued that the condition of the course was not satisfactory, and that they were not prepared to pay increased subscription charges and the £8.0.0 motion was defeated. The Secretary, Bill Dudley-Evans was asked to write to all members in an appeal to contribute to one or more of the four money raising proposals

This meeting was the last one held at Castle Bromwich, and it was agreed that Mr Beaumount Fetherston-Dilke be appointed as President in view of the move to Maxstoke.

As a final severance from the old course, the Castle Bromwich flag pole was taken down and erected at Maxstoke. New wooden Car Park Notices were manufactured at a cost of £6.15.0. and an alloy Badge was fabricated for fitment to member's cars

The original concept for eighteen holes at Maxstoke was to extend the

course to the left of the existing boundary of the original 6th hole (our 7th) towards the Greenkeeper's House, now occupied by our former President, Captain Charles Fetherston-Dilke. Unfortunately, the farmer, who was Chairman of the Land Agricultural Committee would not agree to part with the land. It was therefore decided, to lay out 6 more holes on the Castle Lane side of the Lakes, thus forming 15 holes. This was to be done in two stages, and because of the shortfall in finance, it was to be completed by members.

All manner of additional labour was co-opted. Boy Scouts and boys from Father Hudson's Homes were recruited, and picked up stones. Tom Marks recalls that our present eighteenth fairway was one of the areas where potatoes had been planted. These were collected by the boys and taken to the kitchens of the Clubhouse where John Ralston made 'buckets of chips' which more or less fed the boys during the school holidays.

Most of the course maintenance and preparation at this time was done with the help of member farmers, who used their own equipment for harrowing, spraying, cutting and seeding, at no cost to the Club.

Chris Aldridge, another member, a local Coal Merchant, used his lorries to fetch and carry soil, and to remove most of the unwanted debris, again free of charge.

Frank Blakey, who for some time was Green's Chairman, remembers filling a boggy area with dead tree trunks which were dragged from various parts of the course. He could not recall where this was, but Tom Marks indicated that it was a wet hollow at the far side of the lake which is now well established as our ninth tee. Frank, an octogenarian, came from Castle Bromwich and is probably the oldest member from the old course.

STAGE TWO – ADDITION OF THREE MORE HOLES . . . 12 HOLES COURSE

Three further holes were added which caused considerable re-numbering of the course:

A new short hole of 140 yards was added to the left of the 1st green, this became the 2nd hole.

Another short hole 210 yards was made across the lake, and became the 7th. (now our 9th)

A new hole was laid past the end of the lake. 365 yards long it became the 8th (now our 10th). This hole caused considerable problems, it was invariably wet and during winter months the lake often overflowed and the hole became unplayable. On many occasions large fish were washed on to the fairway and had to be rescued, and placed in the far lake. The existing 2nd hole was extended to 345 yards, and became the 3rd. (this is now our 12th.)

The original 6th became the 9th (now our 7th)
The original 7th became the 10th (now our 15th)
The original 8th became the 11th (now our 16th)
The original 9th became the 12th (now our 17th)

COURSE LAYOUT – 1951

Hole	*Length*	*Par*	*Hole*	*Length*	*Par*
1	375	4	10	330	4
2	140	3	11	159	3
3	345	4	12	420	4
4	407	4			
5	324	4			
6	477	5			
7	210	3			
8	365	4			
9	480	5			
OUT	3123	36	IN	1769	22

Holes 1, 2 and 3 were repeated to give 15 holes.

TOTAL 4892 YARDS (58)

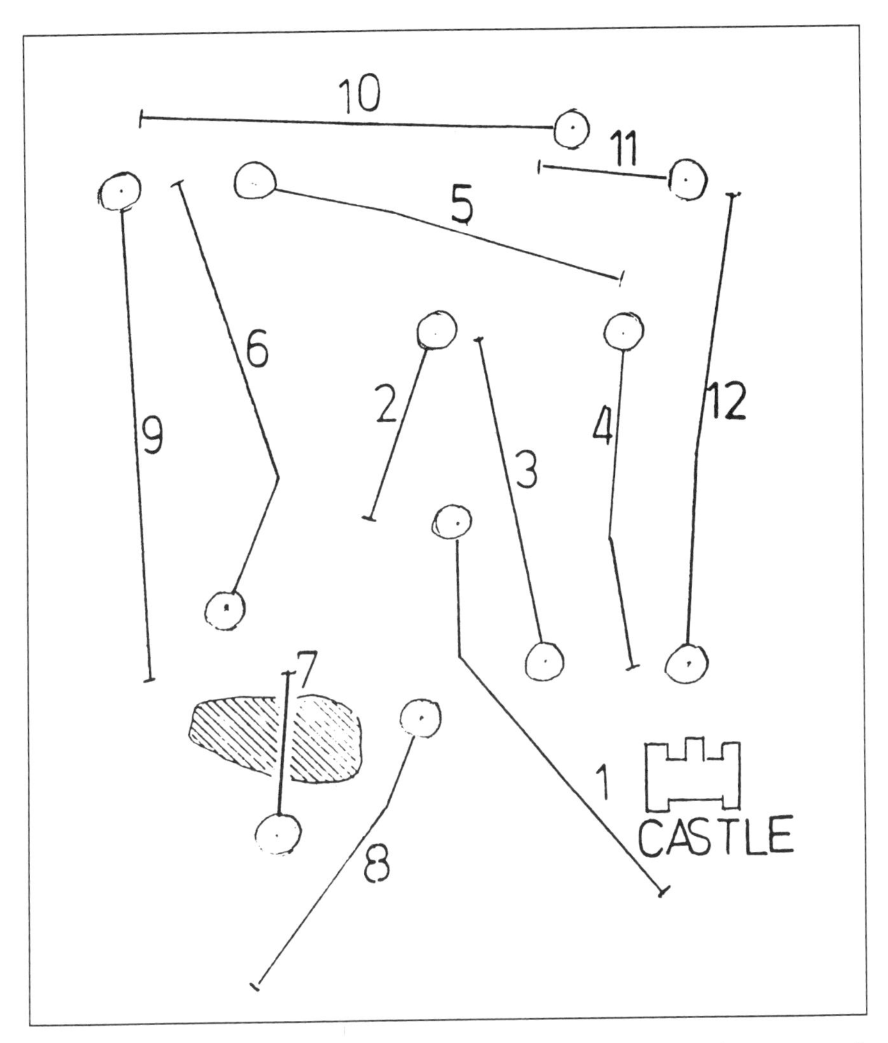

At the AGM of 1951, reference was made to the fact that the greens of the 2nd and 8th holes had needed to be re-constructed, and that the level of the 3rd green had been raised and returfed. The 2nd hole referred to was in fact a new hole, as the original plan was for five additional holes, but in the laying out of the extended course, the Committee took the opportunity to add this additional short hole, and lengthen the original 2nd hole to a par 4. Apparently, all of this work had been done by members.

STAGE THREE – FURTHER ADDITION OF THREE HOLES TO CREATE 15 HOLE COURSE.

The setting out of these additional holes had been in progress at the same time as the earlier three holes were laid out, but there were considerable problems due to the dampness of the areas involved, and the difficulty in achieving satisfactory drainage.

The three new holes were on the Castle Lane side of the lakes, and today they are identified as our 18th, 4th and 6th.

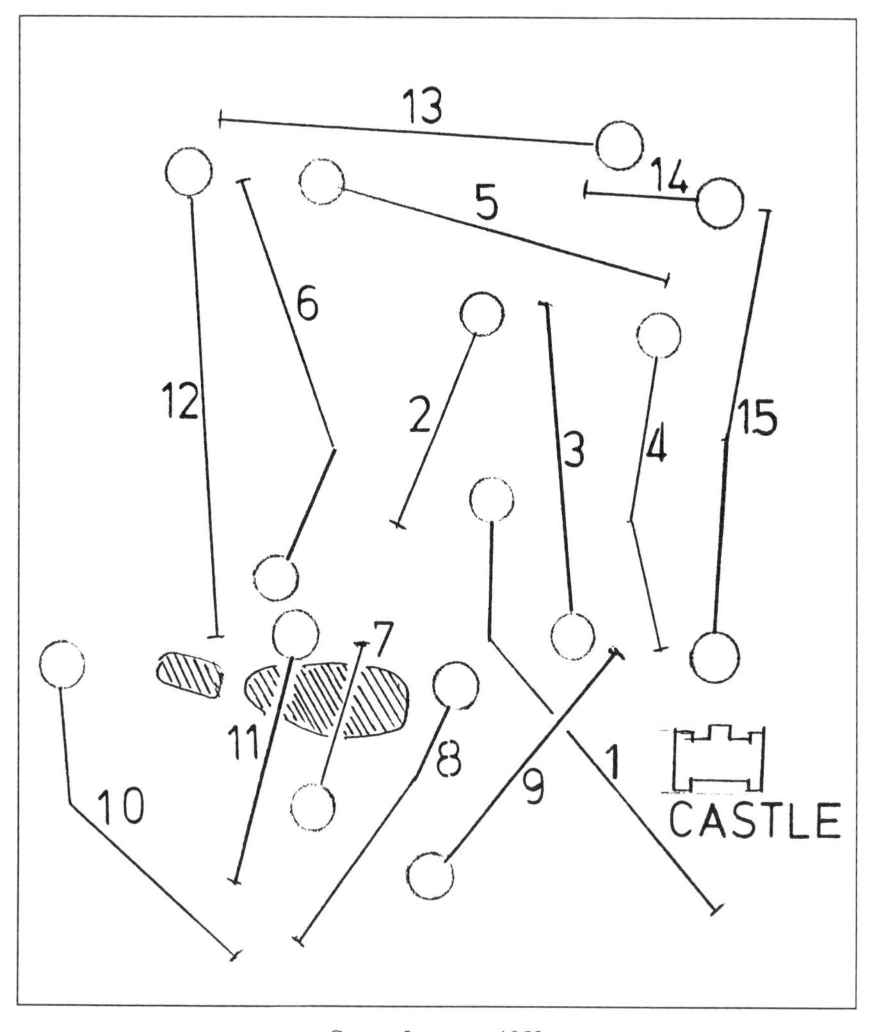

Course Layout – 1953

Hole No.	*Length Yards*	*Par*	*Hole No.*	*Length Yards*	*Par*
1	455	4	10	389	4
2	140	3	11	356	4
3	345	4	12	480	5
4	407	4	13	330	4
5	324	4	14	159	3
6	477	5	15	420	4
7	210	3			
8	365	4	Holes 1, 2 and 3 were repeated to give 18 holes.		
9	356	4			
	3079	35	IN	3084	35
			OUT	3079	35
				6163	70

In those early days at Maxstoke when the course was being laid out, the following gentlemen acted as Green's Chairman and supervised the operation with much support from Club members.

STAGE ONE (9 Holes)
John P. Nicholson, Vernon Wilder and John Ralston.

STAGE TWO (12 Holes)
John Ralston and Frank T. Blakey

STAGE THREE (15 Holes)
Frank T. Blakey and Tom Marks.

At the 1953 AGM, the Chairman Vernon Wilder, made complimentary remarks with regard to the satisfactory progress that the Club had made in the year, and to the fact that a profit of £71 had been made, which he considered to be a better result than that shown by other clubs in the area. What he did not say was that in the middle of the year there had not been enough money to pay the staff wages and the rent.

At an emergency meeting of the Committee which had been called, they were more or less told that 'the Club had probably come to the end of the road'. Fortunately, and today we must be forever grateful to them, most of the Committee Members, felt that to go under after so much hard work was unthinkable. Frank Walker, the Treasurer, apparently threw £20 on the table (more than a week's wages in those days) and invited other members to match it. Most of them did and the Club survived a crisis.

They continued to struggle over the next few years, but towards the end of the late '50s with a boom in the popularity of golf, a significant number of new members joined the Club and at last we turned the corner, after what had been very difficult times.

SETTLING IN AT MAXSTOKE

For a period of time it could be said that the Club stood still in the early '50s. There was not much money to spare, and members carried out tremendous amounts of work, simply to keep the course in reasonable order. The 1954 AGM Minutes referred to the problems that the Committee had experienced during the past year in keeping down the rough to manageable proportions, and as a result a new tractor had been bought to replace the old machine which was deemed unsafe. It was explained that the new tractor would be able to pull a larger number of mowing units and that it was possible to 'mole drain' the 9th fairway which was a major problem with the lakes frequently overflowing during the winter months.

A vote of thanks was extended to Tom Marks and Frank Blakey for the considerable work that they had done on the course in the year.

Despite the criticism of the course, the Warwickshire County 2nd Team played a match against The Warwickshire Assistant Professionals at Maxstoke, and Carl Bretherton, a well known top Midland amateur golfer of the day, and several Warwickshire Professionals, who were present, were all very flattering in their tributes to the condition of the course.

In 1956 a Special General Meeting was called to review the financial situation and after much discussion it was reluctantly agreed that the Subscriptions be raised from 8 guineas to 10 guineas for Full Playing Male Members, and from 4 guineas to 5 guineas for Full Lady Members. Members once again, were not happy about the condition of the course, the operation of the Green Staff, and had doubts regarding the security of tenure.

Parts of the course were obviously not up to standard, as a proposal made under AOB at the 1958 AGM requested that 'the course revert to 9 holes'. This matter was referred back to the Greens Committee who were asked 'to bear in mind the feelings of the members, and to do the best for the Club with the existing facilities'.

The Treasurer of the day Stan Davis, in his report pointed out that the Club could not hope to liquidate its overdraft with the capital position as it stood. Further finance was necessary to carry out minimal work on the course, and an amount in the order of £1,000 was needed if the Club was to remain solvent. The Committee had guaranteed to provide £500 in loan to the Club, providing the the ordinary members subscribed another £500.

This offer, not for the first time, did not meet with much response from members, and it was decided to write to all members, requesting a 'loan' of £10.

The Professional of the day came under criticism following complaints about the neglect and maintenance of the ground equipment – apparently he was employed as Greenkeeper as well as Professional.

In the earlier 'History of Maxstoke Park Golf Club' written by Bert Jolley in 1982, it stated that at the end of the late '50s, an influx of new members, brought some who were willing to serve on Committee and to do what they could to breathe new life into the Club. Apart from himself, he specifically mentioned Norman Taylor and the Trippas brothers, Ron and Arthur.

Upon being elected to the Committee, this quartet began to grapple with the administrative and financial problems that the Club were experiencing. It soon became apparent that the membership total was a rather vague figure. Members of the Committee at that time were more or less volunteers, who in most cases had their own businesses to run, and consequently were not able to devote enough time to carry out their duties diligently.

It was believed that many people who were not members of the Club, found it easy to play on the course without paying. In other cases, there were a number who deemed themselves members, but who had not received demands for Subscription payment for two or three years. With these obvious irregularities, the four gentlemen offered to form themselves into a Membership Sub-Committee to investigate the situation, and attempt to put things in order.

Over the next twelve months, they held 21 meetings, and combed through the haphazard records of the Club, until an accurate assessment of the Club's strength had been reached. During this time they telephoned 'apparent' members, called at their homes, or checked with their friends, until they were satisfied that they were in a position to record the established members on to a register.

'Kalamazoo' a firm specialising in filing systems was approached, and they soon supplied suitable documentation, and this system was used for many years satisfactorily until it became redundant with the introduction of computers. The information so painstakingly obtained, was then transferred to the new filing system, which was then used to clarify the accounting shambles. In one or two cases, members had not received demands for, or paid subscriptions for up to three years, and a considerable number were in arrears to some extent.

As an indication of the problem that the Sub Committee had tackled during this period, a years subscription fees from the apparent membership at that time amounted to £2,500, but as a result of the research and thorough investigation, the following year produced a sum of £7033. Nowadays of course, the income from members subscriptions is more than thirty times that amount, and even societies bring in over four times that figure.

In addition some £1,430 had been received in loans from members, the loan being in units of £25, with each member required to loan £50. Norman Taylor recently told me that some members did actually refuse to make a loan to the Club, and in the minutes there is mention of a 'black list' of those members who at that time had not paid up their loans.

This list was to be presented at the next General Meeting of the Club Committee to decide what action to take regarding these non payments. The deliberations went on for some time, and there were a few resignations from the Club. It fairness to those who did resign, it is pertinent to point out that £50 was in the order of two weeks wages, and apart from those who refused to pay, there were many unfortunates who probably could not afford to pay.

Subsequently, and apparently after all these problems had been sorted, what appears to have been the final of the Sub Committee took place, and it was recorded that the state of Membership stood at:

Fully paid up Male Members	321
New male members not yet paid up	5
Approved applications for membership	16
SUB TOTAL	342
Fully paid up Female Members	53
New member not yet paid up	1
SUB TOTAL	54
Junior Members	28
TOTAL	424

As a welcome relief to the years of not having sufficient finances, additional funds did become available, and the Club were able to spend £1,000 to refurbish the lounge area. The Bar was rebuilt, the high level ceiling was painted, and a false ceiling incorporated, giving an appearance of reducing the original height, walls were repainted, and this completely transformed the original drab outlook. Members were obviously impressed, they brought their wives and friends along, social functions took place, including concerts presented by several of the members, bar receipts rocketed, and in a couple or so years the cost of renovation was recovered.

In what appears to have been a significant change in atmosphere at the Club, members seem to have joined in all sorts of activities. A publication called 'Miscellany' was issued each month which gave details more or less of the happenings during the month. Bert Jolley described himself as the 'scribe' and obviously edited this journal. Contributions were made by Doug Marston, who was Competition Secretary, and in the October issue of 1965 he gave lengthy and rather complicated account of how the Standard Scratch Score for the course was evolved.

Without going into detail, his account related distances, above or below, a 'standard' course of 6300 yards and basic SSS of 70, and took into account 'Course Value' (degree of difficulty), and weather conditions that were assessed on the day. I don't think we have those problems these days. There was a report on the St. Leger evening when members were given a 'fluent and informative talk' on the subject of course upkeep and maintenance by the Head Greenkeeper, J. Ainslow, and the Captain and Lady Captain made the draw for the St. Leger.

'Miscellany' gave details of personal achievements of members,both in connection with golfing activities, but also announcements of weddings, births, and funerals. It emphasised the need for collars, jackets and ties to be worn in the Clubhouse during the winter season, and apparently these requirements were relaxed in the summer months.

Details of all of the Competitions played in the month, for both the men and ladies sections, were included. No doubt, in order to pay for this very informative document, the inside pages of the front and rear covers, were taken by some 19 of member's adverts. Being an advocate of letting members know what is going on, I think it was an excellent publication, and credit is due to Bert Jolley and all of those who contributed to the contents.

During the later years of the '50s, work began on setting out further holes, towards the objective of attaining 18 hole status. Reading the Green's Committee Minutes at that time, it appears that there were many problems. Before any work could begin, Mr Harris a local farmer, had to be advised that we were starting work so that he could remove his cattle, which apparently grazed on most of the land towards Castle Lane.

There was a deep ditch which extended right across the area behind our present 4th tee. The ditch was therefore culverted with 'scraper pipes' and for most part filled in, to give reasonable access to tractors. A green that had already been laid in the far corner for the then 10th hole was not satisfactory due to excessive wetness in that area, and for a considerable period, a temporary green was cut in front of the green.

By 1960, following much endeavour and hard work, again by a number of enthusiastic members, the course finally attained 18 hole status. Three new holes had been added, two down towards Castle Lane, in the area vacated by the clearing of the old Prisoner of War Camp, and a short hole which is now our 5th, teeing from the far corner adjacent to our present 4th green. At the time of setting out these extra holes because of the

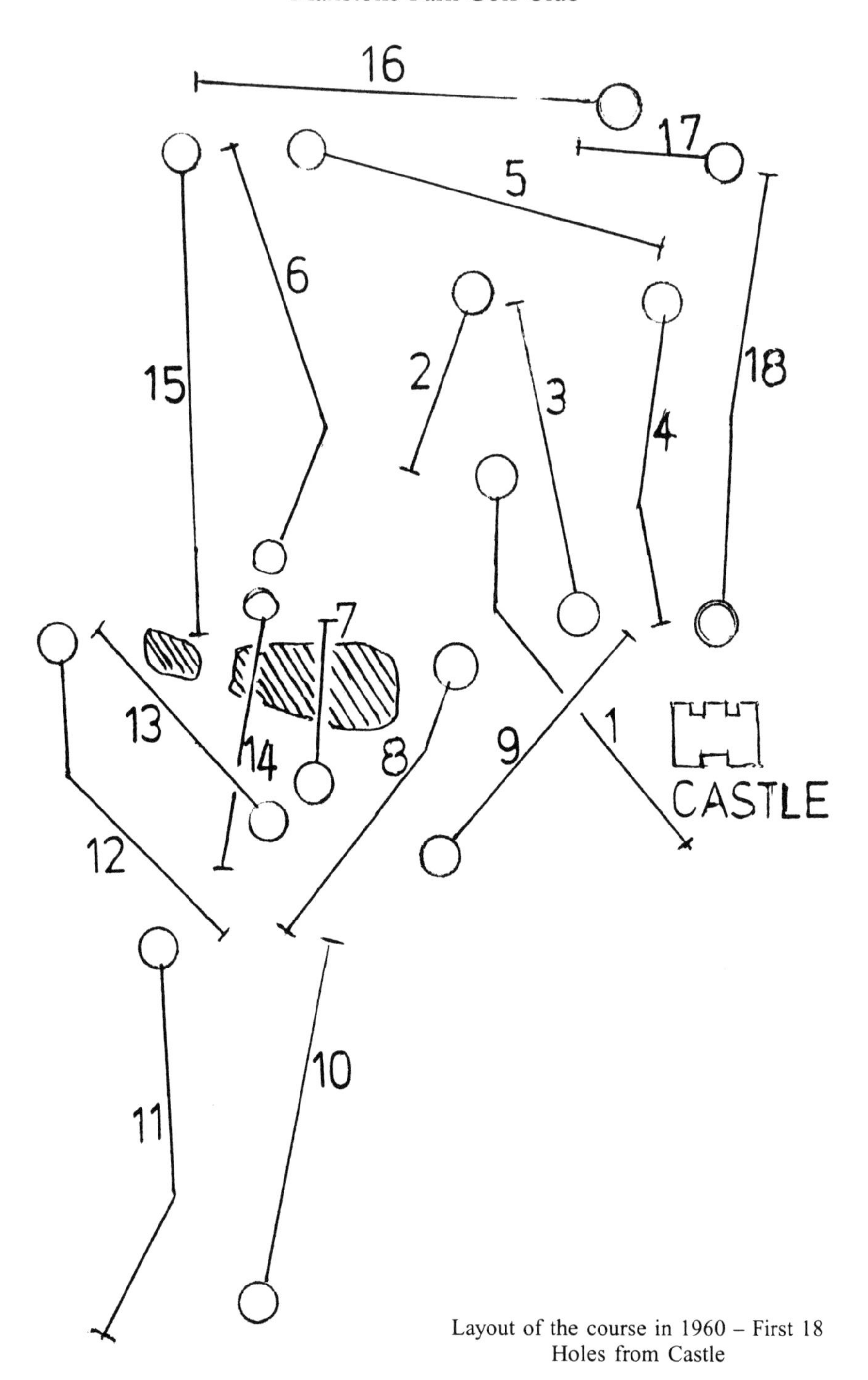

Layout of the course in 1960 – First 18 Holes from Castle

problems mentioned above, it had even been suggested that the 10th (our 4th) should be scrapped and 4 new holes prepared.

It took some 12 months to resolve the problem and this involved a complete rehash of the green which had to be raised considerably, and graded to allow water to run off. The drainage in this area has been a problem for many subsequent years, owing to the level of the water table on this low part of the course. A new raised tee on the short hole was later added, and even recently ditches have been excavated and filled with pebbles to improve the problem.

Again the addition of these new holes caused a re-numbering of the course, but the layout does begin to show resemblance to the present day, albeit with a few minor changes.

Maxstoke Park Golf Club

Name of Player

Marker's Score	Hole No.	Length Yds.	Par	Stroke Index	Bogey	Score	Bogey Result
	1	455	4	7	5		
	2	140	3	17	3		
	3	345	4	13	4		
	4	407	4	1	4		
	5	324	4	15	4		
	6	477	5	12	5		
	7	210	3	8	3		
	8	365	4	5	4		
	9	356	4	11	4		
		3079	35		36		

Marker's Signature

Player's Signature

In Bogey Competitions, Competitors must enter their actual score for all holes won or halved.

Competition

Marker's Score	Hole No.	Length Yds.	Par	Stroke Index	Bogey	Score	Bogey Result
	10	365	4	10	4		
	11	389	4	2	4		
	12	365	4	4	4		
	13	268	4	16	4		
	14	356	4	3	4		
	15	480	5	9	5		
	16	330	4	14	4		
	17	159	3	18	3		
	18	420	4	6	4		
	IN	3132	36		36		
	OUT	3079	35		36		
	TOTAL	6211	71		72		

BOGEY PLAY		MEDAL PLAY	
Holes won (+)		Gross Score	
Holes halved (O)		Handicap	
Holes lost (—)			
Bogey Result		Net Score	

Comparing the card of today with the 1960 one shown, one can see that for many of the holes, the yardages have remained. Several have lengthened, and these are mainly due to 'back' tees being introduced since that time. A couple of holes have been changed considerably by the re-positioning of new greens viz: the 11th and 18th, and of course the introduction of our new 2nd hole.

At this time, the Club were still located in the Castle stable courtyard.

From the courtyard, members walked through a tree covered Car Park, which was well endowed with puddles in wet weather, along a leafy path, and through a five barred gate which led on to the course.

The gate was behind the old competition tee for the then 1st hole, but which subsequently became the 11th when the new Clubhouse was built. When that happened, it became a Par 5, and at 571 yards was the longest hole on the course. This tee was abandoned in the late '70s.

Looking back, Bert Jolley recalls that the catering was very basic, and that 'poached egg on toast' was about the limit of the Steward's capability. There were apparently, a succession of stewards, and they lived in the 'Coachman's House' which was located halfway up the drive to the Castle.

One night, the Club was broken into by an armed gang, and the Steward's dog, which was locked in the Clubhouse at night, was shot with a pistol. The gang entered the Clubhouse, and the Club lost bottles of whisky, cartons of cigarettes, and the contents of the old type 'one armed bandit' – believed to be about £300. The fruit machine took old sixpences (tanners), and next morning many of them were found littering the Car Park.

The intruders were never caught, and the Steward and his wife, Mr and Mrs Evans were given £15 so that they could get another dog. Despite the description given of the basic accommodation of the Clubhouse in the old stables, the photograph does show that even a few Christmas decorations did brighten the place up.

Apart from George Dowse who is squatting in the front foreground and his wife at his side, the only other person that I can identify is Stan Davis, who is wedged between two ladies at the back on the extreme left hand side of the photograph. Other members at that time would have been Bill Dudley-Evans, Doug Marston, Tom Marks, Wilf Martin, Vernon Wilder, John Ralston and Frank Blakey, and comparing Captain's photographs from that era, they do not appear to have been present at this function.

Mention is made elsewhere of a refurbishment of the Clubhouse in the late '50s and one item specified was the lowering of the high ceiling. It is apparent that this had not happened when the photo was taken, so it is reasonable to assume that the period was the early to mid '50s.

When the lease was originally granted on the parkland at Maxstoke, it was for a 50 year period from 1946 until 1996, and one of the stipulations was that a new Clubhouse be built within 10 years, and to cost not less than £5,000. The Committee were of course aware that the use of the Stables, was only of a temporary nature, and that sooner or later, alternative accommodation would have to be found.

Fortunately, the then Landlord, Mr Beaumount Fetherston-Dilke, was a patient man, and as has already been stated, a good friend of the Club. At an AGM bearing in mind the concern regarding security of tenure, he assured the members present that the Club were good tenants, they had improved the parkland, and that as far as he was concerned, they could stay there, in the old Stables, for as long as it suited them.

Nevertheless, following the 1964 November AGM and the subsequent General Committee Meeting, it was decided that a Building Sub Committee be formed to investigate the possible implications of providing new premises. Jack Edwards, and the two Trippas brothers, Arthur and Ron, were elected to this Sub Committee.

After 6 months, in March 1965 an Extraordinary General Meeting was called to hear the report of the Sub Committee, which made the following points:

1. It was not feasible to remain in the Stables, despite the President's offer, as it was accepted they were too limited, would cost too much to renovate, and there was nowhere to expand.
2. A scheme to move into the Castle, was also impracticable.
3. That the Club should consider building a new Clubhouse, on the highest ground available, at a cost of £30,000. The area suggested at the time, was the 13½ acre site which had been occupied by the former Prisoner of War Camp.

The recommendation in Item 3, was adopted and the Building Sub Committee had further meetings to consider the scheme in more detail. The Building Fund was quoted as £2,100, and it was anticipated that by the end of March 1965, it would be in excess of £4,000.

Subsequent to these agreements, the Committee passed a resolution that 'the membership be increased (from 280) and stabilised at 350 Full Male Members, and that after that new applicants shall be placed on a waiting list'.

Congratulations were recorded in the Minutes of the AGM and extended to Club Professional, Don Knight, who had been elected as Captain of the Warwickshire Professional Golfers Association. Thanks were also recorded by the Committee to him and his Assistant T. Munro in appreciation of their services during the year. Most of the references to earlier Professionals over the years, had not been complimentary.

Don Knight had been Assistant to Jack Cawsey at Pype Hayes, and prior to his appointment the Club had been without a Professional for quite a long period of time. Bill Adwick at Marston Green, and Jack Cawsey had both been approached to see if they were interested in moving to Maxstoke.

They both declined, and were then asked to see if they would consider part time appointments, or even be prepared to organise golfing tuition classes at Maxstoke. Obviously the answer was 'no', and Don Knight came to Maxstoke. He was a very popular Professional, and remained with the Club for some 20 years.

OFFICERS OF THE CLUB – MAXSTOKE CASTLE DAYS

During the formative years at Maxstoke, from the late'40s to the early '60s, it is reasonable to say that all members were involved, and indeed, had to be, to set about what must have been a formidable task, in creating a new golf course, with little money, and inadequate equipment.

When the move from Castle Bromwich was made in 1946, only about 70 of the existing members came to Maxstoke. One or two of those, according to information received from the few survivors from those days, did take upon themselves the onerous task of deciding how to go about laying out the course, and organising the 'volunteers' to maintain a logical work plan to achieve the objective.

Unlike the Castle Bromwich Committee of pre war years, it was too early to have a long term continuity of length of service with the Officers of the Club. Nevertheless, certain members of the Committee did accept responsibilty during those early years, and John Nicholson, who was Club Captain in 1947, is one who can be singled out, as having made a significant contribution at that time. John was also Chairman of the Club in two separate spells, 1945–1948, and again 1954 and 1955, and these two periods were associated with the establishment of laying out of the course.

Bill Dudley-Evans was Club Captain in 1945, and also Club Secretary for a 12 year span during the early days at Maxstoke. He later became Chairman for another lengthy spell in the '60s and '70s. The entry in the Golfer's Handbook of 1948 gave very minimal information regarding the course. Bill Dudley-Evans was quoted as Secretary, and it gave his home phone number and address. The figure quoted for a day's golf 'playing with a member', on the then 9 hole course was 2 shillings and sixpence (12½p). If this figure is compared with established courses like Harborne and Moseley, both 18 holes, where 'visitors fees' were quoted as five shillings (25p) per day, then our charges did seem a bit steep. Harborne Church Farm, a Municipal course, only charged 2 shillings (10p), but again it was an established course. Interesting to see that Bill Adwick was the Professional, who of course moved to Marston Green about that time.

Harborne G. C., Ltd., 40 Tennal Road, Harborne. Tele. No. 1728 Harborne. Membership, 325. Sec., J. Watson, M.B.E., 226 Kingsbury Road, Birmingham, 24. Tele. No. Harborne 1728. (p), W. Button. Greenkeeper, W. Firman. Records (a), 65, C. S. Buckley ; (p), 67, W. Button. S.S.S. 73. Par 72. 18 holes. Station—Birmingham (3 miles). Motor bus 2 mins. Visitors' fees, 5s. per day ; 7s. 6d. Saturdays and Sundays.

Harborne Church Farm G. C., Vicarage Road, Harborne. Tele. No. Harborne 1204. Membership, 200. Sec., G. T. Parker, 36 Victoria Road, Harborne, Birmingham. (p), W. H. Adwick. S.S.S. 70. Par 68. 9 holes. Bus Nos. 12, 20 and 20B from Birmingham pass club entrance. Visitors' fees, 2s. per day. Sunday play.

Ladbrook Park G. C.—*see* Ladbrook Park.

Maxstoke Park G. C., Maxstoke Park, near Coleshill (Castle Bromwich Golf Club Ltd.) Tele. Nos. Coleshill 2158. East 0389. Membership, 210. Hon. Sec., W. N. Dudley Evans, 76 Darnick Road, Sutton Coldfield. Tele. No. SUTton 3792. 9 holes. Visitors playing with member, 2s. 6d. per day ; 3s. 6d. Saturdays, Sundays and public holidays.

Moseley G. C., Springfield Road, King's Heath. Tele. No. 2115 Highbury. Membership—gent.'s, 350 ; ladies, 150. Sec., C. Fred Hughes. (p) and greenkeeper, John Morris. Records (a), 68, A. S. Newey ; (p), 67, G. Johnson. S.S.S. 74. Par 73. 18 holes. Bus Nos. 48, 50, 50B from Birmingham. Visitors' fees, 5s. per round ; 7s. 6d. per day ; 10s. Saturdays and Sundays.

Frank Walker, who was Treasurer throughout the late '50s and early '60s obviously had the difficult task of financing the course building programme, and preparing for the long term new Clubhouse objective. He was also Club Captain later in the '60s.

Vernon Wilder and John Ralston, again both Club Captains in 1950 and 1951 respectively, also had spells as Club Chairman.

Frank Blakey, Club Captain in 1954, and Tom Marks were particularly active in those early years, and both had spells as Green's Chairman at the time when the course was being laid out. Frank Blakey did have some influence in the layout of the individual holes, and Tom probably more than anyone else, spent hours upon the course, personally driving the tractor and gang mowers, and was instrumental in recruiting and organising gangs of 'volunteer' labour from the Boy Scouts and Father Hudson's Homes.

Another committeeman who is worthy of mention was Wilf Martin. He was Club Captain in 1960, and then took on the role of Secretary for a period of nine years, from 1962 right up to the time that the Clubhouse was completed in 1970. He would of course have been much involved in the negotiating and drawing up the contracts for the project, as well as administering the day to day business of the Club.

FRANK THOMPSON BLAKEY

Frank Blakey was born in Croydon on July 20th 1913, educated at Bideford Grammar School, but spent most of his working life in the Midlands. An Accountant by profession he had several appointments within the motor industry, and rose to the position of Company Secretary at Armstrong Siddeley and in the later years became Commercial Director at Bristol/ Rolls Royce, and he finally retired in 1976.

He married his wife Joy and they lived at Marston Green. They have 3 children, 7 grandchildren and 2 great grandchildren. Frank and Joy have now retired to Appledore in North Devon, and Frank in his mid 80s, still plays golf at the Royal North Devon Club at Westward Ho.

Frank recalls that he swung his first golf club at Westward Ho Golf Club at the tender age of 3 years and became an 'artisan' member in 1927. He joined Castle Bromwich in 1933 and at that time his handicap was 4 and by 1935, he was down to 1 handicap.

In 1945 he moved North and joined Dinsdale Spa Golf Club at Darlington. He played off scratch and played regularly for Durham County. He then moved back to the Midlands where he played at Marston Green and was a big influence in setting up the Club there. He was also a member of Copt Heath from 1960 until 1976.

I have personal memories of Frank's ability as a golfer at Marston Green. He was over 6 foot in height, and was exceptionally long off the tee. The eighth hole was a 406 yards dog leg to the right. Frank used to go for the green, over a hedge which bordered the out of bounds, some 230 yards from the tee, and often reached the target. When I sent an early copy of this draft to him, he was quite anxious to point out that because of his length off the tee, he rarely had to resort to using low irons, and did not consider himself a good long iron player. On occasions he would play a 'friendly' match against three of us, (all single figure golfers) for 5 shillings and most times took the money.

Frank returned to Maxstoke in 1949 and is one of the 'pioneer' golfers who came to Maxstoke from Castle Bromwich and became involved with laying out the course. He was off plus two for many years and regularly represented Warwickshire at County level. He also won the Club Championship on six occasions, and recalls that in one of those he returned a 36 hole total of 136, which he believes was a record at that time. With retirement pending he rejoined the Royal North Devon Golf Club at Westward Ho in 1965 as a Country Member, and became a Full Member in 1976 when he finally retired. His golfing career has therefore turned 'full circle' after a 50 year gap. Since rejoining Royal North Devon he has served as Chairman and been honoured with the Presidency. Today his other leisure activities are fishing and boating.

During war time he served in the Auxiliary Fire Service for a time and after transferring, reached the rank of Captain in the Home Guard. Frank became Captain of the Club in 1954, and has many memories of playing from the Castle. He recalls a Professional, who he refused to name, who experimented with the concept of playing night time golf. He managed to get a degree of fairway illumination by hanging miscellaneous battery powered lighting and hurricane lamps from the trees on a couple of holes. It was not a success, and Frank suggested that as one or two younger lady members participated, the Professional may well have had other considerations, apart from golf in mind.

In the early '50s, matches were played against a team of Archers from Meriden. The Archers 'holed out' in a marrow. and Frank recalls that they invariably won as they were capable of holing out regularly from 50 yards. The golfers did eventually manage to win once, when cucumbers were used instead of marrows.

Match against the 'Archers of Meriden' in 1953. The Archer is Lord Guernsey, son of the Earl of Aylesford, and behind him were Tom Marks, on his left, and Frank Blakey with a cap.

The photograph was taken at the time when the course was only 12 or 15 holes, and from the background it was probably taken on what is now our 12th. Frank Blakey could not identify the others in the photo' but for those interested in ancient yeomanry, the bow used dated back to Crecy days.

Another match against 'The Archers' – Frank Blakey again with Stan Davis on the left. Lord Guernsey the bowman.

Frank Blakey's Captains Day – 1954

Just after I became involved with producing this book, knowing that Bill Dudley-Evans and Frank were old friends, I was able to inform Bill of Frank's address in Appledore. Bill did manage to visit him and played with him at 'Westward Ho'.

THOMAS MARKS

Tom Marks has had a long association with the Club as he started playing as a 17 year old at Castle Bromwich, where his father was Head Green-keeper. Tom served an apprenticeship with 'Maddox and Walford' who were a company specialising in shop fitting in pre war days. He remembers being instructed by Mr Maddox, who was a member at Castle Bromwich, to erect timber shelters around the course, made from redundant fencing from the Bromford Bridge Race Course.

As a youngster, Tom lived with his parents at 464, Bromford Road, right opposite to the old course, and swung a golf club for the first time when he was quite young. After the war, he moved to Marston Green when he married. He and his wife had two children, Frank and Muriel. Tom worked at Coleshill Hall, where he instructed the boys in wood craftmanship. In his younger days, Tom was a keen cricket and soccer player, and turned out for both Coleshill Hall and Marston Green. He played golf at Marston Green Municipal Course where he was a mid handicap player. He said that he eventually managed to get down to 6 handicap, and claimed that he often played below that.

He recalls that when the move to Maxstoke was made, the first 9 holes were quickly brought into play. The greens were cut straight from the original park land grass with member's hand mowers, Tom recalls that with other Committee members, he spent many hours cutting the fairways with a gang mower powered by the old 1928 'Fordson' tractor.

One event that Tom remembered quite vividly was at a Captain's Day Dance in a marquee, back in the Castle days. Tom was in charge of the Bar, and at the end of the evening it was believed that the takings had been stolen. Fortunately, the next morning it was decided to dismantle the old till that had been used, and to everyones relief it was found that all of the notes had worked their way to the back of the till, and thence underneath the till drawer.

I have obtained much of the detail about the early days at Maxstoke from Tom. He had a wonderful recall for events that occurred some 40 or 50 years ago. He was not always able to put dates to the events but invariably named the particular Club Captain of the day, and by perusal of old minute books, I have in most cases, been able to confirm that his information was correct.

Tom Marks was a hard working member of the Committee of the Club

Tom Marks, Lena and Harry Field with Bill Dudley-Evans taken on the course in the late '80s

Tom Marks taken on his last appearance at Maxstoke on Captain's Day, 2nd August 1997, with long time friend Trafford Stonebridge

for many years. He had three spells as Chairman of the Greens at the time when the original course was laid out, 1957–58 and 1967–69, and again later 1975–82, when the present layout of holes came in to play.

In recent years he always played with Bill Dudley-Evans, and it must surely be some sort of achievement for two octogenarians to turn out regularly in Club medal competitions. Tom was Club Captain in 1970, and was honoured by being made a Vice President of the Club in 1971 in appreciation of his endeavours over the years. At my Captain's Day he was pleased to inform me that he had attended every Captain's Day since 1947, a remarkable record, and at 87 years of age he looked alert enough to attend many more, but it was not to be, and he died suddenly just 12 days later.

WILLIAM NORMAN DUDLEY-EVANS

Bill Dudley-Evans without doubt was the longest serving member of the Club having had a long association both at Castle Bromwich and Maxstoke Park extending to some 76 years.

The Castle Bromwich Golf Club, Limited.

(Incorporated, under the Companies Acts of 1862 to 1907, as a Company limited by guarantee).

I desire to become {~~an ordinary~~ / ~~a Country~~} a Junior Member of the above-named Club, and I hereby agree to submit to, and be bound by, the Memorandum and Articles of Association.

Signature (in full) Wm. Norman Dudley Evans

Address (private) Fair Lea, Castle Bromwich

**Occupation* School

**Ladies please say whether married, widow, or spinster.*

Signature of Member presenting application A Dudley Evans

Signature of Member seconding application [illegible]

Supported by

Date when presented 11 . 6 . 21

Date when posted in Club House 12 . 6 . 21

Date of Election 27 . 6 . 21

Registered No. 886 [illegible] *Hon. Sec.*

This application must be sent to the Hon. Sec., Haye House, Castle Bromwich.

All Applications must be supported by a member of the Committee.

The application form for membership of Castle Bromwich Golf Club submitted by Bill Dudley-Evans in June 1921

Referring back to his early days at Castle Bromwich Bill remembered Dr Pooler who was the first Hon. Secretary of the Club.

The membership of the Castle Bromwich Golf Club, according to Bill, was a social mixture, but mainly professional people, including doctors, solicitors and accountants. Many of them cycled to the course, but most members travelled by train to Castle Bromwich Station, (long since closed) crossed the bridge over the river, and walked down a lane to the Golf Course. He recalled that on one occasion he walked from the centre of Castle Bromwich village to the course, probably a good mile walk.

Bill's father joined the Club in 1909, and Bill recalled that due to his influence, he was able to get into the Club as a Junior in 1921. Juniors were not looked on favourably in those days. There were no Junior competitions, but they were allowed to play in Medals once their handicap was down to 18. He believed that there were less than ten Juniors at that time, and the subscription fee was 2 guineas (£2.10) which remained at that level until you reached 21 years. When he first started playing golf Juniors were not allowed into the Clubhouse, and if a Junior wanted a drink, he would have had to stand in the Porch of the Clubhouse to drink it.

Bill was born in Castle Bromwich in 1910 and went to school at Hallfield Preparatory School at Edgbaston. He travelled by train and pony and trap, but later when bus services improved, he travelled by bus direct to King Edward's. He was at King Edward's from the age of 13 until he was 17, spending two years in the same form as J. Enoch Powell. Enoch Powell was an exceptional pupil, and despite being two years younger than the average age of the class, he always came top of the class.

From the age of 13 golf was the only sport that Bill played, as he was told to give up cricket and football when he was ill with appendicitis.

Bill remembered playing a round of golf with Viscount Newport, who was a very good golfer, when they were both about 21 years of age. After playing they went back to Castle Bromwich Hall and had lunch with Viscount Newport's grandmother.

The Castle Bromwich course was always kept in good condition and Bill recalled that it had the advantage of being built on sand and gravel and drained very well. By today's standards the course might be considered short but nevertheless it extended to some 95 acres.

There were a number of very good golfers from other Clubs who played at Castle Bromwich through the winter months, when their own courses were probably closed. Duncan Sutherland was one, and he was the first winner of the 'Brabazon Trophy'.

The lowest handicap that Bill played off was 2, and this was in the period 1936 until 1950. When the handicapping system was revised his handicap went to 4. Bill was a member of the 'Bears Golfing Society' and to qualify for admittance to this Society, one had to have played at least 12 times for the Warwickshire County First Team. The Society was started in 1958 and Bill recalled that the first meeting was at Hunstanton Golf Club.

One of Bill's favourite memories was being present at Little Aston when Phil Perkins won the English Amateur Championship.

Philip Perkins played off plus 4 at Castle Bromwich, and Bill's handicap was 4 when he first played for the Castle Bromwich First Team. He was convinced that there were many more Club matches in those days which I find hard to believe. Looking at the 1939 fixtures, matches were played against 6 other Clubs as double fixtures with First and Second Teams being turned out on the same day on a home and away basis. 4 other clubs were played as 'B' Team fixtures again home and away, giving a total of 32 matches.

Today with 'Scratch League', 'A' Team, 'B' Team and W. M. L. matches we are close to 50 matches and that doesn't include 'Maxies' and Juniors matches. Bill indicated the the standard of golf in those days was very high despite the equipment used. Bill's clubs were hickory shafted, the golf balls used were smaller than today's and cost about 2 shillings (10p). The balls used were all locally made – 'Dunlop' and 'Penfold'. Bill pointed out that Harry Penfold used to work for 'Dunlop' before setting up on his own, and that he was a good friend of Harry's son, Dick Penfold.

When Bill qualified as an Accountant, he was asked to work for the Club and he becamc Assistant Secretary in 1933. He recalled that he was allowed to attend Committee Meetings but it was a long time before he was allowed to take an active part. He also remembered that he helped the Hon. Treasurer by collecting and recording subscriptions.

There were some 7 people on the staff working for the Club. The Head Greenkeeper was Roland (Harry) Marks, father of Tom Marks. Following him was Horace Shaw, who had worked on the course for many years, and who later became Club Steward.

Bill became Secretary of the Warwickshire Golf Union in 1939, a position he held until 1973. Then he took over as President for 12 years until he stood down in 1986. Bill was always a supporter of Junior golf and he started the Warwickshire Junior Championship and later the Under 15s Championship.

Bill recalled that he was an articled clerk for 5 years, earning 5 shillings (25p) for the first two years, then rising to 10 shillings (50p) before he qualified. His father helped to support him. He married his wife Isabel in 1940 when he was 30, and they had two sons. His youngest son was articled to Price Waterhouse, but died from leukemia at the early age of 32, and his eldest son works at Birmingham University. Isabel died in 1984.

Bill remembered that during the war he often worked 9 hours a day, 7 days a week for the Chartered Accountants that employed him. A fire bomb dropped on the offices in Colmore Row and the firm moved to Sutton Coldfield. In 1949 the Senior Partner retired and the firm were taken over by Michael Stephens and Co. and Bill became a partner in the business.

Bill started the Warwickshire Open Championship after the war which was played at Olton Golf Club. He remembered he played with the winner, George Maisey, who was the Professional at Castle Bromwich.

As mentioned elsewhere Bill was Club Captain in 1945, he served as Assistant Secretary from 1933 until 1943, he became Hon. Secretary in 1944 and remained in that position until 1957. He then served as Club Chairman from 1963 for 14 years. He became President of the Club in 1991, a fitting and well deserved honour which he greatly appreciated, and he held the position until his death in 1996.

Bill's name appears in many places on the Club's Honours Boards and it is certainly a wonderful achievement that he played golf more or less right to his death.

Other aspects of Bill's achievements within the Club are mentioned elsewhere, His winning of the 'Veterans Cup' at 79 and 83, both times with scores to match his age, his 50th Anniversary Party and even more remarkable his 70th Anniversary with the Club.

Bill Dudley-Evans as he will always be remembered – out on the course with his long time partner Tom Marks. Taken in 1995 when they were both well into their 80s

OBITUARY

BILL DUDLEY-EVANS: A LIFETIME OF GOLF

The passing of Billy Dudley-Evans, during the Bank Holiday weekend, deprived both Warwickshire golf and Maxstoke Park GC with a revered link with the past.
Bill was 86 when he died in hospital, after a short illness and, no doubt, he would to that day have been frustrated had he not been able to go around the course with just one stroke for each year of his age.
The president of his club and past president of his county had served in so many offices during his eighty years association with the sport that it would be difficult to recall and list them all.
Basically he was simply a much-loved individual who was always there, a four-ball every Saturday morning, in the chair at AGMs, following county teams around any course, any time.

As an administrator the former accountant's contribution to golf was simply enormous. On the playing side it was no less impressive.
Twice in the last seven years of his life he won the Maxstoke veteran's trophy in a score to match his age, 79 at 79 and 83 at 83.
It all added up to quite some lifetime 'round of golf' bearing in mind that he started caddying for his father at the age of six when Maxstoke was based at Castle Bromwich.
He told me with a chuckle once that though his father allowed him to walk behind with a sawn-down club and a ball it wasn't long before that ball started to whizz past his father's ear.
By the time he was around ten years of age, not long after World War 1, he was a junior member, thus he completed some 76 years of membership of Castle Bromwich/Maxstoke GC.
The offices Bill Dudley-Evans filled for the Warwickshire Union included: 1939-1972: County secretary; 1961 County captain; 1972-74: County chairman; 1974-86: County president. 1986 onward: served on EGU and Midland Union executive. He also represented his county as a player and served in virtually every capacity for his club Maxstoke Park.

BILL DUDLEY-EVANS (1927)

We are indebted to Victor Jones and John Brown for the following:

In addition to his family, a large number of friends — Old Edwardians, Golfers and Freemasons — attended the funeral to pay tribute to "Bill" Dudley-Evans who died on 24th August in his 87th year peacefully after a short illness.

He was born on 24th March 1910 and when he was only 8 suffered the trauma of losing his only brother who was killed in the Royal Flying Corps at the very end of the 1914–18 war; he was thus brought up as an only child.

He went to Hallfield Prep. School and entered KES in September 1923. He and I were "sherrings" together and shared a desk both then and for the whole of our school life until we left in 1927. We did classics — in a small and very select form which included John Enoch Powell in our last two years.

Our friendship continued after leaving School and Bill became a kind of "hon." member of my family. My parents were fond of him and he joined us on all our family holidays from 1928 to 1937. In that year Bill, my parents and I went by car to Austria and there, in Innsbruck, we met Rosabelle (a Sutton Coldfield girl) who became his wife in 1940. I was his "best man" at the wedding.

Bill's father was a keen member of Castle Bromwich Golf Club (later Maxstoke GC) and Bill, following in his footsteps was playing regularly by 1917 (aged 7!) and became a very good golfer. Golf in fact became a great and absorbing part of his life. He was secretary of the Warwickshire Union of Golf Clubs for 25 years and then President for 25 years! He was also President of Maxstoke GC and had a very respectable handicap right to the end.

One of his feats, of which he should have been very proud, was that of winning Maxstoke's Golden Oldies Trophies on two occasions with scores to match his age — a 79 at 79 and an 83 at 83.

By profession he was a Chartered Accountant and became a partner in the Birmingham practice Bowker Stevens and Co.

He had two sons; the elder, Anthony, having taught in many countries worldwide is now at Birmingham University; the younger son, Roger, qualified as a chartered accountant and was advancing his career at Price Waterhouse when he died of leukaemia about ten years ago. This was followed within two years by another tragedy when Rosabelle died of cancer.

Bill was a keen and active Freemason for nearly 50 years. He held honours in the Province of Warwickshire and was appointed an officer of the Grand Lodge of England in 1983 and he was very proud of being the recipient, in 1995, of the Rt. Wor. Provincial Grand Master's Certificate of Merit.

He was a very good family man and an excellent holiday companion — steady, witty, amusing and amused. He was proud of having been at the school, proud of his contact with it to the end, and proud of being a past master and an active member of the Old Edwardians Lodge.

The obituaries are worthy of inclusion, one by Dennis Shaw published in the 1996 October Edition of in 'Amateur Golf' and the other in the 'Old Edwardians Gazette'. Both articles reaffirm the comments that I have mentioned but they do emphasise the respect and reputation that other people apart from our own members, felt for Bill Dudley-Evans. People such as Bill only come along once in a lifetime and we at Maxstoke were all fortunate to have known him during his lifetime.

GEORGE W. DOWSE

George Dowse was one of the longest serving members of the Club having joined on December 8th 1951. During his long years with the Club he was an enthusiastic member and had a long association on Committee. He remembered going to look around the course in 1950, and recalled that he was surprised to see the Captain of the day, Vernon Wilder and a number of Club Officials actually laying out new greens, which was obviously at the time when three more holes were being added to the original nine.

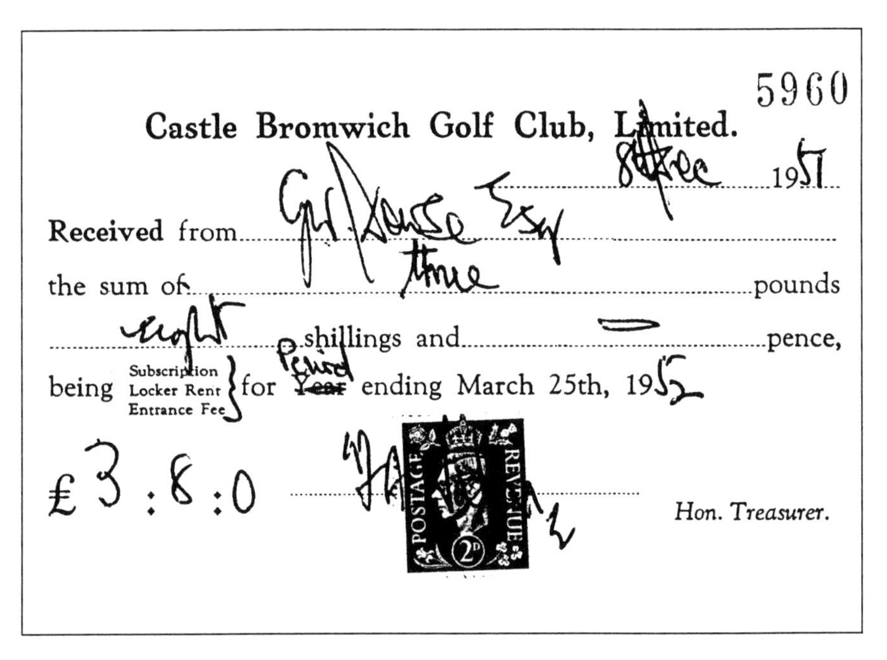

5960

Castle Bromwich Golf Club, Limited.

8 Dec 1951

Received from G W Dowse Esq

the sum of three pounds

eight shillings and — pence,

being Subscription / Locker Rent / Entrance Fee for ~~Year~~ Period ending March 25th, 1952

£3 : 8 : 0

Hon. Treasurer.

George must have been impressed by the enthusiasm shown by senior officials of the Club and he applied to join the Club shortly after. His receipt when he joined shows that he paid three pounds eight shillings which was roughly half of the Annual Subscription rate at that time. He recalled that he took out a Family Membership at some time and paid

£8.00 for two adults and two boys, but it is almost certain that he had got the amount wrong, as a man and wife in 1950 would have paid £10.12.0.

George was born in 1917 and recalled that he played most sports in his youth, except cricket. He left school at the age of 14 and went to work at the Singer Motor Company. Two years later he joined Alfred Herberts employed in the Company's Fire Brigade, and in time played for their football team. He indicated that at some stage he had trials with Birmingham Football Club, but was turned down as he developed rheumatic fever. Later he took up cycle racing and won several prizes.

He met his wife Madeline in Stoke on Trent in 1938 and after they got married they had two sons, Roger and David. Roger has won the Junior's Cup and David at one time worked on the greenstaff. Madeline joined the Club in August 1952 and her receipt shows that she paid £5.00, but on the bottom edge it states '6 pence overpaid'. Being aware of George's infinite knowledge of the Rules of Golf, I have no doubt that if George said she overpaid, then he was probably right.

6107

Castle Bromwich Golf Club, Limited.

31st August 1952

Received from Mrs M. W. Lucke

the sum of Five pounds

— shillings and — pence,

being Subscription / Locker Rent / Entrance Fee for Year ending March 25th, 1953.

£ 5 : – : – [illegible] Hon. Treasurer.

6d overpaid

George recalls that in the early days it was quite normal to play on Sunday afternoons and find that there were probably only four to six members on the course. George and Madeline used to take their two boys around the course with them.

George first went on the Committee in 1962. He was honoured by being elected as Club Captain in 1967, and in that year he gave the present flagpole to the Club.

He also served on the Green's Committee for a number of years, but he will always be remembered in his role of Handicap Secretary. He was involved with the first computer programme used by the Club. This was introduced in 1983 and controls the handicap system which is still used today. It is to George's credit that though computers were new to him, he soon came to terms with them, and was able to set down an acceptable programme.

Modestly, he stated that he was very much involved in keeping members informed of the Rules of Golf – surely the understatement of the year. Those of us who have been with the Club for a reasonable time are fully aware of George's interpretation of the Rules of Golf. He knew them backward, invariably he would quote the rule number, the section reference and even the sub section reference of most of them. We didn't always agree with his interpretation at the time, but usually he was right.

As a golfer he recalled that he only got down to 11 handicap, but nevertheless perusal of the honours boards indicate that he did win one or two competitions in his day.

George was always an active man, gave the impression of having plenty of energy, always carried his clubs, and still played golf more or less right up to his passing in June 1997.

George is in the centre foreground, sitting on the floor with the Captain's

George Dowse's Captain's Day – July 1967

Cup placed in front of him. The photograph appears to be taken on what was then the first tee, but is now our 18th, and it is interesting to note, that 30 years ago there were no bushes or trees evident around the moat.

The photograph below was taken at a Nuneaton Carnival probably in the late'50s. They entered the Carnival under the title 'The Tyroleans' and there was no indication as to whether they received a prize.

Whilst nothing to do with golf, I include it to show George and Madeline as Club members have never seen them before. As mentioned earlier George was a man of many talents and had been a keen racing time trials cyclist. For cycling enthusiasts, the gear change appears to be a simple 3 speed and not one of the 10 speed versions seen on today's more expensive models. The lad in the trailer was Eric Hickman, but whether he was ever a member of the Club is not known.

LOOKING AHEAD AT MAXSTOKE

Following the 1965 E. G. M. Arthur Trippas visited the Market Research Department at Aston University, and they produced a questionnaire which was forwarded to all Club members. The object was to ascertain exactly what the majority of members felt should be included in building plans for a new Clubhouse. The results of this survey were incorporated into a full report which was presented to the Building Sub Committee in June 1965.

Plans were then prepared by an Architect, and these were presented to the General Committee in November 1966. It is worth recording that the Building Sub Committee had grown substantially since it was set up in 1964, and at the meeting Arthur Trippas paid tribute to the 'work and efforts of the Building Sub Committee' and cited the additional names of Les Brock, Frank Cartwright, Bill Hawley, J. Pagett and Ray Watkins. He also praised Messrs F. Parkin, Henry Locker-Marsh, Peter Blundell and Mr and Mrs W. G. Black for 'their valuable assistance in the matter of fund raising'.

An Extraordinary General Meeting was then called for all members, and this was held at the 'Arden Hall' Castle Bromwich in March 1967. Considering earlier reluctance on the part of members to dig into their pockets at times when the Club was in serious financial trouble, the Committee were naturally concerned that the proposals would not be accepted by a majority at this meeting. For two weeks prior to the meeting, members of the Sub Committee and 'pro' supporters of the project actually adopted 'electioneering' type canvassing, and went round to members' homes, urging them to attend the meeting if they wished the Club to proceed.

The tactics apparently worked, as a signed attendance register indicated that 153 members attended the meeting, which equated to 60% of the membership. Detailed plans and costings were shown to the members, and more importantly, the proposals as to how sufficient funds could be raised to finance the building programme.

After some considerable discussion, with the meeting swayed by the enthusiasm shown by the Committee, the proposals were carried by a small majority on a show of hands.

In October of the same year, £15,000 was invested in Building Societies to gain interest until such time as the building work went ahead. This figure came largely from loans which had been levied on members in £25 units, and which each member had to guarantee a minimum of £50. As an incentive, for every £25 unit, members were given a £1 reduction in their Annual Subscription which continued for many subsequent years. At that stage the Club had also been promised a grant of £10,000 from the Sports Council.

With the financial obligations more or less guaranteed, the project was then put out to tender, and the one accepted, being the lowest was from 'Rix (Contractors) Ltd'. with a figure of £42,313. The breakdown of this figure revealed that £2,600 for drainage, was chargeable to Maxstoke

Castle, and the Club would therefore have to find £39,713 plus some £4,000 in fees to Architects and Quantity Surveyors.

At that time the Club had £25,673 in cash at the Bank and in Building Societies, plus £2,500 which had been received from member's loans. It was felt that this amount, with a bank overdraft, ensured that the Club were in a position to go ahead with the building of the new Clubhouse.

The contract was signed on August 13th 1968, and on August 30th, at a small ceremony, new President Captain Charles Fetherston-Dilke. R. N. cut the first sod. It is rather sad to note that Beaumont Fetherston-Dilke had passed away at this time, having been so much involved with our early days at Maxstoke.

I do not wish for this to read like an obituary column, but unfortunately several of the Committee Members who had been involved and had worked so hard to get the Club established had also died, and were never able to witness the results of their endeavours. John Ralston who was a Committee man for over 8 years as Chairman of the Green's Committee and Club Captain in 1951, died in 1953. James S. Luke, Club Chairman, 1956–1960, and Captain in 1957, died in 1961. C. B. Hatton, Club Captain 1963, died in his year of Captaincy, Alf Blundell, who completed Mr Hatton's year of Captaincy, then died the following year in his year of Captaincy 1954, and finally Frank Walker, Treasurer from 1947–1954, and 1961–1967, and Club Captain 1959, died just about the time that building work commenced in 1968.

It is of interest to give details of the specification that had been drawn up and presented to the members for approval. The project had been split into three distinct phases, and it is evident that there have been many improvements over the years when you compare todays Clubhouse. Obviously, also at that time, there must have early changes of mind as Phase 2 was never completed to the original concept and Phase three was never carried out.

DESIGN CRITERIA

PHASE 1: Site Layout

When the site was used as a Prisoner of War Camp, the topsoil was bulldozed to the western boundary, where it formed a large mound, slightly higher than the golf course on one side, and considerably higher than the remaining field on the approach side. The Clubhouse will have extensive views over the course, and an elevated approach from Castle Lane.

The existing ditch will be culverted to provide unobstructed access from the Clubhouse to the course. *(Trafford Stonebridge indicated that this ditch, parts of which still remain, ran from the far side of the 3rd fairway, right across to the trees on the Northern boundary, and was in reality a 'deer's leap' intended to deter the many deer on the park land from straying.)* A new sewage disposal plant to take advantage of the levels created by the mound, with access provided for maintenance via the Car Park in the most screened portion of the site.

Car Park

A shale surfaced car park will be provided for 120 cars. The maximum number of players on the course at any one time will be 120, allowing play from 1st and 10th tees at 10 minute intervals.

Cars will be screened from the course, and the relatively flat area of the remainder of the site, can be developed later for other recreational activities. Access to the site will be made at the existing gateway on Castle Lane. Roads will be shale surfaced with tarmac surfacing at turning spaces only, having concrete curbs.

Locker Rooms

As golf clubs will not be stored in the Locker Rooms, small timber or metal lockers will be provided along the walls, 6 tiers high, for 200 men and 75 ladies. Seating and hanging space will be provided for 120 men and 30 ladies. Floor surfacing will be rubber belting.

Ablutions

Adequate hand basins, footbaths and showere are provided, together with toilet accommodation, which will serve the golf and social functions of the Club.

Professional's Shop and Facilities

The shop and office are placed to have unrestricted views to both starting tees and the 18th green. Although temporarily housed in the future Ladies Lounge in Phase 1, the fittings are designed for complete re-use in Phase 2.

The Professional's workshop has direct access to the Club Store, and a window controlling access to the Locker Rooms is in both Phases.

Floor surfacing will be rubber belting.

Social Facilities

A Mixed Lounge, with view over the course, direct access from the Mens Locker Room, and a covered way from the Ladies Locker Room, will cater for functions of up to 100 people. A moveable screen will sub-divide the room for normal use, and will set aside dining space for 20 people. Provision is made for a Buffet Counter and direct service from the Kitchen.

A Committee Room, accessible from the Dining area will seat 14 people.

Steward's Quarters

The Steward's Quarters provide a Living Room, one Bedroom and a

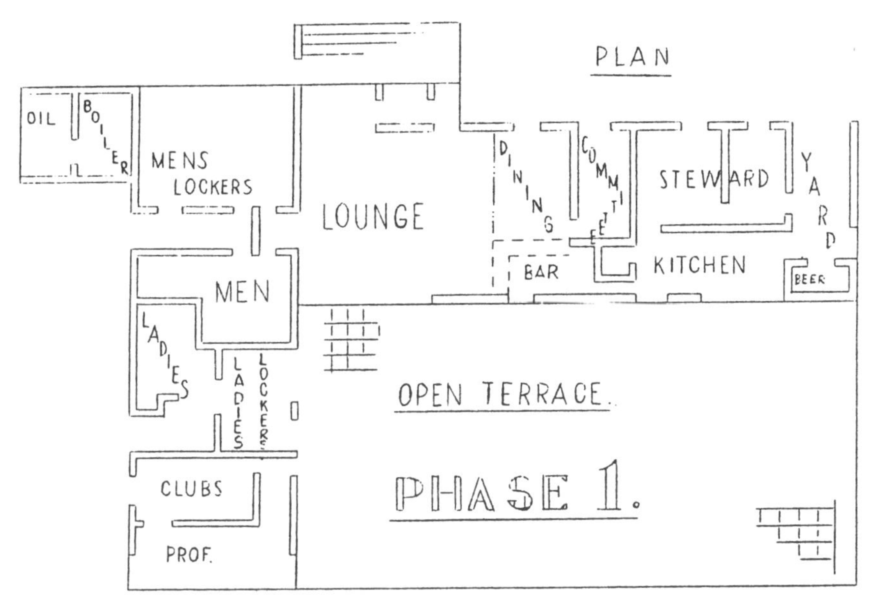

Bathroom. The kitchen and beer store will be provided in Phase 1, and no costly alterations or additions will be needed in Phase 2.

PHASE 2

The intention is to provide extensions to the Lounge and Dining Room areas, allowing space for 150 to attend any function. It will also incorporate extensions to the Steward's Quarters, allow room for a Manager's Office, and space for a Gentleman's Bar and Billiard Room.

Additions at this stage will include a Club and Trolley Store, at one end of which will be a drying area, and the Professional's Shop will be moved from its position in Phase 1, making that space available for a Ladies Lounge.

Social Functions

Mixed Lounge to be extended, with direct access to the Ladies Lounge, Dining Room, Mens Bar, Terrace, Locker Rooms and Committee Room. The sliding doors will enable the combined Lounge and Dining Area to be used for functions up to 150 people.

Dining Room will cater for 52 people.

A covered Terrace with service from the Kitchen and Bar, directly overlooking the Putting Green and course.

Mens Bar and Billiard Room – this small compact Bar leads into a one table Billiard Room, both with direct access from the Bar. The Billiard Room will have an external door and is so designed that it may be used after the rest of the Club is locked for the night, and the Steward has gone off duty.

A Committee Room, accessible from the Lounge, will seat 14 people, and sliding doors will convert it for use as a Band Platform or Stage, for social functions. A small Hall will act as a draught lobby to the main social areas, and will accommodate Club notice boards.

Ladies Lounge

This Lounge is adjacent to the Ladies Changing Room, with views over the course, and accessible from the Main Lounge for social functions and the area will serve as changing space for performers.

Manager's Office

An office is provided for a Manager, as at this stage of development, a full time Manager will be needed by the Club, in addition to the Steward.

Store

A store is provided in this phase, for the stowage of tables and chairs, in addition to separate cleaning material storage cupboards.

Club and Trolley Store

Conventional stowage of clubs vertically, is wasteful of floor space, and lock up storage in metal framed wire mesh units, arranged horizontally, four tiers high, is proposed for 200 bags. Heating pipes under the units will ensure that clubs are dried during storage, and the Professional will have access to the locker of any member with whom he has a contract for maintenance.

The drying room will be situated at the end of the Club and Trolley Store, adjacent to the central heating plant. Ample provision will be made in this drying room for the drying of both ladies and gents clothing and shoes. Trolleys will be stowed on the walls.

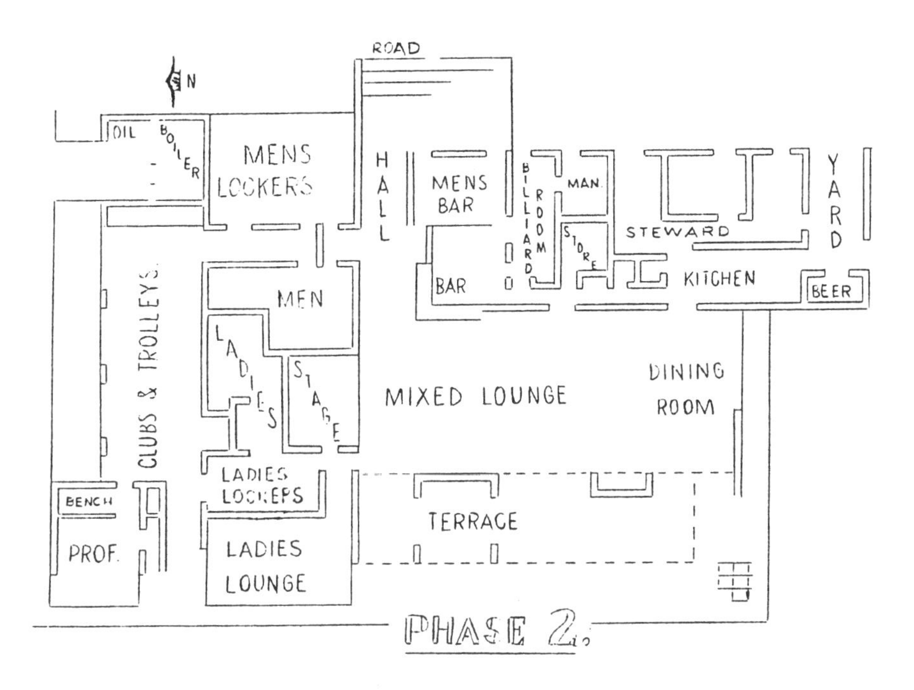

PHASE 3

Range of Activities

In addition to the established golfing activities, greater mobility and increased affluence in the future, suggests that facilities for other recreations such as tennis, bowls, driving range, archery etc., could be catered for, and indoor activities, such as squash, badminton, etc.

Phase 3 was never carried out, but for interest the draft plan is shown. It can be pointed out that not all of these facilities have been offered by our neighbours at the 'Forest of Arden Golf and Country Club'.

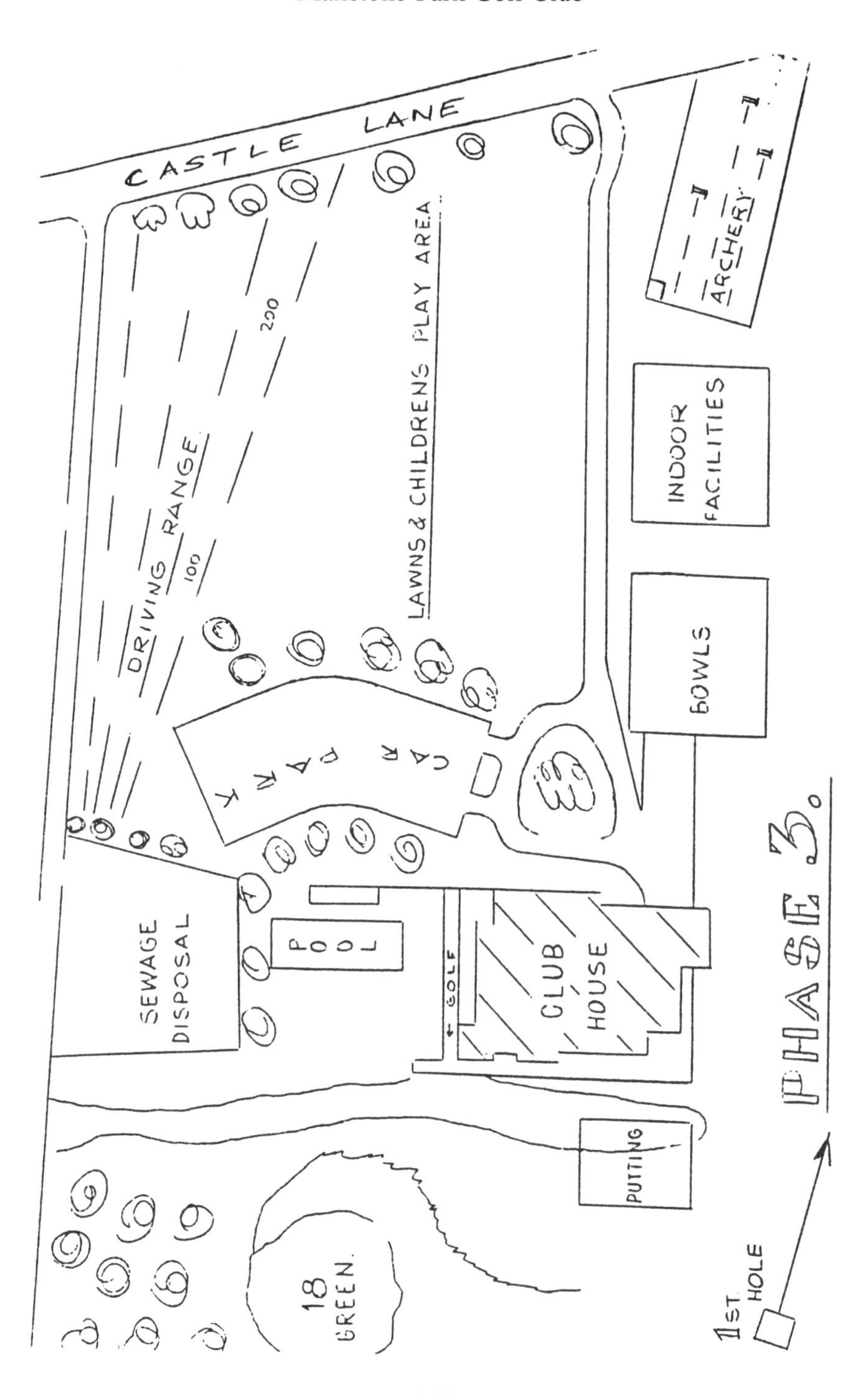
CASTLE LANE
DRIVING RANGE
100
200
LAWNS & CHILDRENS PLAY AREA
ARCHERY
INDOOR FACILITIES
BOWLS
CAR PARK
SEWAGE DISPOSAL
POOL
← GOLF
CLUB HOUSE
PHASE 3.
PUTTING
18 GREEN.
1ST HOLE

COST ESTIMATES

EXTERNAL WORKS

Including the access roads, turning areas, external pavings, steps, ramps and sewage disposal plant – £13,000.

PHASE 1 – Clubhouse

All building costs, inclusive of fittings in the Changing Rooms, Club Store, Professional's Shop, Bar and Kitchen. The cost of loose furniture and furnishings is not included – £30,000.

PHASE 2 – Clubhouse

The cost of additional work to complete the Clubhouse – £20,000.

It is apparent that not all of the proposals in Phase 2 were carried out. The Billiard Room, Manager's Office and Men's Bar were never included, and the efficient and well thought out Club and Trolley stowage area with drying facilities incorporated never materialised.

The work was completed, and finally handed over by the building contractors on August 8th 1969, and an official Opening Ceremony took place on September 20th 1969, with Keith Speed, the Member of Parliament for Meriden performing the actual ceremony.

Once the new Clubhouse was in use, it became essential to review the lease of the course which had been negotiated for the 50 years from 1946 until 1996. A tentative approach was made to the new President, Captain Charles Fetherston-Dilke and he readily agreed, and the new lease was arranged from 1972 until 2022, for the original 105 acre course, with an option of a further 25 years. It was also agreed that should the lessor require the course to give up the lease, then the Club would be paid compensation of such a sum as would be required to lay out a new 18 hole course in Warwickshire.

The lease on the land occupied by the old Prisoner of War Camp was negotiated when the new Clubhouse was being built, and this was for a longer period of 99 years from 1967 until 2066.

Chapter Four

New Beginnings at Maxstoke

The new Clubhouse heralded exciting and more stable times for the Club. After the trauma of the closure of an excellent course at Castle Bromwich, followed by some 20 years of financial problems, temporary residence in the Castle stables, a lot of hard work and fortunately some positive thinking by an active Committee, Maxstoke Park Golf members could finally look forward to a brighter future.

The Clubhouse was 'officially' opened on Saturday 20th September 1969 by Keith Speed, the Member of Parliament for Meriden. A large marquee was hired and an evening's dancing was enjoyed by those in attendance, which included a buffet.

In a foreword to the brochure, Bill Dudley Evans pointed out that in the 71 years since several doctors first started the Club in the Ward End area, there had been four previous buildings used by members, none of which were built for the purpose.

An acknowledgment was made on the brochure which stated that 'It is impossible to name all those who have given valuable assistance. However, without the generosity of the sponsors and advertisers, the events for the opening could not have been staged on such a scale. We thank them all most sincerely for their support'.

For what was believed to be the first such competition in the Club's history, a PRO/AM Tournament was held on the day after the opening of the Clubhouse. Almost certainly the biggest name amongst the Professionals was Charlie Ward from Little Aston. Charlie Ward played in several 'Ryder Cup' teams in the immediate post war era, and in 1960 was still a formidable golfer. Other well known Midland names were Jack Cawsey, Frank Miller, Michael Skerritt, Tom Hassall and of course our own Don Knight.

Looking at the members names who played that day, many of them are no longer with us. Fortunately a good few have survived, a little older, a little greyer, but still enjoying their golf.

In what was apparently the last edition of the 'Miscellany' published by Bert Jolley from the Castle, it is interesting to note the names of several of the competition winners. Jim King won the 'Smevans Cup', the 'Final

Maxstoke Park
Golf Club
Souvenir Brochure
2/6
COMMEMORATING
OPENING OF THE NEW
CLUBHOUSE
THE NEW CLUBHOUSE
ARCHITECTS : A.G.SHEPPARD FIDLER & ASSOCIATES
QUANTITY SURVEYORS : SILK & FRAZIER
MAIN CONTRACTOR : RIX CONTRACTORS LIMITED

Gala Opening Night

SATURDAY, 20th SEPTEMBER, 1969

AT 7 p.m.

BY KEITH SPEED, R.D., M.P.

Dancing in the Large Marquee

TO

JOE ROYAL AND HIS MUSIC

from 9 p.m. onwards

Gala Buffet will be served at 10 p.m.

Medal' resulted in a tie between Ted Feeley and Ralph Souster, and a replay was called for to decide the winner. Harry Poynton won Division 2 with Arthur Poole a close runner up, and Division 3 was won by Sid Watts with Henry Locker-Marsh in second spot.

The 'Hewlett Trophy', a greensome foursomes competition was won by M. Simmonds and a 'new' member Harry Wood, described as " coming to us, as an established middle handicap player". Doug Marston the Competition Secretary of the day, each month provided a comprehensive record of all the competitions that were ongoing at the time.

With the occupation of the new Clubhouse, it became necessary once again to alter the sequence of play for the 18 holes. The 10th hole down to Castle Lane was re-numbered as the 1st hole. It was interesting to note that the preliminary layout for this hole showed an alternative position to

Pro-Am Tournament

2 p.m. SUNDAY, 21st SEPTEMBER, 1969

For details of Competition starting times, etc.
please see pages 12 and 13

PRIZES :

- WINNING CARD
- 2nd BEST CARD
- 3rd BEST CARD
- BEST FIRST NINE HOLES
- BEST SECOND NINE HOLES
- LONGEST DRIVE
- HOLE-IN-ONE AT THE 16th
- NEAREST THE PIN AT THE 16th

An official photograph will be taken and all Members are invited to be in attendance no later than 1.30 p.m.

where it is today. The intention was to make a dog leg to the left, with a green virtually positioned where the Steward's bungalow is located.

The short 2nd hole from the Castle was abandoned but the green was retained to extend the old 1st hole which then became the 11th, and at 517 yards became the longest hole on the course. A new short hole, our present 2nd was added, and the 11th hole became the new 3rd hole. The rest of the holes then followed on in the sequence played today.

Considerable tree planting took place in tandem with the new course layout, particularly on the holes on the Clubhouse side of the lakes. Looking at the specification, I am not sure that all the trees quoted were ever planted, but nonetheless, it is interesting to read what was intended.

Twenty Silver Birch and Mountain Ash were planted on the right hand side of the 1st fairway, from the telegraph pole down to the oaks, in groups

PROFESSIONAL–AMATEUR GOLF TOURNAMENT, SUNDAY, 21st SEPT

Match No	AMATEUR	PROFESSIONAL	Starting Hole	Time	Score
1	A. BROCK	A. SADDLER of Whittington	1	2.00	
2	R. G. R. CARTER		1	2.00	
3	P. COLGAN	J. WIGGETT of Kings Norton	5	2.00	
4	P. BLUNDELL		5	2.00	
5	G. W. DOWSE	M. SKERRITT of Nuneaton	10	2.00	
6	N. E. TAYLOR		10	2.00	
7	E. C. FEALEY	D. R. KNIGHT of Maxstoke	13	2.00	
8	J. W. LAND		13	2.00	
9	W. J. MARTIN	T. HASSALL of Handsworth	1	2.08	
10	H. W. ROSE		1	2.08	
11	W. A. HARRISON	D. RATTY of Leamington	5	2.08	
12	H. W. POYNTON		5	2.08	
13	A. CARTWRIGHT	T. COLLINGE of Olton	10	2.08	
14	F. CARTWRIGHT		10	2.08	
15	M. D. SIMMONDS	M. NOTLEY of Sandwell	13	2.08	
16	R. E. SHARPE		13	2.08	
17	A. MILLAR JNR.	H. McDONALD of Droitwich	1	2.16	
18	R. SOUSTER		1	2.16	
19	L. C. R. HEMMINGS	J. H. CAWSEY Unattached	5	2.16	
20	A. WENMAN		5	2.16	

12

BLACK & WHITE
OFFICIAL STARTERS: W. G. BLACK,
ALL PROFESSIONALS PLAY OFF SCRATCH

Match No.	AMATEUR	PROFESSIONAL	Starting Hole	Time	Score
21	H. S. BADLANDS	E. LARGE of South Staffs.	10	2.16	
22	L. H. BROCK		10	2.16	
23	R. WRIGHT	E. BOOY of Fulford Heath	1	2.24	
24	D. W. BRENNAN		1	2.24	
25	W. ROBINSON	D. FITTON of Walsall	5	2.24	
26	A. NANSEN		5	2.24	
27	E. CARS	R. JOHNSON of Brockton Hall	10	2.24	
28	K. M. REHMANY		10	2.24	
29	G. SHERRATT	R. WELDON of Bloxwich	1	2.32	
30	B. BECKETT		1	2.32	
31	R. FEENEY	J. RHODES of Walsall	10	2.32	
32	K. H. BOOTH		10	2.32	
33	E. WYATT	R. LIVINGSTONE	1	2.40	
34	G. HITCHMAN	Unattached	1	2.40	
35	R. CLARKE	W. BYARD of Gay Hill	1	2.48	
36	R. G. CARTER ×		1	2.48	
37	A. A. TRIPPAS	C. H. WARD of Little Aston	1	2.54	
38	S. C. HILL		1	2.54	
39	G. BRENNAN	F. MILLER of Moseley	1	3.00	
40	A. POOLE		1	3.00	

MARKERS
J. KING, J. F. EDWARDS
AMATEURS PLAY OFF ¾ HANDICAP

13

of threes, fours and fives at a cost of £1.85 each. On the left hand side, another forty trees of the same type were planted.

On the 3rd hole, ten Plane, five Silver Birch and five Chestnuts were planted on the right hand side some 150 yards out, to drift towards the 1st green.

On the 4th hole, down to the large trees on the right hand side of the fairway, twenty Silver Birch, five Mountain Ash and five Plane, and on the right hand side of the 5th hole, five Silver Birch, five Mountain Ash, five Acer Platanoides and five Whitebeam. Also on the left hand side of the 5th, at 45 degrees from the tee, thirty Silver Birch And Mountain Ash.

On the left hand side of the 7th hole, thirty five Scarlet Oak, Pink Chestnut, Tilia, Whitebeam and White Chestnut. At the back of the green, thicken up existing Silver Birch with twenty more. On the 8th hole create a spinney on the right hand side, some 210 yards out, with fifty Silver Birch to form a better dog leg. On the left hand side, 250 yards out, twenty Scarlet Oak and Chestnut.

On the 10th hole, 70 yards out, to the right of the 1st tee, ten Silver Birch, five Mountain Ash and five Crataegus. Between the 10th and 18th fairways, fifty Weeping Willows which were recommended with the moist nature of the soil in that area.

Down the left hand side of the 11th hole, two drifts, 200 and 300 yards out, comprising Chestnut, Tilia, Crataegus and Oak, ten in each drift.

The 13th hole, three drifts on the left hand side, six Ailanthus, six Crataegus, six Whitebeam, six Silver Birch and six Mountain Ash.

On the 14th hole, behind the 12th tee, create a copse of thirty Silver Birch and Mountain Ash, and towards the 8th fairway, another group of thirty comprising Mountain Ash and Silver Birch.

On the 17th hole, 2 drifts running the full length of the hole on the right hand side, each with ten Silver Birch and ten Mountain Ash.

Finally on the drive from Castle Lane, it specifies seventy assorted trees, including Silver Birch, Mountain Ash, Flowering Cherry, Crab, Acer and Golden Weeping Willow. The total expenditure quoted for 815 trees was £1290.

I joined the Club in 1972 and in that year the conifers along the left hand side of the 17th fairway were planted. For probably some five years, it was not difficult to recover your ball if a misdirected drive went out of bounds. An item in the Green's Meeting shortly after the planting, referred to a request by our Landlord of the day, that golfers should not be allowed to enter the newly planted area. Nowadays of course it is almost certain that a lost ball is the most likely outcome of hooked drive.

Since that tree planting exercise of 30 years ago, many more trees have been planted around the course, and the trees described earlier have now grown considerably and realised the potential of their intended planting.

Thirty years ago, the course was wide open and one could get away with misdirected drives, but now many of our fairways are tree lined and have definition to them – errant drives do get punished.

Unfortunately, over the same period of time, many of our mature trees have perished, and in my time I recall that probably about ten magnificent old trees have gone. Many of the visitors to Maxstoke do comment on our old trees. Most of them have been brought into play, and many holes are designed around them, such that they deter the majority of golfers from attempting short cuts round intended dog legs. Many have been utilised to good advantage to tighten wayward approach shots to a number of greens.

THE 'SEVENTIES'

Once the Clubhouse was opened, many considerable changes occurred over the next few years, and the Club began to improve in many ways. More attention was paid to the course, but there were still problems, particularly with drainage which continued for many years.

In 1971 a new class of membership was recommended – 5 day. It was restricted to a maximum of 50. Although this proposal came from the General Committee it did not get the approval of the members at the AGM and two years elapsed before it was introduced.

Reserved car parking spaces were allocated to Officers of the Club for the first time. The year of office was added to the Captain's badge for the first time.

A commemorative dinner was held to celebrate the 50 years membership of Bill Dudley-Evans, and a former Captain of the Club, A. J. Wenman who had retired to Ross on Wye, called his house Maxstoke XIX. '

A 'decimalised' cash register was bought. In January of 1971, concern was expressed at frequent locker room thefts. The Steward of the day complained that he could not cater for 24 people due to shortage of crockery. Apparently doubts already existed about deficiencies in stock and with crockery and cutlery also going missing, an inventory of all equipment belonging to the Club was undertaken. Stewards came and went frequently about this time.

A robbery took place at the Clubhouse on Sunday October 10th 1971. I had mentioned earlier that the intended Phase 2 of the Clubhouse building programme never went ahead as planned. This robbery probably had much to do with the change in plans. Harry Field who was on the Committee of the day, recalled that Mr Spanton was the resident Steward at the time, and that he and his wife lived in the area now occupied by the dining room. The area nearest to the Club Lounge being their living quarters, and further on was a bedroom and a bathroom.

On the night in question, an armed gang thrust a double barrelled shotgun through the bedroom window, threatened the Steward's wife and ordered the Steward to turn off the alarm and open the door. Not surprisingly, the Steward complied with their demands, the gang then ransacked the Club, leaving Mr and Mrs. Spanton in a state of shock. According to the account given by the Treasurer, the loss was in the order of £194 in cash, and some £233 in stock, cigarettes and spirits.

At the eventual enquiry, the police recommended that the Steward be housed as far away from the Club premises as possible. At the next Committee meeting, it was decided to follow the police recommendation and it was agreed to delay the Phase 2 of the Clubhouse project, and to build a bungalow instead.

On 24th October 1971, another PRO/AM took place and many of the local well known professionals took part including Peter Butler, who at that time was the Professional at Harborne Golf Club, and also a regular member of the 'Ryder Cup' team.

His card which is shown below was at that time, the record score made by a Professional at Maxstoke. His 8 at the old 11th hole, 571 yards, spoiled his card. Wayward tee shots from the competition tee, right back to the hedge, often strayed on to the 12th fairway and were deemed out of bounds.

SSS71

Handicap SCR — Maxstoke Park Golf Club — Date 24.10.71

Name of Player P.J BUTLER — Competition PRO/AM

Marker's Score	Hole No.	Name	Length Yards	Length Metres	Stroke Index	Par and Bogey	Score	Bogey Result
3	1	Camp	389	356	[illegible]	4	4	
3	2	Hawthorns	167	153	[illegible]	3	3	
3	3	The Foxes	433	396	[illegible]	4	4	
4	4	Stella's	365	334	[illegible]	4	4	
3	5	Pooltail	268	245	[illegible]	4	3	
4	6	Lakelands	356	325	[illegible]	4	4	
4	7	Keepers	480	439	[illegible]	5	4	
4	8	The Warren's	485	443	[illegible]	5	4	
2	9	Coot's Lair	210	192	[illegible]	3	3	
30	OUT		3153	2883		36	33	

Marker's Score	Hole No.	Name	Length Yards	Length Metres	Stroke Index	Par and Bogey	Score	Bogey Result
4	10	Dilke's Bluff	376	344	7	4	4	
4	11	Blyth Drive	571	522	2	5	8	
4	12	The Oaks	345	315	14	4	4	
4	13	Turkeys	407	372	4	4	4	
3	14	Old Road	324	296	11	4	4	
4	15	Birchwood	336	307	13	4	4	
2	16	Old Park	171	156	17	3	2	
3	17	Castle	421	384	3	4	4	
4	18	Old Manor	356	325	10	4	4	
32	IN		3307	3021		[illegible]	38	
		OUT	3153	5904		36	33	
		TOTAL	6460	2883		72	71	

Marker's Signature G. Sheppard

Player's Signature P. Butler

In Bogey Competitions, Competitors must enter their actual score for all holes won or halved.

BOGEY PLAY

Holes won (+)

Holes halved (O)

Holes lost (—)

Bogey Result

MEDAL PLAY

Gross-Score

Handicap

Net Score 71

The subscriptions for 1972 were increased to the following levels:

	MEN	LADIES
Full playing members	£37.00	£19.00
Full playing member (age 21–25)	23.00	13.00
Full playing members (juniors)	7.50	5.00
Country membership	15.00	9.00

It was also agreed at the AGM that members on attainment of age 65 years, being fully retired, with not less than 15 years membership, their Annual Membership be reduced to £25.00.

At this AGM it was decided to consider the building of a bungalow for the Steward, thus enabling the Clubhouse to be used to greater advantage, rather than proceed with Phase 2 of the Clubhouse building programme.

Other plans being discussed in the early '70s were 'pop up' sprinklers, a swimming pool, the laying out of a driving range and the feasibility of providing squash courts facilities.

On the course, the new 2nd green had to be lifted and relaid, the 4th green was also lifted, and soil added to raise the level, and the level of the 7th and 15th greens were raised to give improved definition for approach shots from a distance.

An apprentice groundsman, who had been sent on a groundsman's course had received a high grade pass mark, and the Head Greenkeeper reported that the lad's performance and enthusiasm since returning to work had been exceptional. As a 'reward' the Committee presented him with 2 tickets for the Coventry v Hull City FA Cup tie.

The Professional, Don Knight reported that there were problems with Competition Start Sheets, as some members were booking times on the sheet but did not play in the Competition. In those days the Start Sheet was pinned to a board in the entrance to the Gent's Locker Room and payment was made when you went out to play. After discussion at Committee, although the practice was deplored, no action was taken.

In 1972, the Club applied for entrance to the Bainbridge Shield Competition for the first time. An Invitation Open Competition was held for the first time. Harry Field organised the event and a vote of thanks was recorded in the Minutes in appreciation. A trophy for this Competition had been presented by Bob Beckett which was also commended.

In 1973 Professional Don Knight, resigned after some 13 years service to take up a similar appointment at Newbold Comyn, near Leamington. Roy Young was appointed to take his place

The Steward and his wife who had been the victims of the armed raid left the employ of the Club. L. R. C. (Dick) Hemmings who was already

Hon. Treasurer was scheduled to take over from Arthur Trippas as Hon. Secretary, and his wife Dora temporarily took over.

Dick Hemmings had earlier been House Chairman and E. W. Hemmings, his brother succeeded him in this position. There was unease amongst members about their role with the Club, and rumours were circulating that a faction of the Committee had the intention to propose that Dick Hemming became the 'salaried' Manager of Maxstoke Park Golf Club, and that his wife take over as the Stewardess of the Club. Furthermore, that they would move into the proposed new bungalow. With so many controversial issues being discussed, it was inevitable that there was considerable difference of opinion on the Committee. Matters came to a head and an Extraordinary General Meeting was convened in February 1974. At that meeting, Ron Trippas who was Club Captain, gave a speech that was intended to justify the proposals being put forward, in an attempt to persuade members that the 'many duties and work involved in running the Club gave little option but to appoint a full time Manager, and that L. C. R. Hemmings be appointed to this role'.

The climate of opinion expressed by the majority of the Committee, was that bearing in mind the financial position of the Club at that time, it would be difficult to sustain a paid Manager. The membership obviously felt the same way and the resolution was defeated, firstly, quite convincingly by a show of hands, and then by a postal vote which did not receive the required majority of 75% of the membership.

But that was not the end of the matter. A few days later, Dick Hemmings resigned from his positions of Hon. Secretary and Hon. Treasurer of the Club. At a Committee Meeting held a week later Ron Trippas – Club Captain, Bill Dudley-Evans – Club Chairman and Arthur Trippas – Green's Chairman, also resigned.

The remainder of the Committee endeavoured to continue the management of the Club's affairs, but after a period of two weeks reached the conclusion that to serve the best interest of the Club, they also should resign. It was however agreed that the resigning officers together with Norman Taylor – Captain Elect, Tom Marks and Doug Marston – Vice Presidents and Vic Johnson – House Chairman would manage the Club's affairs until the next AGM scheduled for July.

In the interim period of 4 months, Ron Trippas the former Captain collapsed and died on the course, the Bungalow was completed and officially handed over, and a new Steward, G. Wigley and his family took up residence.

At the AGM a new Committee was formed, Norman Littleford became Hon. Secretary, Arthur Trippas retained the Green's Chairmanship, Vic Johnson the House Chairmanship, and after a ballot from a list of 17 valid nominations, John Barber, Dennis Brennan, Les Brock, Les Buonvino,

George Dowse, Jack Edwards, Ted Fealey, Harry Field and Bert Jolley were elected and made up the new Committee.

Subsequently, Harry Field took over the vacant position of Hon. Treasurer, and in September L. C. R. (Dick) Hemmings was appointed as General Manager. Arthur Trippas once again resigned as Green's Chairman and was replaced by Tom Marks.

The new Committee soon had problems. The new Steward and his wife, despite excellent references, soon had problems in meeting the Committee's requirements as to their duties. Differences of opinion frequently occurred, and after several exchanges which resulted in a somewhat strained relationship between them and the Committee, the Steward and his wife left after just six months' service with the Club. Club member Les Buonvino took over as Steward.

An indication of the deficiencies of the Clubhouse were apparent when it was decided not to run a Mixed Open due to lack of changing room space for the Ladies. On the occasion of a Ladies Charity Meeting the Gent's Locker Room was given over to the Ladies for the day.

After years of comings and goings of Greenkeepers, a new Head Greenkeeper took over, Trafford Stonebridge who was to give over twenty years continuity to the position.

In 1975 after so much upheaval in the previous two years, life appeared to return to normal. The drainage problems still persisted in parts of the course however, and a new raised 5th tee was brought into play. It is interesting to note that a quotation for spring and summer maintenance of all greens and tees which included power scarifying and sweeping, slit tining and aerating, and application of fertiliser came to just £516.

For the first time since Castle Bromwich days, the Club had no overdraft at the Bank. However, concern was expressed at the AGM at the Club's finances, the balance of income over expenditure was £5,537 less than the year before and expenditure had risen by £6,000. The Hon. Treasurer, Harry Field in his report pointed out that Visitor's Fees, Fruit Machine takings, Bar profits and Competition receipts had all risen substantially, without which there would have been a loss on the year.

It was also pointed out that entrance fees and subscriptions had only risen by £360 over the previous year, which indicated that the members had made very little extra contribution to the increased expenditure.

The Committee indicated that there was no alternative but to increase subscriptions:

	MEN	LADIES
Full Members	£44.00	£27.00
Full Members (21–25)	34,00	19.00
Full Members (18–21)	26.00	16.00
Full Members (under 18)	11.00	9.00
Five Day Members	30.00	
Country Membership	18.00	12.00
Social Membership	8.00	

However all was not gloom, many improvements were made to the course and reasonable confidence was felt by the Committee that the Club was going in the right direction.

Sprinklers were introduced for the first time on the greens, not the present 'pop up' variety, but basic garden lawn revolving type which had to be moved around the green manually, and were powered from long hoses fed from taps situated at points around the course.

The lake was dredged and deepened, and the 6th and 9th holes were not played for some 3 months whilst the dredging operation took place. It was estimated that some 10,000 cubic yards of silt were removed and that the increased water storage potential would provide a back up supply for the proposed automatic sprinkler system scheduled for installation in 1976.

At the bar of the clubhouse prior to the extensions. Les Green and Arthur Trippas on the left, and on the right Roy Young, Club Professional, and Trafford Stonebridge, Head Greenkeeper

The cost of the drainage of the lake was £3,444.00 and the silt removed proved to be of great benefit in the cause of course management.

After several arguments over a long period concerning casual dress and permitted hours restrictions, and indeed many instances of transgressions, it was decided to increase the time that casual dress be permitted to 6.00 p.m.

CONSOLIDATION AT MAXSTOKE

By 1976, events at Maxstoke improved, the Clubhouse Building Fund stood at £43,505 and there was a belief that the Club would be able to go ahead with enlargement of the Clubhouse.

An honour was bestowed upon Bill Dudley-Evans by being elected as President of the Warwickshire Union of Golf Clubs, whilst Maxstoke Park Golf Club claimed the headlines with Tony Allen and Alan Cartwright becoming winners of the 'Bainbridge Shield' and Roy Young winning the Shirley Pro/Am Tournament.

Alan Cartwright and Tony Allen with the 'Bainbridge Shield' that they had won for the second time

Club members were asked to volunteer to adopt a hole and become responsible for filling in all divot holes on their specific fairway. This was a wonderful idea, especially as 1976 was a dry summer, the actual time

Standing: Gary Knight, Tony Allen, Alan Brock, Adrian Harrison, Robert Frost, Martin Buxton and John Gough. *Seated*: Alan Cartwright, Barry Robb, Pat Colgan (Captain), Bill Baker and F. Rennie

spent was relatively short, and if three or four members operated at one time, it normally only amounted to twenty to thirty minutes at the most. It was a good way to raise a thirst anyway and it's a pity that it can't be re-instated.

A painting of the President was displayed in the Clubhouse for the first time. Tony Allen also won the 'Howitt Bowl' for the second time in three years. There were some excellent golfers in the Club at that time and the Scratch League Team won the Championship. The members of the squad who played during the succesful year are shown above;

On the debit side, catering available at the Club was more or less confined to the odd sandwich and there were many complaints. In an attempt to remedy the problem, the Steward was allowed to engage a part time chef at a wage of £15 per week.

The Subscriptions had risen sharply by some 33% from the previous year and for 1976 were fixed at:

	MEN	LADIES
Full playing members	£65.00	£27.00
Full playing members (21–25)	49.00	29.00
Full playing members (18–21)	38.00	24.00
Full playing members (Under 18)	18.00	15.00
Country membership	27.00	19.00
5 day membership	45.00	

By the following year the Building Fund had increased to £60,504, and agreement was given to go ahead and prepare up dated plans for Phase 2 of the Clubhouse improvements. The general concept was to extend the Locker Rooms, Main Lounge area and the Bar. The automatic sprinkler system was installed on the course.

The General Manager L. C. R. (Dick) Hemmings and his wife left the Club to manage North Foreland Golf Club and Lou Hatton took over as Club Manager. Former Hon. Secretary and Past Captain Norman Littleford passed away.

An item of interest indicated that a sponsored walk was going to take place on Sunday April 16th at 2.30 p. m. and that they would provide their own Stewards to ensure safety across the 4th and 5th holes. It did not mention crossing the 3rd and 2nd holes, so presumably the walkers kept behind the hedge on that section of the walk.

Shortly after, the Club had a letter from the Public Footpath Preservation Society indicating that they had been establishing the correct route of the public footpath, particularly the section which crossed the 2nd and 3rd holes. After some discussion the Committee decided to repair the two stiles on the section, but not to signpost the route.

George Dowse the Competition Secretary gave a comprehensive report to the Greens Committee indicating that 319 Full Members had handicaps, whilst 22 had not, 20 Five Day Members had handicaps and 22 had not. 9 Five Day Members had been refused Full Membership, and 15 Full Members had requested transfer to 5 Day Membership, and 11 of them had handicaps.

One of our original members who moved from Castle Bromwich, Doug Marston, was presented with a Colour TV to commemorate his 50 years service with the Club. Doug in his younger days was a very fine golfer and played off 2 handicap for some years.

In his later years, Doug was badly affected with arthritis but he still served the Club in the capacity of Competition Secretary. He needed transportation to the Club, and every competition day he waited patiently for cards to be handed in, and then would enter them meticulously into his record book, this before the days of computers. Nonetheles if you had a handicap query, Doug would produce his book and could give information on every competition that you had ever played in. The ditch across the 18th fairway was ducted and filled in.

It was decided that only wide wheel caddy carts would be allowed on the course after 1st November, but this requirement ran into trouble fairly quickly as the Professional, Roy Young, was not able to meet the demand from members.

Tony Allen won the Warwickshire Amateur Championship, and it was announced at the 1978 AGM that this was the first time that a Club member had won the award since 1928. This was not strictly true, as reference to any copy of the 'Golfer's Handbook' would have indicated. Philip Perkins won the award every year from 1921 until 1929 and in 1931 another Castle Bromwich golfer Harry Hall, took the title. Tony was however the first Maxstoke member to win the award.

During 1978, the long awaited improvements to the Clubhouse took place. The lounge area was extended from the old alignment where the dividing screen is now situated, forward to the present patio doors. The 19th hole bar was added, the old Steward's Quarters were demolished and the area vacated became the new dining room. The Bar was extended and the Gents Changing Room was enlarged.

The door from the Ladies Changing Rooms thereby opened into the Lounge whereas before it was an external door opening on to the patio.

The Clubhouse extensions were officially opened by the President, Captain Charles B. Fetherston-Dilke on Saturday 14th April 1979, and representing the Club at the simple ceremony were Harry Poynton the Club Captain, Carol Patterson the Lady Captain and Victor Johnson the House Chairman.

Reference to the earlier plans indicate that there were significant omissions from that which had previously been envisaged. The earlier plans had indicated that the main Lounge area would be a Mixed Lounge, with separate Ladies Lounge and a separate Mens Bar. Neither of these segregated options took place which was probably just as well with today's modern outlook on sex discrimination.

The Club and Locker Storage Area which was intended to be an integral part of the Clubhouse never happened, and the Manager's Office and Billiard Room never materialised. The original concept of a Dining Room was for it to be a section of the Mixed Lounge but of course the removal of the Steward's Quarters gave the opportunity for the area to be sited there, and allowed the 19th Casual Bar be be introduced.

Recognition of the Club came with Maxstoke Park 'hosting' two major Midland events, the 'Courage Trophy' and the 'Howitt Bowl', and our players winning in important competitions. Alan Cartwright and Tony Allen won the 'Bainbridge Shield' for the first time and Tony Allen also won the 'Howitt Bowl' as mentioned earlier.

Pat Colgan became the new Club Captain in 1979, and his Captain's Day photograph was the first one taken at the new entrance to the Clubhouse.

Captain's Day of Pat J. Colgan, 1979

With the members now occupying the extended Clubhouse the Club were able to hold 'in house' functions, and the improved facilities and additional Lounge was used more often than hitherto. Unfortunately, within a very short time there were calls for further improvements, especially to the Ladies Changing Rooms.

Apparently the Committee already had plans produced but these seemed to confirm rumours that were circulating at the time. A few of the Committee had notions of forming a Sports Club, with squash courts, badminton, saunas and swimming being amongst the activities offered.

The British Squash Association were prepared to build squash courts and offered to pay the Club £1000 per annum rental, providing that their members had free use of the Club's facilities. Members had not been given the opportunity to see the plans, they had not been discussed at AGM level, and considerable doubts were being expressed by the members. Eventually the plans were displayed on the notice board and as a result, an Extraordinary General Meeting was called by the membership and the proposals discussed.

The resolution placed before the membership at the EGM asked for approval of the the plans so that the further extensions could go ahead. There was a heated meeting, the costing figures for the proposals were queried and in the event the resolution was defeated.

On the course there were several changes proposed. The most important was a proposal to eliminate the crossover between the 11th and 18th fairways by abandoning the old 11th tee and utilising the forward tee position. This would result in a loss of some 79 metres to the course. and would have brought the SSS down to 70.

This was not acceptable and it was decided to implement alternative changes that would recover the lost distance. The 18th green was repositioned some 40 metres nearer to the Clubhouse, the 6th and 10th tees were moved back some 15 metres, the 11th 'forward' tee was moved back 25 metres and a new 12th tee was built again 25 metres further back.

These proposals were carried out during the winter months of 1979 /80 and preliminary investigations were also instigated with a view to eliminating the 5th and 6th fairway crossover, and to consider the laying of a new 11th green some 25 metres further on.

After continued complaints with regard to the reluctance or inability of the Steward and his wife to offer acceptable catering, Angela Reading was appointed to provide full catering services. Angela lived locally and immediately the standard and range of catering improved.

On the Balance Sheet, members subscriptions realised £52,210, whilst fruit machine takings at £13,049 had overtaken visitor's fees which amounted to £11,096.

Another Maxstoke member who brought the name of Maxstoke Park into the spotlight was Malcolm Scott. Malcolm won the Club Competition which was sponsored by Willis-Faber, and went forward to the Midland Regional Finals at Kings Norton.

There were 20 qualifiers from various Midland Clubs and on the course they were joined by an impressive array of sports celebrities including Peter May, David Brown, Dennis Amiss and Ken Barrington from the world of cricket, soccer's Chris Balderstone and George Curtis, and former British Lion's and English rugger international Peter Robins.

The level of subscriptions had risen considerably for 1981 / 82 were set at the following levels:

	MEN	LADIES
Full Members	£140	£95
Full Members (21–24)	112	70
Full Members (18–20)	88	60
Full Members (16–17)	40	35
Full Members (under 16)	25	
Five Day Members	100	

An unusual occurence, but nevertheless almost certainly the only time that it has ever happened in the history of the Club, Alan Cartwright recorded two holes in one in the same round. With Ray Barrett marking his card he had 'aces' at the old 5th hole (par 4) 259 yards, and the 9th (par 3) 196 yards, on 16th August 1981.

In 1981 the PGA ran a Golf Clinic at Maxstoke, and this was well supported and of considerable interest to Club members. Vic Johnson who was Club Captain at the time does not remember the names of the Professionals, but it is of interest to spot the Club members who are still with us today, albeit a lot older but with less hair. Paul Mayov went round in 70 which apparently is still the course record for a professional.

During 1982 further improvements were carried out to the Clubhouse which more or less brought it up to the 1997 level.

Malcolm Scott receiving his qualifier's prize of two dozen golf balls from Gordon Denman of Wills-Faber with Vic Johnson, 1980 Club Captain

Club members with the professionals following the PGA Golf Clinic in July 1981

Again the specification that was originally drawn up was not carried out and several proposals were dropped. The main change affected the much needed enlargement to the Ladies Changing Rooms, which had a knock on effect of requiring a new Professional's Shop to be built.

The Gents Toilet and Shower facilities were enlarged and refurbished, changes were made in the Dining Room area which enabled private functions to be held segregated from the Lounge area, alterations were made to the kitchen area, beer store and the yard storage area.

Proposals deleted from the original concept were the provision of a snooker room, enlargement of the Dining Room and a small Club Room, which was intended to cater for Committee meetings, small functions such as whist drives, bridge matches etc.

At the A.G.M. held in February 1983, members queried that the snooker room had not been built and that this had been agreed when the plans were approved. The Treasurer of the day replied that 'the immediate objective of the Committee was to stabilise finances, and that once this happened, then consideration would be given to such building'.

At the same meeting, a resolution was passed that . 'the new plantation to the right of the 18th fairway would be known as 'Marks Wood'. Am I alone in not being aware of this appreciation bestowed on Tom Marks for his many years service as Green's Chairman.

Charles Turner's Captains Day – 1981

Watery outlook with newly planted 'Marks Wood' trees providing separation between the 10th and 18th fairways

THE MOST RECENT YEARS

As an appreciation of the amount of endeavour and time spent on behalf of the Club, two past members of the Committee were given due recognition of their hard work. Pat Colgan was granted a Hon. Life Membership of the Club and Arthur Trippas was made a Vice President.

Rather sadly, Pat did not survive very long after accepting the Life Membership. Club Captain, Tony Reading generously provided a trophy in memory of Pat, and recommended that the trophy be played for between Maxstoke 'A' Team and Walmley Golf Club 'A' Team. This was accepted and the match between the two clubs has been played each year ever since, and is certainly one of our most enjoyable inter club fixtures.

At the AGM held on 23rd March 1984, Tony Reading announced another sudden death, that of Arthur Trippas. Arthur in his long service with the Club had been Club Captain, Hon. Secretary, Club Chairman and Greens Chairman, and over the years had been a significant figure in ensuring that the Club survived the troublesome early years at Maxstoke. Fortunately, Tony was able to report that he had spoken to Arthur informing him of the appointment before he was taken ill, and that Arthur had been delighted to accept the honour.

At the AGM, Bill Rendall objected to the fact that competition start sheets went up on the board on a Wednesday, some 10 days before the event. Bill, not for the first time, complained that as a working man, he was not able to attend on Wednesdays and could not add his name to the list. He requested that the Start Sheets should be displayed on Saturday or Sunday, two weeks in advance.

The reply given was that 'Bill rarely missed a Competition, and in spite of the problem his name always appeared on the start sheet'.

Not a very sympathetic reply. Nowadays of course, the present Competition Secretary does put start sheets up two weeks in advance at weekends, and we can thank Bill for his perseverance in pursuing what he thought was a reasonable complaint.

On the course, the 11th hole was lengthened by laying the new green 25 metres further along. This was not a popular improvement as many members regarded the old green as one of the best on the course.

A notice was positioned on the 14th tee requesting members not to drive from that tee whilst the competition back tee on the 12th hole was occupied. Today when you note the size of the well established trees protecting the 12th tee it is easy to forget that the area in that part of the course was quite open not so many years ago, and wayward drives off the 14th could well have caused problems. 1983 was the year that the pond on the 10th came into play, and was also the year for the introduction of the 1.68 'big' ball.

The winners of the 'Chelpers Cup', the Winter League Competition were Gordon Hitchman and Bill Griggs seen here with their trophy. In the background to the left can be seen the building contractor's hut used when the Clubhouse extensions were carried out earlier.

In 1984, Alan Brock was selected as Captain of the Warwickshire County Second Team, and with Tony Allen as partner, they won the Warwickshire County Foursomes Competition.

The Balance Sheet for the year showed that £87,442 was received in Entrance Fees and Subscriptions which is more or less five times greater than the 1974 total. Thank goodness for fruit machines, with a net profit of £13,187. They still brought in more money than visitor's fees at £12,053. In 1974 however, the fruit machine takings were roughly 22 per cent of the entrance fee/subscription totals, whereas in 1984 the figure had dropped to 15 per cent. At the AGM, Norman Taylor was presented with a lead crystal decanter which was given as an appreciation of his services to the Club over a long period of time.

Owing to concern regarding the financial state of the Club, a Finance Committee was convened to investigate all aspects of the Club's income and expenditure. Apparently, according to comments appearing from time to time, it was not always clear to members of this committee exactly what their role was, and indeed what action would be taken upon their findings.

Members were once again not enthusiastic about proposed increases in subscriptions and it was decided to run a 'lottery' in an attempt to bring in additional revenue.

After a troublesome tenure in the position of Club Steward, mainly in connection with complaints regarding the standard of the catering, Les Buonvino resigned early in 1986 after some 10 years in service. He was replaced by Mr Bloomfield, but unfortunately he too left very quickly as it soon became apparent that he and his wife were quite unsuitable. Mr and Mrs. Peter Brown were then taken on.

Firstly Mr Brown did not get off to a good start. He was mugged whilst on the way to the bank, which obviously did not help. Unfortunately, the culprits were never caught, and this did cause considerable annoyance and upset to members of the Committee. Mr Brown seemed to lose some enthusiasm about the role of Steward, and once again the Committee felt the Club's interests would be better served with another change of Steward.

With the Club finances still not exactly flourishing, the Finance Committee recommended that the purchase of new machinery and the installation of extra drainage should be deferred.

	NAME(S)	H'cap.	Allow	Competition Par Bogey	189
A	T. Allen	+1	+1	Date 12th July 1986	
B				S.S.S. – White Tees 71 Yellow Tees 69	GENTS CARD

Marker's Score	Hole No.	Name	White Tees Yards	White Tees Metres	Yellow Tees Yards	Yellow Tees Metres	Par	Index	Gross Score A	Gross Score (B)	Nett Score (or nett best ball)	Win + Loss - Half 0 Points
		–·7 –·1 / –1·4 +1										
4	1	Camp	384	351	377	345	4	[illegible]	3			+
3	2	Hawthorns	165	151	156	143	3	[illegible]	2			+
4	3	The Foxes	431	394	378	346	4		4			0
–	4	Stella's	367	336	355	325	4	[illegible]	4			0
3	5	Pool Tail	268	245	259	237	4	[illegible]	3		4	0
4	6	Lakelands	362	331	355	325	4	[illegible]	4			0
5	7	Keepers	491	449	479	438	5	15	3			+
5	8	The Warren's	481	440	477	436	5	12	4			+
3	9	Coot's Lair	204	187	196	181	3	[illegible]	2			+
	Out		3153	2884	3032	2776	36		29			
–	10	Dilke's Bluff	373	341	363	332	4	7	3			+
5	11	Blythe Drive	458	419	409	374	4	2	5			–
4	12	The Oaks	379	347	338	309	4	11	4			0
4	13	Turkeys	406	371	400	366	4	4	4			0
4	14	Old Road	317	290	308	282	4	14	4			0
4	15	Birchwood	351	321	338	309	4	13	3			+
–	16	Old Park	171	156	161	147	3	17	3			0
4	17	Castle	448	410	403	369	4	3	4			0
4	18	Old Manor	422	386	399	365	4	10	4			0
	In		3325	3041	3119	2853	35	In	34	0		
Plus Strokes Taken at 5th & 7th Holes		TOTAL	6470	5925	6151	5629	71	Out	29	0		
							Total		63	0		
Marker's Signature	A H Brock						Handicap		+1	Bogey	Won	7
Player's Signature	T. Allen						NETT SCORE		64		Lost	1
REPLACE DIVOTS – REPAIR PITCH MARKS ON GREENS – RAKE BUNKERS											RESULT	+6

Tony Allen set a new course record with an excellent score of 64 off plus 1 handicap. The competition was a Par/Bogey and he returned a card of +6. Alan Brock marked his card.

Tony Allen was again in the limelight by winning the prestigious ‘Champion of Champions Competition’ for the third time. Dean Bradley, assistant to Professional Roy Young left the Club to take over as Professional at North Warwickshire Golf Club.

Yet another Steward was appointed, and as we all appreciate today, the choice of Bob and Sheila Cardwell was an excellent one, albeit not in the manner that was originally intended.

With regard to the Club Championship in 1988, which was won by Adrian Harrison, Dr K. M. Rehmany generously donated a new trophy which would be given to the member with the best net score in future Championships. Bob Beckett volunteered to run the 'Invitation Open' after the success of the earlier competition.

Bert Jolley was honoured by being awarded an Honorary Life Membership of the Club, as an appreciation of many years of service as Club Captain and as an active and hard working Committee man.

Subscriptions for 1990/91 were set at the following levels:

	MEN	LADIES
Full Member	£315.00	£210.00
Full Member (18–20)	203.00	141.00
Full Member (16–17)	86.00	74.00
Full Member (Under 16)	30.00	28.00
Five Day Member	225.00	210.00
Country Member	150.00	107.00
Social Member	13.00	

THE 'NINETIES'

As the Centenary landmark approached, it is reasonable to say that thanks to prudent 'housekeeping' and good management by a hard working and diligent Committee, the Club were at last in a sound financial state, and had a course which was getting better every year.

It is worth recording that the Officers responsible for this excellent state of affairs at the start of the decade were Hon. Secretary – John Evans, Hon. Treasurer – Harry Field, House Chairman – Harold Evans who had also been Hon. Secretary during the late '80s, Greens Chairman – Trevor Maddox and Jim McCulloch who had taken over as Competition and Handicap Secretary. Added to these names one must add Bob and Sheila Cardwell who were at last giving members excellent service and catering facilities.

At the 1990 AGM, Captain Charles B. Fetherston-Dilke, the Club President presented the Club with an oak gavel to be used at future AGMs. This ceremonial gavel had been cut from a beam taken from a tithe barn at the Castle demolished in 1957 and which had been built in the reign of Elizabeth I, and was therefore at least 400 years old.

An item of interest from the 'Golfer's Handbook' indicated that one Neil McEwan won the Warwickshire Stroke Play Championship in 1990 and also the Warwickshire Professional Championship.

The following year we had a change of presidency, as Captain Charles Fetherston-Dilke had written offering to give up the role after some twenty years in the position.

There was unanimous agreement at the AGM that long serving member Bill Dudley-Evans be appointed to this prestigious position. This was particularly appropriate as 1991 marked the 70th year of Bill's membership with the Club which he had joined as an eleven year old Junior way back in 1921.

The Club commemorated this incredible length of service by holding a Celebration Evening on Friday 5th July when a considerable numbers of friends and members attended and enjoyed an excellent meal laid on for the occasion. The President of the Warwickshire Union of Golf Clubs Chris Dixon was pleased to attend and gave details of Bill's enormous contribution to golf over the years. The menu for those with culinary interests is shown below:

Prawn Cocktail with Brown Bread

Braising Steak with Onions cooked in Red Wine
New Potatoes, Roast Potatoes
Cauliflower au Gratin
Carrots and Garden Peas

Melon with Stawberries and Vanilla Ice Cream

Cheese and Biscuits

Coffee and Chocolate Mints

Bill Dudley Evans joined Castle Bromwich Golf Club
as a junior at the age of eleven in 1921 where
his father was a member. The club moved to Maxstoke
in 1948 where he still competes in club competitions.
In fact he won the Veterans Cup in 1990 for the
second time returning a card to match his age.
An honoured life member of Maxstoke Park Club,
his loyal services have included stints as Assistant Secretary,
Secretary, Chairman of the committee & Captain in 1945.
He also captained the county second team off a two
handicap, and was non playing captain of the county first team.
He was the unions first Secretary in 1939, Chairman,
Deputy President then President of the Warwickshire Union.

The tribute to Bill detailing his achievements

Front cover of the leaflet commemorating Bill's 70th anniversary

During recent years considerable improvements had been made to the course and in 1991 probably the most significant came into play when the 5th hole was completely altered. A new green was built to the right of the older one which had always caused problems with the crossover on the 6th fairway. The new green had a water hazard on the approach which considerably increased the degree of difficulty resulting in a change of stroke index from 18 to 14.

Doug Hayward the Club Captain of the day was persuaded to officially open the new hole on his Captain's Day as can be seen in the photograph.

In his Captain's Newsletter Doug recalled that at the time of his taking an early bath, Dennis Hall, Frank Hubble and Frank Smith were noted to have been in the vicinity at the time.

An item of unusual interest at the Captain's Day was that with the usual 'shot gun' start, John Hobday playing the 16th, immediately holed his tee shot. John and his partner Frank Pritchard then went on to win the Captain's Cup. Doug indicated that 144 members supported his day and that this number is believed to be a record turnout. Quite a day for the Hobdays as Sylvia Hobday, the Lady Captain also managed to finish up testing the water.

Also in 1991, Hon Treasurer Harry Field stood down after six creditable years during which he ensured that the Club's finances were kept in good order and tighter control over expenditure maintained. Harry had an earlier seven year spell as Treasurer in the '70s.

The Club also were honoured by being host to the Coventry Lord Mayor's Charity Day held at Maxstoke on August 19th. The organisers were obviously most pleased with the hospitality and facilities offered and they have returned to Maxstoke every year since.

There were many well supported social events, and Doug Hayward in his Newsletters gave frequent complimentary comments at the success of these functions. Quiz Nights were held, a 'Music Hall' night, a Cabaret Evening with Mike Gerrard was a particular success, and special mention was made of a 'Karaoke Evening' with the Peter Taylor 'fan club' in attendance. The outstanding performance of the evening however went to Sadie, Caroline and Leanne for their brilliant rendering of 'Like a Virgin' which apparently brought the house down. Later in the year a Carol Concert by the 'Fillongley Choral Singers' was well supported and was another enjoyable experience for those in attendance.

Tony Allen won the 'Howitt Bowl' again, the Warwickshire Amateur Championship for the 3rd time, the Warwickshire Open Championship for the 5th time, and even more prestigious he won the English 'County Champion of Champions Trophy' at Clitheroe by four clear shots. He received the Trophy at the Warwickshire County Union of Golf Clubs

ROTARY CLUB OF COLESHILL

COUNTY OF WARWICK

ENGLAND

Headquarters:
Swan Hotel, Coleshill
Coleshill 62212

Luncheon Day
Monday 12.45 p.m.
Except Bank Holidays

"SERVICE ABOVE SELF"

In 1986 A great deal of discussion took place in Coleshill Rotary Club as to the merits or otherwise of holding a golf AM/AM competition to raise money for charity. I am delighted that interest has been maintained and that we are now holding our fifth fixture.

The event would not be possible but for the support from many people. Tony Reading of Coleshill Club, the original initiator of the competition, puts a great deal of hard work into making the day successful, together with Adrian Harrison and many Club Members. I thank them. The Club extends its thanks to Maxstoke Golf Club for allowing us to use the Course and Club Facilities, we much appreciate the generous gesture and are truly grateful. A last but special thanks is extended to all those sponsors , professionals and amateurs who gave their time and money to make the AM/AM actually work.

Teams For The 1991 AM/AM

NEWTOWN INDUSTRIAL PAINTS
D. Penrice (19)
G. T. Carless (21)
A. N. Other

BRADLEY MILLER JONES & DOCKER
J. Jones (24)
R. Gazey (15)
D. Alford (15)

HARBEN BARKER
Peter Scott (20)
Jim Harben (21)
John Baker (3)

PANDA PRE-PACKS
S. Morris (16)
E. Mold (13)
D. Dicken (11)

A. W. R. CONTRACT FLOORING
Alan W. Roberts (14)
G. Ryan (14)
P. Hutton (22)

HARCROS
Bill Hampton (20)
John Parry (18)
A. N. Other

SUTTON VESEY ROTARY
David Dedicoat (9)
Rob Willis (13)
Elizabeth Dedicoat (24)

CROWN ACCOUNTING SYSTEMS
George Kettrick (6)
H. Ashton (11)
W. Stewart (11)

SOLIHULL SWINGERS
Brian E. Beattie (15)
A. Niall Beattie (5)
Mark T. Hopton (12)

ERDINGTON ROTARY
Richard Parker (12)
Ian Hawkins (7)
Mark Needham (11)

STRAWBERRY BANK RESTAURANT
Eloy Marin (16)
Manuel Francos (18)
Pepe Frutos (10)

CAMBRIAN ENVIRONMENTAL SERVICES
W. Reading (20)
W. Waddington (24)
D. Pugh (12)

A. W. CONSTRUCTION P.L.C.
P. Goodwin (24)
M. Booth (24)
I. C. Bertchin (11)

POLYPIPE
J. Swindell (12)
M. P. Cowman (12)
A. Lawson (24)

PEARSON & WHITFIELD 'A'
L. B. Pearson (9)
G. Dean (16)
E. Jones (18)

PEARSON WHITFIELD 'B'
E. Pearson (20)
A. Allen (11)
M. O'Donnel (3)

DENNIS WALKER INSURANCES
Dennis Walker (18)
Andrew Walker (6)
John Ambler (13)

BLYTHE HILL
Roy Clarke (13)
D. Scott Miller (7)
M. Scott (24)

THE RUBBER MEN
L. Bramall (19)
J. Poxon (18)
S. Farmilow (13)

P. & M. EAGLE
Derek Winnett (13)
Jon Twigg (14)
E. Sercomb (5)

A. G. R. BUILDING CO.
Tony Reading (12)
Peter Henderson (12)
James Reading (11)

Annual Dinner at Copt Heath from the President of the English Golf Union, Dr Norman Bradford. It was pointed out that Nick Faldo and Ian Woosnam were previous winners of this trophy.

The Committee were delighted that the Club was honoured by the Rotary Club of Coleshill who selected Maxstoke Park to host an AM/AM on the course. A figure in excess of £2000 was raised for a local charity and many Club members participated as can be seen in the list of teams shown.

1992 started badly. There was a break in to the Trolley Shed on the night of January 5th/6th when many members had clubs stolen. Almost immediately after, the prefabricated Club Office was burnt down, Roy Young, the Professional, lost quite a lot of equipment, and Trafford Stonebridge the Head Greenkeeper, lost all of his records and golf clubs. Much of the Office Equipment including the Computer, some of the Club's records, etc, were lost in the fire. Fortunately, the Club's Insurance covered most of the cost of the equipment lost, but the information destroyed was irreplaceable.

By the start of the new season, the latest round of Clubhouse extensions and refurbishments had been completed. The main extension involved a completely new enlarged Professional's Shop, which included a small kitchen, toilet facilities and an office overlooking the course. Improvements were also made to the Ladies Changing Room where a Visitor's Cloakroom had been added with Toilets and Vanity Basins. In the Mens Changing Room six open plan Italian type Showers were added and three new wash hand basins.

In the Clubhouse new seating and tables were purchased and existing chairs re-upholstered. Considerable lighting changes were introduced in the Lounge area and in the event much re-wiring was carried out. Both the Ladies and Mens Changing Room Entrance Doors had a new covered way extending between both entrances.

The Starter's Hut which had been donated by Stan Howell following his year of Captaincy, came to grief following a particularly stormy night, and finished in an ungainly position, upside down in the pond adjacent to the walkway to the 1st tee. Stan has since generously replaced the hut and it has been re-located in a 'safer' position to the rear of the tee.

After much discussion over a long period of time in connection with the building plans for the addition of a Snooker Room and a Club Office, it was decided to take no action for the foreseeable future. As a temporary measure it was decided to consider the use of a 'Portakabin' as an Office, and one was obtained at no cost to the Club with the help of the Lady Captain, Barbara Wooley.

Following the death of Tom Curry, a popular member of the Club, the Committee received an unexpected surprise when it was made known that the Club was the main beneficiary in his will. It was known that Tom had intended to bequeath a figure of some substance to the Club in appreciation of his many happy years spent at Maxstoke, and of the many friendships that he made. The size of the legacy however was quite surprising.

Further bequests to the Club were made by Roy Clarke the retiring Captain who donated the Captain's Bell, and by Tony Reading who provided the Trophy Cabinet.

Changes within the management structure, Doug Haywood took over as Hon. Secretary, and Ray Barrett came in as Green's Chairman after Trevor Maddox had stood down after four years. Bob Cardwell, the Steward left the Club, and after a three month trial period, Sheila Cardwell was confirmed as Stewardess of the Club.

Tony Allen won the Warwickshire Stroke Play Championship, and the Club held the first 'Seniors Open'.

THE MID 'NINETIES'

During 1993 Trafford Stonebridge reached retirement age and was succeeded by Andy Ross. Trafford had been Head Greenkeeper for some twenty years, but he had an association with the Club back in the Castle Bromwich days. His father was employed at the old Bromford Bridge Racecourse which was adjacent to the Golf Club, and Trafford and Tom Marks more or less grew up together. Norman Taylor was awarded an Honorary Life Membership as appreciation of his many years service on the Committee, including being honoured as Club Captain way back in 1974. On the course the nature of the 13th hole was changed forever when two diseased mature trees were cut down thus easing problems with hooked drives off the tee.

After trials had been carried out successfully, it was decided to purchase 'vert-drain' equipment so that the standard of the fairways could be improved. There had been much criticism of the condition of the fairways for a long time. Successive dry summers had left the ridges on the fairways almost devoid of grass in places. It was anticipated that the use of the equipment two or three times a year with simultaneous application of seed and fertilisers should achieve improvement within two to three years. A further attraction was that the equipment would pay for itself within three to four years, taking into account the high cost of hiring such equipment.

In 1994 the Club appointed a new Professional Neil McEwan. Neil had come with high expectations being a qualified golfing coach. He soon settled in at Maxstoke, is very popular and there is little doubt that since his arrival many members, and indeed golfers from considerable distances have come to Maxstoke, and have benefitted from Neil's tuition.

The Clubhouse received yet another major refurbishment. A new ceiling was introduced, patio doors were added, a sliding partition to segregate the casual dress area from the main body of the Lounge as and when functions are held was incorporated. Bench seating was put into the 19th hole bar, new carpets with the Maxstoke logo laid, new curtains were fitted and a second archway was built in the centre of the Lounge. New and additional ceiling lighting was provided.

Club Captain of the year was Dr K. M. Rehmany. In the early days at Castle Bromwich, the Club was monopolised by doctors. The Captain, the Hon Secretary, the Hon Treasurer and the Vice President were all doctors. Perusal of the Members List indicated that quite a percentage of the members were doctors.

'Doc', as he is generally called, is almost certainly the first doctor to hold office at Maxstoke. He was born in Pakistan, and those who only know him as a competitive golfer might like to know that in his youth he was an enthusiastic table tennis player and did represent his country at that time.

With regard to the Tom Curry legacy some £123,000 had been received to date and it was agreed that a Memorial to Tom should be erected at a cost of no more than 10% of the legacy. Good news for members, in 1994 the subscriptions were pegged at the same level as the 1993 level, and even better news was a ruling from the Income Tax Hierarchy, indicating that members of golf clubs should be re-imbursed the VAT that had been added to subscription charges.

In 1995, David Goodman and Brenda Hindle were employed in the Office. with David as Administrator. Immediately they got to work with the new computer system, and soon had programmes giving immediate detail on Member's records, their handicaps, subscription details, Club's expenditure, budget requirements and monthly analysis, which has made the Committee more able to monitor every aspect of the day to day running of the Club.

As a tribute to Tom Curry a new entrance to the Golf Club was laid out in Castle Lane, amounting to two landscaped gardens with ornamental brick walls added, positioned at each side of the drive.

An unusual yet amusing occurrence happened at the AGM, when it was pointed out that President Bill Dudley-Evans, as a Past Captain of the Club, had been incorrectly dressed at a Past Captains meeting. Bill had turned up wearing a old faded blue jacket which apparently had been the jacket colour in days gone by. However, the rest of the Past Captains did offer to pay for Bill to be measured for a new green jacket, which was well appreciated by Bill.

Club Captain Dennis Walker cuts the ribbon to officially open the 'Tom Curry Memorial' new entrance to the course

Tony Allen won the prestigious 'Howitt Bowl' for the 5th year in succession, and this apparently caused considerable consternation to quite a few people. At the time, for whatever reason, the trophy was displayed on a shelf behind the bar in full view for several weeks. Dennis Walker, who looks after the Club's insurance enquired as to what the trophy was and what was it's worth. Nobody, including North Warwickshire Golf Club, who owned the trophy knew, and so it was valued.

Panic then ensued when it was valued at £23,000. It was quickly returned to North Warwickshire and apparently since then it has remained in the vaults of a bank for 364 days of each year. Nowadays it appears only on the day of the competition, when it is presented to the winner, photographed and smartly returned to the vaults.

Boys' Amateur Championship
at Dunbar, East Lothian

Quarter Finals
S Walker beat C Lee 2 and 1
G Fox beat D Lucas 2 and 1
S Young beat S Chapman 3 and 2
S Whiteford beat P de Salvatore 5 and 4

Semi-Finals
S Walker beat G Fox 1 hole
S Young beat S Whiteford at 22nd

Final
S Young beat S Walker 7 and 6

Tony also won the 'Bainbridge Shield' partnered with Sam Walker. Sam represented Warwickshire and England Boys, and came close to achieving greater recognition finishing as runner up in the Boys' Amateur Championship at Dunbar.

Trafford Stonebridge, the retired Head Greenkeeper was honoured by having an 'Honorary Social Membership' of the Club awarded to him and, also being given the courtesy of the course.

Age was also given a recognition when it was agreed that members over the age of 75 years would be allowed to use their caddy carts all year round. Whether this was to reduce the chances of potential heart attacks on the course was never explained, but nevertheless it is encouraging to see our octoganarians playing regular golf throughout the winter months.

To improve the drainage problems particularly below the lake, ditches were re-opened from the 10th fairway right across the 18th and to the far side of the 17th. Whilst these have increased the difficulty of the holes, the ditches have achieved the required effect. Good news for the members in 1996 was that VAT payments that had been charged in earlier years was to be repaid, and this amount was deducted from the Annual Subscription for the year. Whilst most members were appreciative of this deduction there were unfortunately some apparent anomolies which a number of members did object to, and at the AGM when the announcement was made, the discussions did get rather heated.

Out on the course there were mixed feeling about the gorse patches that had been introduced and it was decided to review the retention of these areas at the end of the year.

Club members were saddened at the passing of two long serving members Alan Cartwright and Bill Dudley-Evans.

Alan had joined the Club as a Junior in the mid '60s and had over the years established himself as one of our leading golfers. He was Club Champion on three occasions, 1966, when still a Junior, and also in 1971 and 1972. He represented Warwickshire on many occasions and in partnership with Tony Allen won the 'Bainbridge Shield' a couple of times. He won many other trophies during his golfing years at Maxstoke as perusal of the Honours Boards indicate.

Alan served on the Club Committee over a long period of time and was Green's Chairman for six years between 1983 and 1988. At the time of his illness he was still an active member of the Committee and would almost certainly have received due recognition of his services at some time. His death after apparently recovering from a brave fight against cancer was unexpected and came as a shock to all members. Alan has been sadly missed, and his funeral at Coleshill Parish Church was well attended by Club members.

Bill more or less played golf right to the end of his life, having regular Saturday fourballs with old colleagues. He was a popular and well loved character who had had been around so long that he gave an impression of being capable of immortality.

Bill died after a short illness and apart from the many Club members who attended his funeral, a considerable numbers of prominent figures from the County Amateur Golf Circuit came to pay their last respects to Bill, who had contributed so much to amateur golf throughout his lifetime.

It was typical of Bill that just a short while before he was admitted to hospital, he travelled to Peterborough Milton Golf Club to support the Warwickshire County Team in the Midland Regional Qualifying Competition for the English County Championship.

1996 was the Club's 50th year at Maxstoke Park and an Anniversary Ball was held to commemorate this milestone in the Club's history. To mark the occasion, which obviously had much to do with the good attendance, was the well advertised fact that all drinks at the Bar would cost just 50 pence.

As a commencement of the Club's Centenary Year programme, new engraved Captain's Boards were introduced to the Lounge area. These were designed so that the names of some 150 years of Captains could be added and with the same arrangement for all of the major competition boards.

Bill Dudley-Evans talking to Tony Allen at Peterborough Milton in June just before being admitted to hospital

The widow of Roger Bacciochi presented an outdoor clock which has been placed in a prominent position on the patio wall, in memory of Roger, who died at an early age after a long illness.

The Tom Curry legacy more or less finalised at the figure of £188,000 and the Committee wisely invested the money received in a Memorial Trust Fund which will be allowed to mature for the foreseeable future.

At the time of writing significant returns have been made on the fund, and members are kept informed of 6 monthly progress by statements shown on the main notice boards. On the lounge wall in the Clubhouse is a framed commemorative tribute to Tom which shows a typical range of stamps that were in his collection.

In the catalogue at the Auction when Tom's Collection was put on sale there was a wonderfully worded testimonial to Tom which read as follows:

Maxstoke Park Golf Club

OFFERED ON BEHALF OF MAXSTOKE PARK GOLF CLUB LTD

Geoff Manton recalls how, some years ago, Tom Curry said to him "One day, when I have gone, you will be surprised by what I have got". In the event there were several surprises last year when Tom died of a heart attack, and the event was even noted in the National Press. The reason for the press interest was that Tom (a bachelor and retired Tax Inspector) had no close relatives, and he had decided to leave his entire estate – his house, his savings and his stamp collection – to his adopted family, the members of his local golf club. The Club were as surprised as the rest of us when Tom's Will was made public, but a year later its members are making plans to put their windfall to good use.

Tom was quite a shy man – a bit of a dark horse in fact – and it seems that no–one knew exactly what his stamp collections included. At one time he exhibited both British Commonwealth and British Postage covers to Societies, but during the last thirty years of his life he began to build specialised scollections of British and German Africa. Whereas the emphasis was on stamps at first, he gradually became interested in Postal History, and in 1984 he became an Associate of the Society of Postal Historians. It seems that Tom built some collections and then sold sizeable groups of material in Cavendish's Auctions. He once had specialised studies of the Rhodesias and of Bechuanaland, but eventually he had honed the collections down to those favourite areas that are recorded in the 220 lots that follow.

The British East Africa, South West Africa and Nigerias Collections were the areas that Tom never stopped pursuing, but many of the other studies are also impressive. His collection of New Zealand, the only other area that he continued with throughout his life – will be found in the Australasia section of the catalogue. The principal surprise was finding so many countries within Tom's overall collection, and examining the 50 or so albums – all neatly mounted up and beautifully written up – one was frequently surprised. If Tom was here today, he would enjoy watching the faces of those reading the descriptions of these lots.

James Grimwood-Taylor
20th January 1994

Just two samples of some of the stamps that Tom collected over the years

Regrettably, several other members of the Club passed away during the year, and Les King the Club Captain did acknowledge that the deaths in his year of Captaincy was rather excessive. The other losses to the Club were Dick Chipman, Richard Davies, Ted Feeley, Howard Figures, Ken Walsh and Ernie Wyatt. All of these gentlemen had been members for lengthy periods, were all well known and popular members, and in the case of Ernie Wyatt had served on the Committee and had been Club, Captain in 1987.

Michael C. Fetherston-Dilke the son of our former President, Captain Charles B. Fetherston-Dilke was invited to become our new President following the death of Bill Dudley-Evans, and he was pleased to accept the honour. The Committee of the day were invited to attend a very enjoyable cheese and wine evening at the Castle, when the new President was able to become acquainted with the Officers of the Club. During this pleasant evening the new President presented a splendid cut glass crystal vase to the Club to be given as an appropriate award for our Junior golfers.

Our new President attended the Club's AGM in November for the first time and he expressed his feeling of honour in following his father, and mentioned the appropriateness of the occasion, being the 50th year of the Club's tenancy at Maxstoke, and the 650th Anniversary of the history of Maxstoke Castle.

Into 1997 and my year of Captaincy. At the start of the year I appreciated the honour that had been bestowed upon me. To be Captain of a Golf Club is a privilege that does not come to many people and even today as I write this, I am still flattered to think that I was chosen.

Like many Captains before me, I have been pleased by the courtesy shown to me by all members at all times, have appreciated the involvement in so many activities, and admit that I have enjoyed every minute of it. I have been amazed, and at times quite bewildered by the honours that have come the way of Maxstoke Park Golf Club this year. To be writing the Centenary Book and to be able to comment on the achievements that our golfers have made is an added pleasure.

Early in April, Tom Whitehouse, finished as runner up in the 'Warwickshire Boys Championship' and won all of his games in the 4 Counties Championship. Ben Senior was honoured by being selected as Warwickshire Youth Team Captain. In May Tom went even better by winning the 'Warwickshire Amateur Championship' at Coventry.

Also in May, Maxstoke won the Warwickshire Team Championship with Tony Allen, Tom Whitehouse, Ben Senior and Anthony Gascoigne being the members of the team. Tom also played in the winning 'Warwickshire Boys Team' in the EGU Qualifying Competition at Hawkstone Park. the team going forward to the final. Tom was joint individual winner with scores of 71 and 72, and his splendid form was recognised by selection for selection for the English Boys Team to play in the European Championships.

Even more eventful for the Club was the choice of Maxstoke Park to host the County Match between Warwickshire and Worcestershire, and the inclusion of three Maxstoke golfers in the Warwickshire Team. Sam Walker, Tom Whitehouse and Tony Allen (seen below) were selected and it is almost certainly the first time that the Club has received such recognition.

Following the match I was delighted to receive letters of appreciation from the Captains of both teams both very complimentary of the hospitality extended to them and generally praising everyone concerned in making the day one to remember. I think it appropriate that the words of Bill Nicolson the Warwickshire Captain be noted when he wrote;

"We, the team – consider Maxstoke to be one of our premier venues, if not the premier venue. There are a number of reasons.

- a number of the team play at Maxstoke and look likely to continue
- the course is always well presented and in excellent condition for our matches
- we are better supported by Maxstoke members than at any other club that we play at.

Could you pass on our thanks

- to your members for allowing us to use the course and in particular

to those members that offered their support
- to your Greens Committee and Greens Staff for the excellent early season condition of your course
- to your Catering and Bar Staff for their enthusiasm and efficiency".

Whilst not collecting any awards, Sam Walker finished 4th in the Midlands Amateur Championship at Sandwell, competed in the 'Brabazon English Match Play Championship' at Saunton, and finished 6th in the 'Links Trophy' at St. Andrew. Not many Maxstoke golfers have even qualified for those events.

Continuing the success story, Tom Whitehouse added the 'Warwickshire Match Play Championship' to his 'Amateur Stroke Play Championship'. Tony Allen won the 'Kenilworth Classic Competition' with Tom Whitehouse in 3rd place, Sam Walker 4th, Tony Gascoigne 5th and Ben Senior 8th.

Tony, Sam and Tom were again selected to represent Warwickshire in the County Championship Qualifier at Robin Hood. Sam Walker won the 36 hole 'Peugeot Trophy' at Coventry after a 4 way play off and came 5th in the 'Midlands Amateur Open' at Little Aston/Sutton Coldfield.

Tom Whitehouse, representing England in the 'European Boys Championship' won 3 of his games on the way to the final, when England lost to Spain. Sam Walker easily qualified in the Midlands section for the 'Open' but missed out in the final qualifier at Prestwick. Ben Senior came 2nd in the Warwickshire Youth Championship at Copt Heath.

Tom Whitehouse reached the 5th round of the English Youths Championship at North Devon but went out to Sergio Garcia, the ultimate winner. Garcia, just 17 years of age plays off plus 5. Sam Walker won the 'Midlands Order of Merit' and has been recruited to the England squad. He finished as leading amateur in the 'Warwickshire Open Championship'. He also recorded a 64 at Maxstoke which is probably a new record since the course was altered. Ben Senior and Lee Lawrence played for the Warwickshire Youths versus Leicestershire at Lutterworth, both winning their matches in a Warwickshire victory.

Not to be outdone by the exploits of the younger players, Bob Cooper, Frank Pittaway, Ray Curzons and Trevor Lewis won the 'Lutterworth Seniors Open'. Frank Smith partnered by the Walmley Captain won the 'Four Ball Better Ball Open' at Walmley.

Into September, and I with a few other Maxstoke members supported Tom Whitehouse and Steven Brotherhood playing for Warwickshire in the 'English Counties Finals' at Sandwell. Both played well and had good wins but Warwickshire had to settle for 2nd place behind Essex.

Tom also came close to claiming a bigger prize, being runner up in the 'English County Champion of Champions' at Woodhall Spa just one shot off the leader. However as consolation he won the 'T. P. Cooke Salver' for the best aggregate in the 'Warwickshire Open' and Warwickshire Amateur Championship' events.

Ben Senior the Warwickshire Youth Captain won the Midlands 'Champion of Champions' at Enville after a three way tie, and Anthony Gascoigne won the coveted 'Howitt Bowl' the trophy that Tony Allen made a habit of winning.

More sadly, during the year another three long serving members passed away, George Dowse, John Bethell and Tom Marks. All three had been members of the Committee in the past, George, serving for many years as Competition and Handicap Secretary, had an encyclopaedic knowledge of the Rules of Golf. Tom was also an enthusiastic member of Committee with course maintenance and greens being his main interest. John served on the House Committee and was involved in many social activities.

Jack Andrews, a former member of the Club, who had been in poor health following a stroke suffered several years ago, left £2250 to the Club, with half to be spent on the course, and the rest in the Clubhouse. Two ornamental benches were purchased and placed behind the 6th tee with flowering shrubbery being placed around them. These were put in position in time for Captain's Day, were much appreciated on the day and have been admired since by most members.

On the course the new ditches have been brought into play and surely

Harold Evans (Vice President) Tom Sutcliffe (House Chairman), Les Cookson, Ray Barrett (Greens Chairman) and Ron Wookhead admiring the benches received from the Jack Andrews legacy

have added to many golfers misfortunes from time to time. The appearance of the 15th hole has been enhanced by the addition of the line of three bunkers added to the right of the fairway to replace the gorse mentioned earlier.

The entrance to the changing rooms however has been improved by the installation of a new Notice Board which has many features which give detailed information as to what is going on for each individual day, and what restrictions, if any, are in force. During the year there have been many events and competitions that have been pleasing to me, but more importantly have brought credit to the Club. The Charity Events - the 'Brain Damaged Childrens', the 'Jim Holton Memorial Tournament' and of course the 'Coventry Lord Mayor's Golf Tournament' have all been well supported and the Club have received much praise for hosting these events.

Many societies have visited Maxstoke and I have always tried to speak to them if possible with a few words of welcome. Generally I think that has been appreciated by most of them. Our own 'Open Competitions' are always well supported and again complimentary remarks are passed on by most of those competing.

The most enjoyable event though, of course, was my Captain's Day. Some 108 members supported me on the day, the weather was ideal, it was a fun day and I am sure that everyone enjoyed themselves. The day started with the traditional short course competition and the putting competition laid out on the putting green. Neil McEwan and his assistants Tony Gascoigne and Lee Laewrence made sure that it was not too easy which was apparent when 7s and 8s were recorded on a couple of holes by quite a number of those competing. It was particularly pleasing to see a considerable number of lady members turning out for the morning activities.

We had an excellent meal afterwards and I was able to meet and talk with many members that I normally would not have come into contact with.

Standing with early morning contestants in the putting competition – Doreen and Roy Robinson, Mary Clarke, Teresa Marklew (Lady Captain), Joan Hall, Kay Williams, Sylvia and John Hobday

Captain's Day 1997 – taken on the bank of the eighteenth green rather than in the traditional position on the entrance steps of the clubhouse

Having written about the achievements of our better golfers, I would mention that I was pleased to play for the 'A' Team and was given the honour of receiving the 'Pat Colgan Cup' from the Walmley Captain after Maxstoke recorded a victory based upon the home and away scores. Not so pleasing though to receive the 'Lew James Trophy' after the match with Robin Hood', when the losing Captain 'carries the can'.

I did receive a cut glass crystal tankard for my 'hole in one' at the 11th hole at Leamington and County in their 'Seniors Open'. Have there been any other 'aces' achieved by a Club Captain in his year of office.

Congratulations must be extended to Vice President Harry Field who in September took over as Captain of the Union of Warwickshire Club Captains. This is a tremendous honour for Harry and he is particularly pleased that his year of office will co-incide with our Centenary Year.

One of the last events of the season was the 'Committee Away Day' at Telford when 16 members of the Committe played an 18 hole Stableford. The whole complex is a Hotel and Golf Country Club with a well appointed and interesting course, and a very expensive catering facility. Everyone enjoyed the day and David Newman won the event for the second year in succession.

The final event of the year was the keenly fought Celts versus English Match this year played on a very wet damp afternoon. Nonetheless it was an enjoyable occasion and whilst some of the Celtic ancestory was in considerable doubt, the banter and company made it all worth while.

At the AGM, there were a few changes of personnel on the Committee. Ray Barrett who has been Green's Chairman for some 5 years was the most significant, and he stood down. His place was taken by Gordon Hancock, a popular member who seemed very enthusiastic about the challenge. Neil Mutter who has done so much in establishing a sound financial policy to ensure the Club's stability over the forthcoming years

'Committee Away Day at Telford'
Standing: David Haynes, George Kettrick, John Hannon, Adrian Harrison, Ted Robinson, Dennis Walker, Peter Kirby, Neil McEwan, Anthony Gascoigne and Bob Cooper. *Seated*: David Goodman, Doug Haywood, Neil Mutter, Graham Crawford, David Newman and Jim McCulloch

was re-elected as Club Chairman. Long serving committee man David Newman stood down after 9 years also on the Green's Committee, and Peter Kirby who withdrew from nomination just before the meeting. Their places were taken by Michael Conroy and Richard Glynn.

By the time that members read this book I shall be a Past Captain, and it is therefore appropriate that I extend my best wishes to my successor Frank Williams, and indeed to his wife Kay, and they will be leading the Club through our Centenary Year. Current 'Maxies' Captain Ted Robinson has been selected as Vice Captain to Frank Williams.

There are exciting events planned and it is hoped that everyone joins in at least some of the 'once in a lifetime' activities.

THE PLAYERS – PAST AND PRESENT

If you compare the history of the Club at Castle Bromwich and Maxstoke Park, it is really quite remarkable how identical they are. At both locations enthusiastic members started from scratch and built themselves a golf course. Then, for entirely different reasons the members needed to reconstruct their course.

The similarities do not end there. As the courses improved so did the standard of golf played, and within relatively short periods of time some very good golfers began to emerge. As mentioned elsewhere, the golfers at Castle Bromwich established themselves, and the Club as being amongst the best in the Midlands. They won the Warwickshire Club Championship frequently in the '20s and '30s, their players regularly appeared in the Warwickshire County Teams, and more than one of them achieved personal honours by winning County Championship titles.

But amongst these excellent golfers there was one who surpassed them all, and no one could have received greater acclaim than Thomas Philip Perkins. Castle Bromwich, Warwickshire and Midland titles came to him from the age of sixteen years onwards, taking the 'Amateur Championship' at Prestwick in 1928 and representing Great Britain in the 'Walker Cup' in America, along with Club mate Archie MacCallum.

Looking at the Maxstoke Park Honours Boards, a similar pattern has emerged. Many excellent golfers names appear, J. H. Sangster and F. T Blakey in the early days at Maxstoke more or less shared the Championship honours. They were followed by Pip Whitehouse who took the Championship title nine times in a twelve year period, and Alan Cartwright who had three successes.

One should note that golfers like Bill Dudley Evans, Kevin McDonagh, Trevor Maddox, John Gough, Adrian Harrison, Alan Brock and many others were all making their presence felt around this time. Many of them played for the County and their names appear frequently on the Club's Honours Boards

Again history repeated itself at Maxstoke Park. A young man appeared who has virtually dominated the Club's silverware since the mid '70s came along. A. M. Allen who had started in golf as a young assistant was reinstated as an amateur and immediately changed the golfing attitudes at Maxstoke. Scribes in local newspapers have called him 'the most gifted golfer to have come to prominence in the Midlands area for the last twenty years'.

At Maxstoke there is no one who would deny that. Tony, as he is better known, became the man to beat. Perusal of the Honours Boards indicate that whatever competition he has gone in for, he has won it at frequent intervals. The Club Champion on 14 occasions so far, extending back to 1975 and the most recent 1996. In 1977 as well as the Championship, he won the 'Newport Cup', the 'Gold Medal', the 'Captain's Shield' partnered by Alan Brock and quite surprisingly the 'Winter League' again with Alan Brock as partner. I say surprisingly because Tony very, very rarely plays winter golf.

In recent years there have been other names on the trophies, but one must sympathise with them. Golfers like Alan Brock, Alan Cartwright, Neil Connolly, John Gough, Derek Greenfield, Adrian Harrison, Peter Stokes, Trevor Maddox, Walter Mason, Colin Wykes, and many other fine golfers in recent years would have achieved far greater recognition but for Tony's consistency and level of performance.

But on the plus side, Tony has been the role model that everyone has tried to match. Play away from Maxstoke and everyone asks about Tony, his reputation is known and many golfers from other clubs mention his name with awe, almost as though he is invincible.

His record outside Maxstoke gives that impression. He has represented Warwickshire on a regular basis for twenty odd years, but despite enquiries I have not been able to establish exactly how many. Tony himself admits that he has appeared 'quite often' but couldn't or wouldn't say how many – how about in the order of 50? He was Warwickshires No. 1 for several years and people that I have spoken to do not remember him losing very often.

Tony has won the 'Warwickshire Amateur Championship' three times in 1978, 1988 and 1991; he has won the 'Warwickshire Open Championship' an astonishing seven times (this Championship is open to professionals) in 1981, 1982 (shared with Paul Downes), 1988, 1989, 1991, 1994 and 1996. He has won the 'Bainbridge Shield' four times, with Martin Buxton in 1975, with Alan Cartwright in 1976, with Alan Brock, (he thinks it was 1984) and Sam Walker in 1995. He won the 'Warwickshire County Foursomes Cup' in 1984 with Alan Brock as partner. He has taken the 'Howitt Bowl' eight times, 1974, 1976, 1978 and five times in a row from 1991 to 1995.

He has won the 'Midlands Champion of Champions' title three times in 1973, 1986 and 1987, and in 1991 went even better winning the 'English Counties Champion of Champions Trophy' at Clitheroe, adding his name to that of Nick Faldo and Ian Woosnam as previous winners.

I believe it is impossible to quantify the local trophies and events that Tony has won over the years, but again quoting a local golf reporter, 'Tony has won almost everything there is to win in his parish'. One thing is for certain, if Tony had started a scrap book all those years ago, he would probably have been on the third or fourth volume by now. It is known that this year, 1997 he has won the 'Whittington Bowl' and the 'Kenilworth Classic' and memories seem to recall that he has had them before.

But are things going to change. Credit must be given to the standard that Tony has set, but also to the coaching expertise of Neil McEwan that Maxstoke's hopes for the immediate future are particularly exciting. We have some tremendous young golfers coming through, Sam Walker, Tom Whitehouse, Ben Senior, Tony Gascoigne and Lee Lawrence are currently amongst the group of teenagers at Maxstoke who could well provide even more credit to the Club's name in the not too distant future. At the recent prize presentation evening, even younger lads were receiving awards. Paul Brennan, Richard Cartwright, James and Ben Harrison, Tim Hearn, Richard Kendall, Neil Thomas, Simon Turley are all young lads showing tremendous potential.

Club member Dennis Shaw, writing in the 'Birmingham Evening Mail' recently indicated that the Maxstoke Park Golf Club at the present time were the 'Kings of the Castle'. This accolade was due to the outstanding success that Maxstoke golfers had achieved during the year. Tony Allen with Tom Whitehouse, Ben Senior and Tony Gascoigne representing Maxstoke won the 'Warwickshire Club Championship'. This is the 3rd time that the Club have achieved this honour, Tony naturally being involved in the previous wins, 1980 with Alan Brock and Adrian Harrison and 1992 with Alan Cartwright and Adrian Harrison.

The Warwickshire Union of Golf Club's Championship Shield

A final word on Tony, considering what he has achieved over the years, he apparently takes it all in his stride, he is so relaxed, he makes golf look so easy, it makes one wonder – have we missed out on another Philip Perkins in terms of a Maxstoke 'Walker Cup' player.

Warren Bladon from Kenilworth won the 'Amateur Championship' in 1996. I do not believe that his track record bears comparison with Tony's. Whilst not wishing to become monotonous, I think it is worth repeating some of the extraordinary achievements of the younger team members.

Sam Walker first came to prominence in 1995 when he represented Warwickshire and England Boys, and was runner up in the 'Boys Amateur Championship' played at Dunbar. He has now progressd to Warwickshire's

No. 1 spot in the county team, and his consistency was rewarded when he came 4th in the 'West Midlands Amateur Championship' at Sandwell, which won him the 'Midlands Order of Merit' which goes to the golfer with the best average over 10 qualifying County Events and Sam won with two more competitions not then played.

To reward his excellent golf over a long season, Sam was called into the England First Team squad. At Maxstoke he returned a 64 gross in the August Wednesday Medal which in effect is a course record due to the changes that have taken place since the same score was recorded by Tony Allen way back in 1986. These are the high points of Sam's year but he has been close on many other occasions. Seventeen year old Tom Whitehouse, who joined the Club in 1994, had in 1997 a season that every golfer must dream about. He started the year as top qualifier in the Warwickshire Boys Championship at Stratford, he won all 3 of his games in the '4 Counties Match' also at Stratford, came 4th in the County trials at Ladbrook and finished 5th in the 'Peter McEvoy Trophy' at Copt Heath.

He then went on to win the 'Warwickshire Amateur Stroke Play Championship'at Coventry after a 3 hole play off with previous winner Peter Chalkley. The 'Warwickshire Club Championship' came next, followed by a leading role in the 'Warwickshire Boys Team' which won the E. G. U. Qualifying Competition at Hawkestone Park, Tom was joint winner of the Individual Award. This success was the first time Warwickshire had reached the Finals for 23 years. He was then selected for the England Team to play in the European Championships in Slovenia.

Not content with the 'Warwickshire Stroke Play Championship' Tom then went on to complete the double by becoming the 'Warwickshire Match Play Champion' as well – I wonder if that has been done before, certainly not by a Maxstoke golfer. Tom was then given his first game for Warwickshire in the County Match played at Maxstoke. He was also runner up in the 'English Champion of Champions' and also runner up in the 'Warwickshire Under 18 Championship'. More near misses, a member of the 'Warwickshire Under 16 Team' that finished runners up in the English County Championship played at Sandwell.

In the 'European Championship' Tom won 3 of his 4 matches helping England to the Final when they were defeated by a very strong Spanish Team.

For any golfer, the achievements listed above above are to be envied, for a 17 year old they are quite remarkable. I followed Tom for most of two rounds at Sandwell in the 'English Counties Championship' and I was astonished at the precision of his shots, and the maturity shown by him. He seemed completely at ease, no signs of nerves (I know mine were fluttering at times) and some of his shots were unbelievable.

Tom has indicated that one day he would like to have a try at the professional circuit, but when asked about that he simply replied "My objective at the present time is to get my handicap down from one, I am not thinking of turning professional for a long time. I don't think I'll be ready for that for a few years yet".

That attitude really emphasises the quality of Tom as a golfer. He hits wonderful shots, he sometimes gets into trouble, he thinks out his next shot, plays the percentage shot if needs be, and more often than not his game is back on course. A potential Philip Perkins – I wouldn't bet against it.

Ben Senior was honoured at the start of the season by being selected as 'Warwickshire Youth Captain' which in itself is a great honour, both for Ben but also for the Club. Ben has taken this honour in his stride, from reports received he has lead the squad well and invariably lead by example which is always a good judge of a Captain. Ben works hard at his golf, probably spends more time on the practice area than anyone else, which is to be admired.

In the first match of the season Ben lead the Warwickshire Team to a convincing 7½ to 4½ win against a formidable Nottinghamshire Team. He came close in the 'Warwickshire Youths Championship' finishing as runner up, then progressed to the Semi Final of the 'Warwickshire Match Play Championship' at Copt Heath.

Lee Lawrence, assistant to Neil McEwan joined Ben in the 'Warwickshire Youths Team' against Leicestershire at Lutterworth and both won their singles matches in a good 7 to 5 Warwickshire victory.

To cap his season Ben won the 'Midlands Champion of Champions' at Enville after a three way tie. Back at Maxstoke Park, he won the Club Championship which considering the opposition lined up for this event was no mean performance. He also won the Best Nett Award Trophy and it is believed to be the first time that anyone has won both awards.

Anthony Gascoigne who is 'learning the trade' as assistant to Neil McEwan, whilst not receiving the prominence that others have done, has nevertheless played a lot of good golf. He made a significant contribution in the Maxstoke Team which collected the 'Warwickshire Club Championship', he also represented the Club in the 'Bainbridge Shield' partnered by Ben Senior winning through a couple of rounds.

Ben Senior

Anthony Gascoigne

Almost as a 'postscript' to the year was the news that the Scratch Team captained by Adrian Harrison had become Champions of Division 3 and will be promoted to Division 2 for our Centenary Year. The team won 8 of their 10 games and no less than 16 members turned out during the year. In alphabetical order they were Tony Allen, Peter Allen, Nigel Cowles, Tony Featherstone, Anthony Gascoigne, Derek Greenfield, Adrian Harrison, Ben Harrison, George Kettrick, Lee Lawrence, John Morris, Ben Senior, Peter Stokes, Andrew Walker, Sam Walker and Tom Whitehouse.

As Captain of Maxstoke Park during 1997, it has been for me, amongst the most enjoyable experiences of the year, to hear and read about the achievements and victories of our younger players. I have followed them around on occasions and have been thrilled to witness the wonderful golf that they have all been capable of, and which they have so often produced.

A wonderful finale to the Centenary Book. Castle Bromwich became the best Club in Warwickshire – Maxstoke Park have arguably done it again.

AN ODE TO MAXSTOKE PARK GOLF CLUB

A hundred years have passed since a few gentlemen
Decided to form a golf club, not knowing where or when
With real enthusiasm they searched and found
In Castle Bromwich – the ideal ground.

With considerable effort, patience and consideration
Hard work plus a few tinctures of liquid medication
They bought, and dug, and levelled each hole
And finally achieved their hard worked for goal.

The course was lost because of World War Two
They built aircraft nearby for the first of the few
But when the war ended, it was quite a strain
To find somewhere else to begin again.

New Beginnings at Maxstoke

Maxstoke Park was the place they sought
Maxstoke Park was the place that was bought
At a rent that was beyond belief
It was grabbed by our founders with relief.

Once more they set to with enthusiasm keen
Skirmishing stones where paths might have been
Laying out greens and measuring each hole
Once again finally reaching their goal.

There's been a few changes over the years
Yet somehow as our Centenary nears
Maxstoke at last feeling so safe and secure
What is the attraction, what is the lure.

We all know St. Andrews, Turnberry and Troon
Birkdale, Carnoustie and golf on the Moon
Little Aston, the Belfry of Ryder Cup fame
But there's more to a Club than just a name.

They call Maxstoke a friendly Club
A warm atmosphere, like your favourite pub
Members and visitors all love the place
So many would join, but sorry no space.

Chelping with colleagues after the game
Praising your partner, accepting the blame
For that awful shot that put us two down
And caused us to end up losing the game

The names of those to whom we owe this pleasure
For those hours of joy, those moments to treasure
There's Dougie and Dennis and Jim and Les
And Bill and Brian and Michael our Pres.

So many people we can name just a few
But all are remembered both old and the new
Who have made Maxstoke Park the place that we love
We drink to them all, be they Below or Above.

MAXSTOKE WE DRINK TO YOU.

Jack Cooper.

BACK ROW: (left to right): George Kettrick, Lee Lawrence, John Morris, Tony Allen, Tom Whitehouse, Peter Stokes and Peter Allen
FRONT ROW: Anthony Gascoigne, Ben Harrison, Graham Crawford (Club Captain), Adrian Harrison (Team Captain) and Tony Featherstone

Tom Whitehouse with the two Warwickshire Championship Trophies: 'Amateur Stroke Play' and 'Amateur Match Play', plus the T. P. Cooke Trophy for the best aggregate for the two competitions.

Chapter Five

The Course Development

Since the Clubhouse was opened in 1969, the course has more or less retained the format of the holes as originally set out at that time. Individual holes however have changed from time to time. Three holes have had new greens laid, other holes have been lengthened by adding new competition tees further back, and new bunkers have been added to several fairways around the course.

Winter rainfall has always caused problems with flooding and additional drainage has been introduced in several locations which feed into new pools which have been excavated to create new water hazards. More

A typical example of problems associated with inadequate drainage in days gone by – this was the scene one Friday morning and unbelievably the 1988 'Invitation Open' was played the next day.

It is interesting to compare the size of the early clubhouse, and also to note the route of the old pathway to the 1st tee.

recently the 10th, 17th and 18th holes have had ditches reopened with the intention of improving the drainage potential.

Over the years unfortunately we have lost several mature trees many of which came into play, and their loss has significantly altered the character of particular holes. Several thousand trees have been added around the course in recent years, and whilst they will in time make their own contribution to the beauty of the course, they can never adequately replace those that have been felled.

In 1976 several significant changes took place on the course. It was decided to abandon the old back tee on the 11th which had the advantage of eliminating the cross over on the 11th and 18th fairways. This had the effect of losing some 70 metres and would have resulted in a lowering of the Standard Scratch Score down to 70. To offset this loss a new green was laid on the 18th some 40 metres nearer the Clubhouse. The photograph opposite shows the location of the old green.

More or less around the same time, a new green was laid on the 11th hole some 30 metres further on, and the hole probably more than any other has seen most changes over the years.

When the hole was originally set out, the tee was adjacent to the Castle Moat and the green was roughly where the 150 yard marker is now placed. Immediately in front of the green were several mounds which are still evident today. At that time when the course was just 9 holes, the hole was

The new 18th green under construction.

No. 1 and the length was 375 yards. When a further 6 holes were added, the tee was moved back to the trees forming the course boundary and the length increased to 455 yards.

Shortly after the Prisoner of War Camp was demolished the course became 18 holes, and about this time the original green was abandoned and the fairway extended to the old 2nd green. This brought the length of the hole up to 571 yards which was the longest on the course.

The decision to eliminate the cross over of the 11th and 18th fairways meant that the old back tee was no longer required, and the forward tee was then utilised. With the length of the hole considerably reduced it was decided to build the new green to retrieve some of this lost length.

The hole length was 430 yards and the tee was then extended to provide a competition tee facility, and the hole finally settled after all the changes to today's length of 444 yards.

The course for many years suffered from flooding. Different remedies were applied and there is no doubt that most have brought about considerable improvement. A new 5th green was brought into play and land drains fed into the water hazard which extended right across the front of the green.

18th Green Nearing completion with turfing proceeding and the bunkers awaiting sand.

A more recent photograph obviously taken on 'Captain's Day' with Trafford Stonebridge's caravan in the background.

The 11th green under construction

Similarly extensive drainage was laid across the 18th fairway which fed into a new pool opened up on the left hand side of the fairway some 270 yards from the competition tee.

In more recent winters significant flooding took place in front of the 7th green right across from the left hand boundary fencing to the 8th fairway as can be seen from the photograph taken in 1992.

To remedy this annual problem, a pool was excavated to the right of the fairway some 100 yards from the green, which does appear to have eliminated the problem.

The 10th fairway was always the one to take the brunt when the lake

The 11th green nearing completion with newly laid turf receiving a good soaking from sprinkler system.

5th green under construction with the water hazard extending right across the approach in front.

At the same time that the new 5th green was laid, land drains were introduced to the 6th fairway which drained into the moat.

Excavation of the pool close to the out of bounds on the left of the 18th fairway.

Flooding of the 7th fairway.

The pool as well as solving the flooding problem does look extremely attractive when the water lilies are in bloom.

overflowed and a few years ago the pool adjacent to the green was dug out to provide an additional water hazard.

Most of the improvements described have been carried out over the past ten years or so. Whilst they in some cases were essential in order to keep the course open during severe weather conditions, others were seen as being genuine improvements to enhance the appearance of the course.

It is appropriate at this time to point out that over this period we have been fortunate in having three extremely conscientious Green's Chairmen in Alan Cartwright, Trevor Maddox and Ray Barratt. These three with responsibility for ensuring that the course remained in good order, were able to appreciate the needs of most club golfers. All being single figure

Excavating for the pool adjacent to the 10th green.

golfers, they were able to address the problems associated with providing a tough yet fair test of golf. Again, they also have had the foresight and imagination to see where improvements were required, and when changes would be appropriate to toughen up the course.

Trafford Stonebridge was the Head Greenkeeper whilst most of the changes took place and with his many years of experience was always capable of ensuring that the work was carried out to a professional standard. It should be borne in mind that not so many years ago the greens staff did not have the equipment that is readily available today and much of Trafford's work was of a manual manner.

Andy Ross who has taken over from Trafford has carried on with the same enthusiasm and the course today is in excellent condition, and much appreciation has been expressed by many of our visitors who have played at Maxstoke.

In the process of toughening up the course the number of trees planted is probably in excess of three thousand. Some holes have been lengthened by providing new competition tees and of course the new pools and open ditches have added to the degree of difficulty.

Bunkers have been added on many fairways. On the 4th adjacent to the tree on the right of the fairway, to deter long hitters from cutting out the

Looking across the pool with the ornamental bridge added to give access to the 11th tee.

The bunker on the right of the 4th fairway – when the bushes beyond the bunker increase in size long hitters may think twice about avoiding the dog leg.

The new bunker on the left of the 7th fairway introduced to replace the untidy gorse patch.

The competition tee on the 12th hole introduced in the late '70s to regain lost yardage when the back tee of the 11th hole was abandoned.

The bunker on the right of the 12th fairway, this was brought into play to replace the original bunker on the left hand side which was out of reach from the repositioned competition tee for most golfers.

The bunker on the right hand side of the 14th fairway introduced to replace a mature tree which was struck by lightening some 20 years ago.

The line of three bunkers added to the 15th hole again to replace untidy gorse planted earlier.

More recently – A section of the reopened ditch which extends from the 10th fairway, across the 18th and to the far side of the 17th fairway.

The 18th – Surely one of the most attractive holes on the course and a good finishing hole.

The same hole – A wintry scene

intended dog leg, on the left of the 7th fairway instead of the gorse planted earlier on a good drive length, on the right of the 12th fairway when the competition tee was moved back, thus making the earlier bunker on the left obsolete, and to compensate for the tree struck by lightening on the right hand side of the 14th.

More recently a line of three bunkers have been added to the 15th hole, again in place of the gorse which was quite out of character with the natural vegetation around the course.

With environmental considerations in mind, several areas around the course have been allowed to grow unattended. Whilst generally not in play, apart from the odd wayward drive, these areas have tended to give definition between adjacent fairways, but more importantly have added to the beauty of the course.

Someone with a penchant for stating the obvious though how the notice was placed there without footprints is not too clear.

Computer No.	COMPETITION		
DATE	TIME	Handicap	Strokes Rec'd	PAR 71 SSS 71
Player A				PAR 71 SSS 69
Player B				

Hole	Marker's Score	Name	White Yards	Yellow Yards	Par	Stroke Index	Gross Score A	Gross Score B	Nett Score (or nett best ball)	W = + L = - H = 0 POINTS		Stroke Index
1		CAMP	370	366	4	5						4
2		HAWTHORNES	163	153	3	16						14
3		THE FOXES	432	364	4	1						10
4		STELLA'S	361	340	4	9						8
5		POOL TAIL	292	280	4	14						6
6		LAKE LANDS	364	355	4	6						18
7		KEEPERS	491	469	5	15						12
8		THE WARRENS	477	467	5	12						2
9		COOTS LAIR	205	196	3	8						16
		OUT	3155	2990	36							

Hole	Marker's Score	Name	White Yards	Yellow Yards	Par	Stroke Index	Gross Score A	Gross Score B	Nett Score	Points		Stroke Index
10		DILKE'S BLUFF	374	365	4	7						7
11		BLYTHE DRIVE	444	430	4	2						3
12		THE OAKS	373	334	4	11						11
13		TURKEYS	407	399	4	4						1
14		OLD ROAD	316	302	4	18						15
15		BIRCHWOOD	349	325	4	13						9
16		OLD PARK	167	161	3	17						17
17		CASTLE	448	404	4	3						5
18		OLD MANOR	409	398	4	10						13
		IN	3287	3118	35							
		OUT	3155	2990	36							
		TOTAL	6442	6108	71							
		HANDICAP									Holes won	
		NETT									Holes lost	
											Result	

STABLEFORD POINTS OR PAR RESULT

Plus Holes
1 - Hole 8
2 - Hole 14

Markers Signature .... Players Signature ....

MARKER POSTS 150 YDS FROM CENTRE OF GREEN

MAXSTOKE PARK GOLF CLUB

1898 1998

CENTENARY CARD

LOCAL RULES

OUT OF BOUNDS
Over boundary hedges. On the line of or over fences. The Castle Moat, or where marked by white stakes.

WATER HAZARDS
Marked with yellow stakes, lateral water hazards marked with red stakes.

MOVABLE OBSTRUCTIONS
Stones in bunkers. *Rule 24-1 applies.* A ball stopped or deflected in flight by electricity pylons or wires, when playing the first and fourth holes must be replayed WITHOUT PENALTY.

IMMOVABLE OBSTRUCTIONS, PATHS & TRACKS
Drain covers, water covers, fixed seats, pop-up sprinkler fittings, electric poles. All bridges, all made up paths and tracks, *Rule 24-2(b)* applies full relief not nearer hole.

NEWLY PLANTED TREES
If newly planted trees (MARKED BY STAKES) interfere with the player's stance or area of the intended swing, the ball shall be deemed interfered with by 'ground under repair', and the player MUST take relief as provided in *Rule 25-1(b).*

PRESERVATION OF COURSE
A ball coming to rest on the Ladies' sixth tee (except in a mixed competition) MUST be lifted off the tee and dropped as near as possible to where it lay but not nearer the hole, WITHOUT PENALTY. G.U.R. *Rule 25-1 (b).*

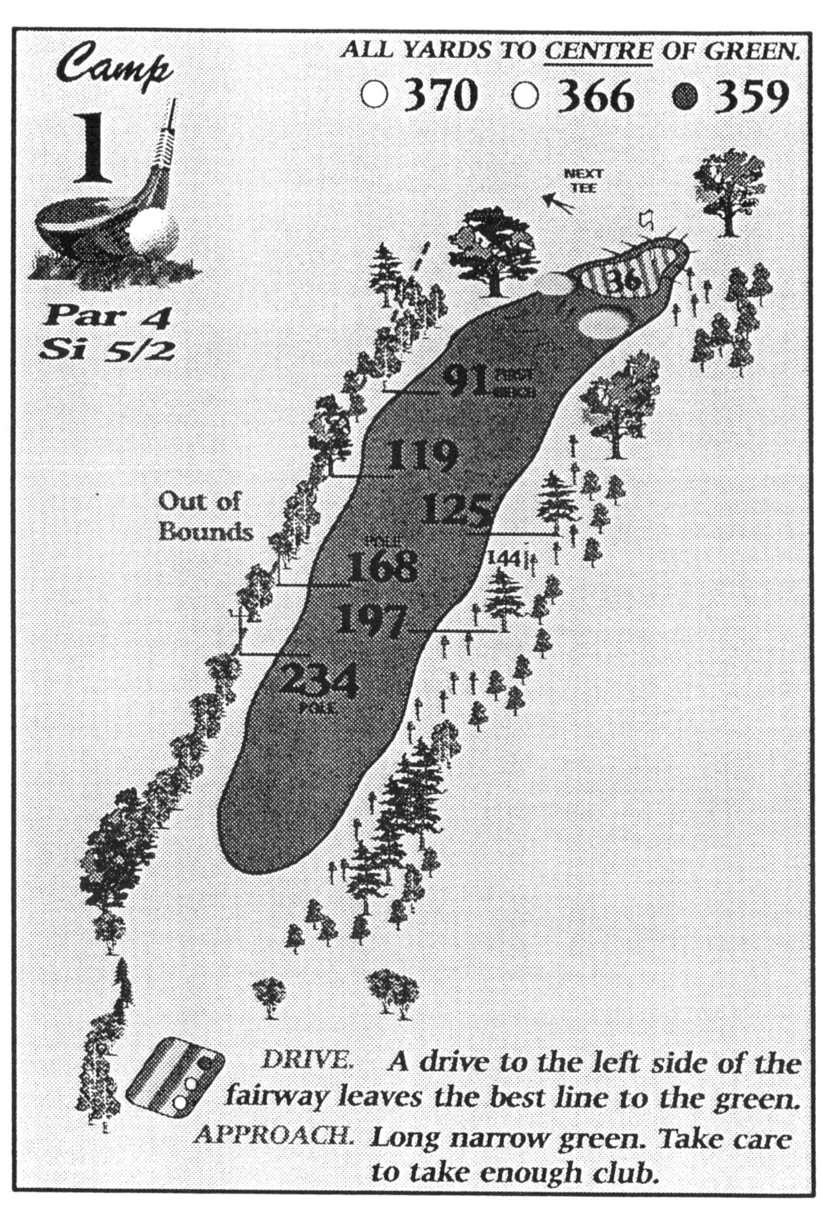
Camp
1
Par 4
Si 5/2
ALL YARDS TO CENTRE OF GREEN.
370
366
359
NEXT TEE
36
91
119
125
144
168
197
234
Out of Bounds
DRIVE. A drive to the left side of the fairway leaves the best line to the green.
APPROACH. Long narrow green. Take care to take enough club.

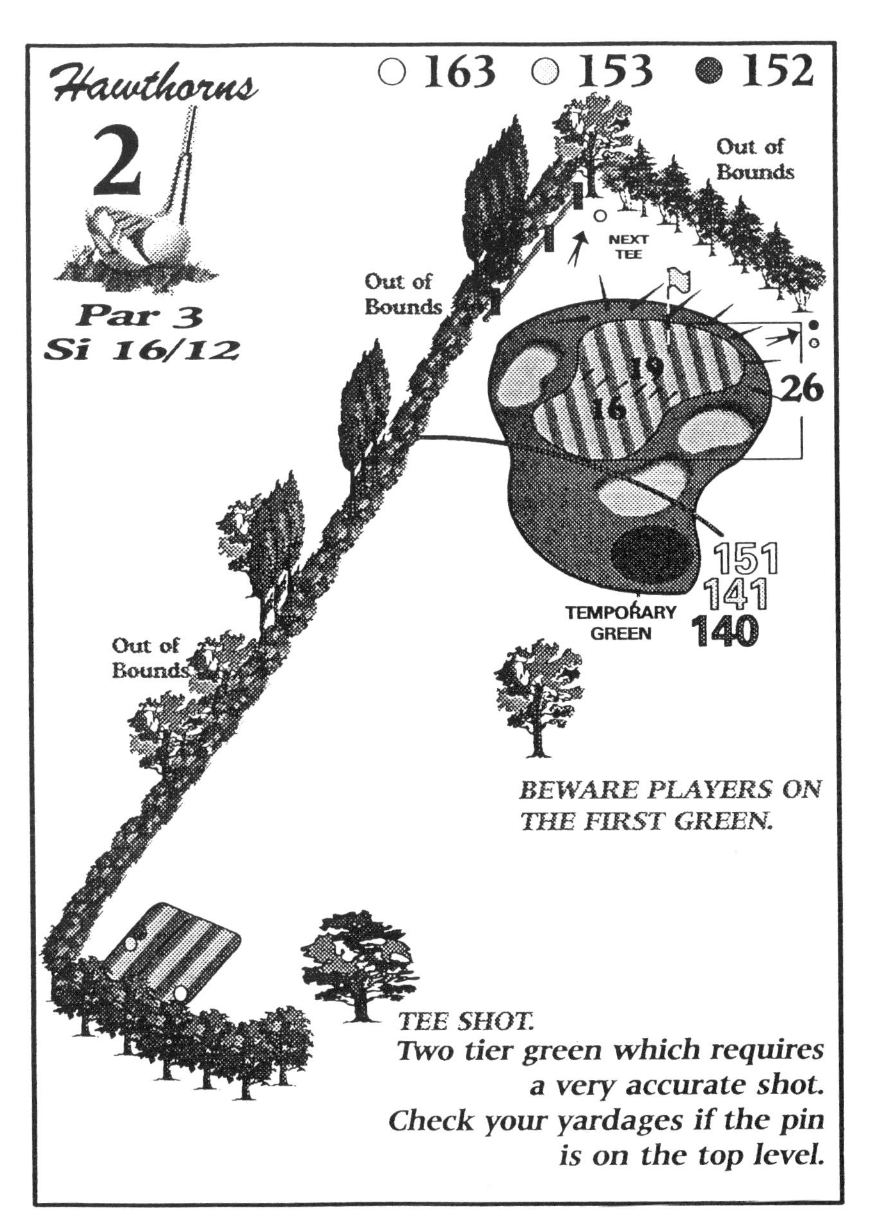
Hawthorns
2
○ 163 ○ 153 ● 152
Par 3
Si 16/12
Out of
Bounds
NEXT
TEE
Out of
Bounds
19
16
26
151
141
140
TEMPORARY
GREEN
Out of
Bounds
BEWARE PLAYERS ON
THE FIRST GREEN.
TEE SHOT.
Two tier green which requires
a very accurate shot.
Check your yardages if the pin
is on the top level.

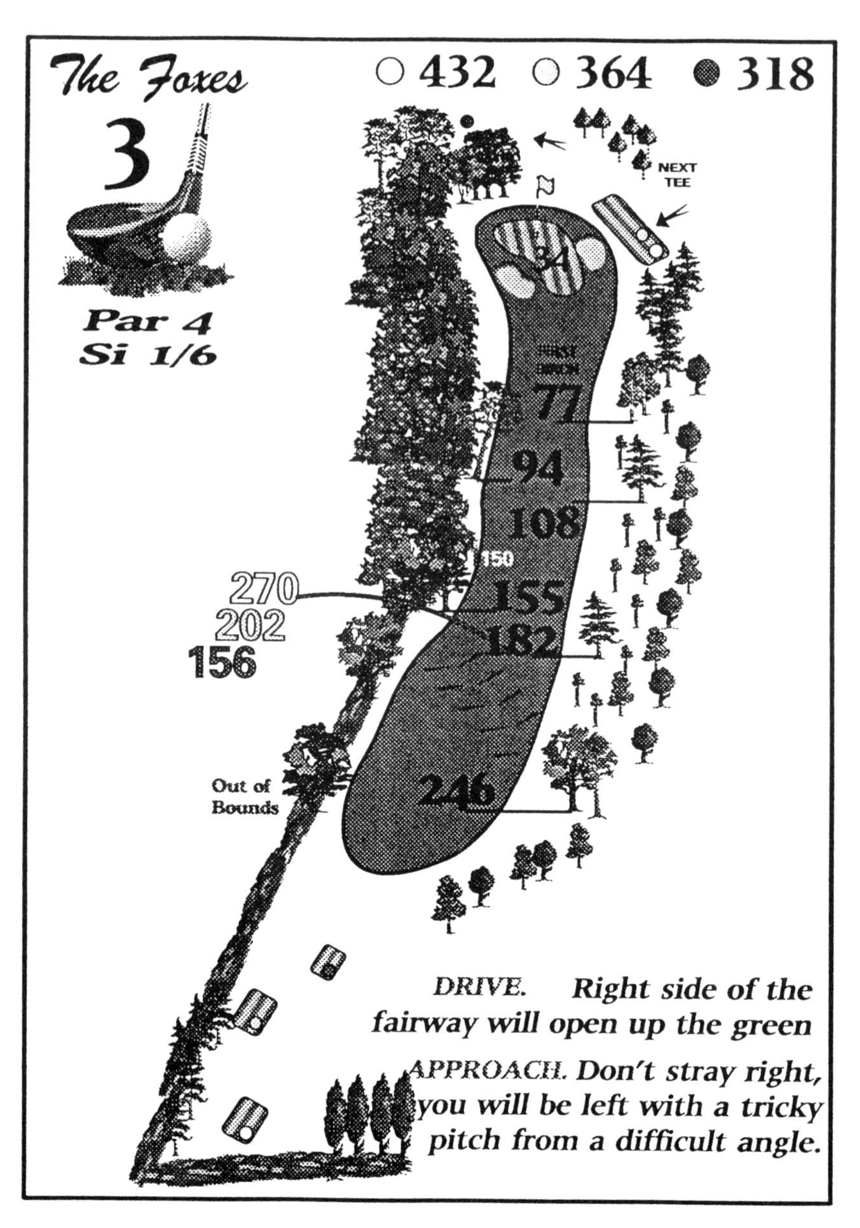
The Foxes
3
○ 432 ○ 364 ● 318
Par 4
Si 1/6
NEXT TEE
34
77
94
108
150
155
182
270
202
156
Out of Bounds
246
DRIVE. Right side of the fairway will open up the green
APPROACH. Don't stray right, you will be left with a tricky pitch from a difficult angle.

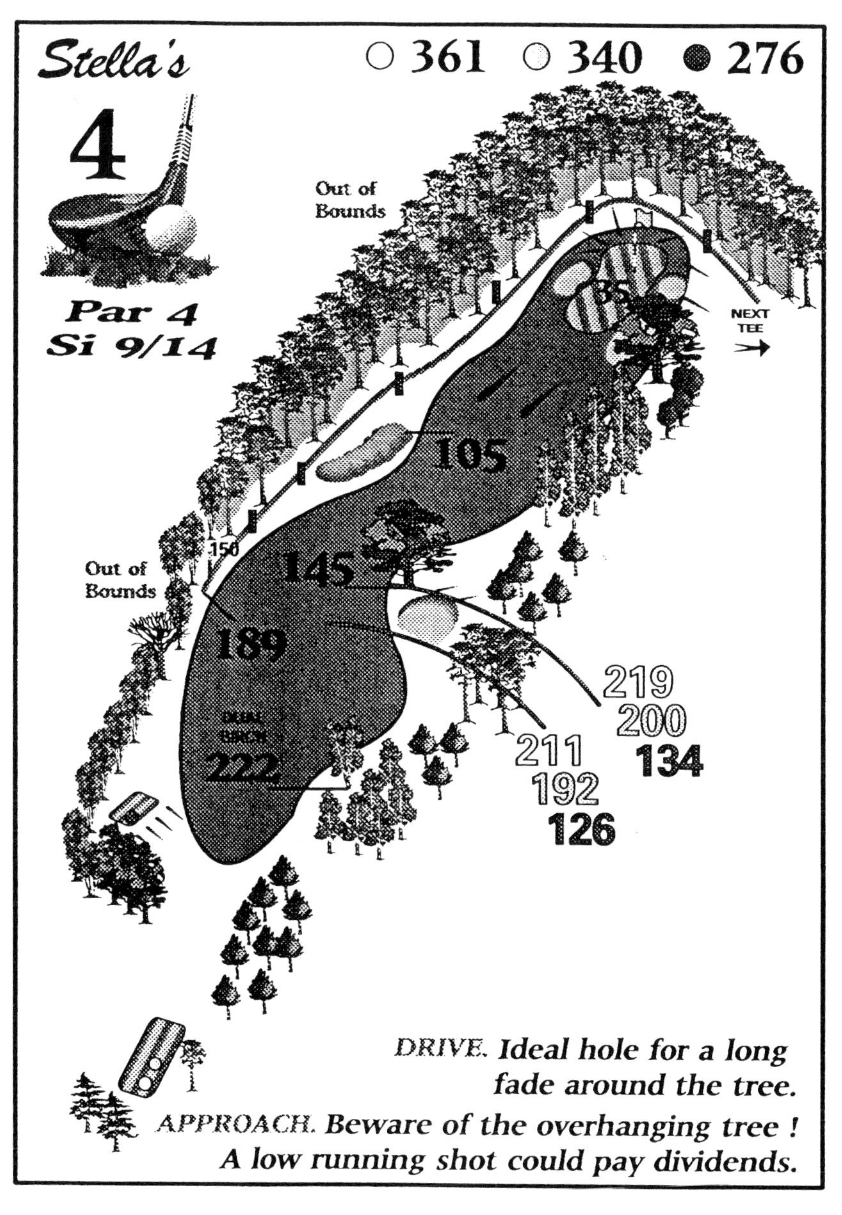
Stella's
○ 361 ○ 340 ● 276
4
Par 4
Si 9/14
Out of
Bounds
Out of
Bounds
NEXT
TEE
105
145
150
189
222
219
200
134
211
192
126
DRIVE. Ideal hole for a long
fade around the tree.
APPROACH. Beware of the overhanging tree !
A low running shot could pay dividends.

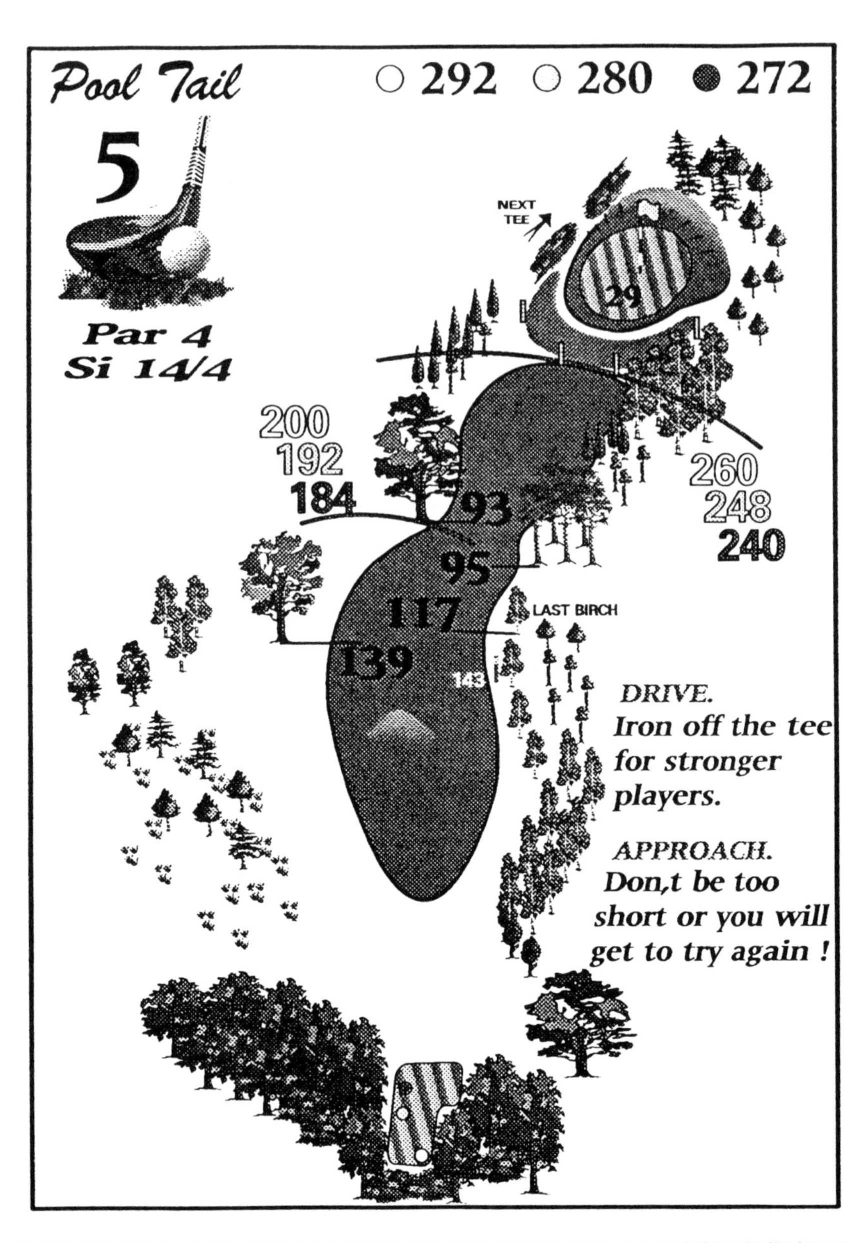
Pool Tail
○ 292 ○ 280 ● 272
5
Par 4
Si 14/4
NEXT TEE
29
200
192
184
93
95
117
139
143
260
248
240
LAST BIRCH
DRIVE.
Iron off the tee for stronger players.
APPROACH.
Don,t be too short or you will get to try again !

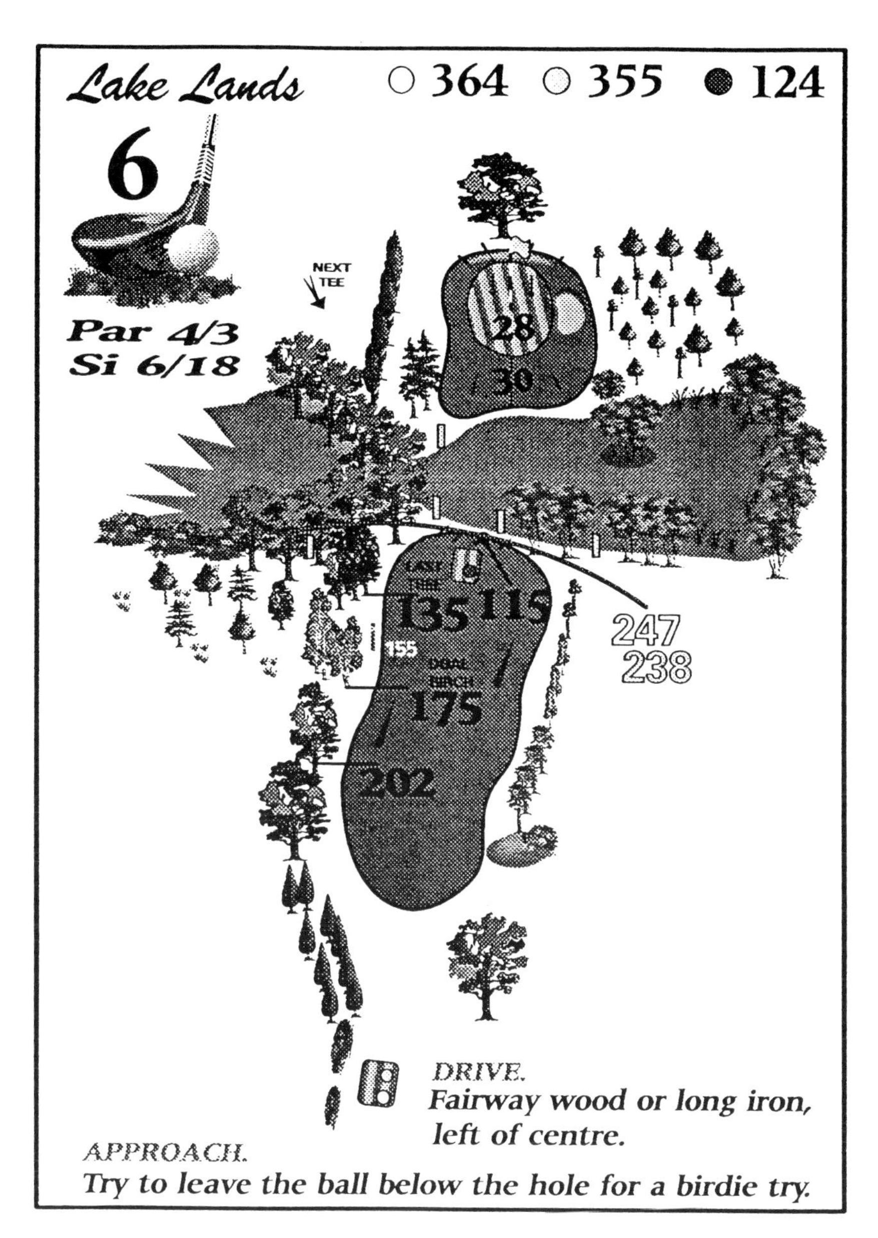
Lake Lands
364 355 124
6
Par 4/3
Si 6/18
NEXT TEE
28
30
135
115
155
175
202
247
238
DRIVE.
Fairway wood or long iron, left of centre.
APPROACH.
Try to leave the ball below the hole for a birdie try.

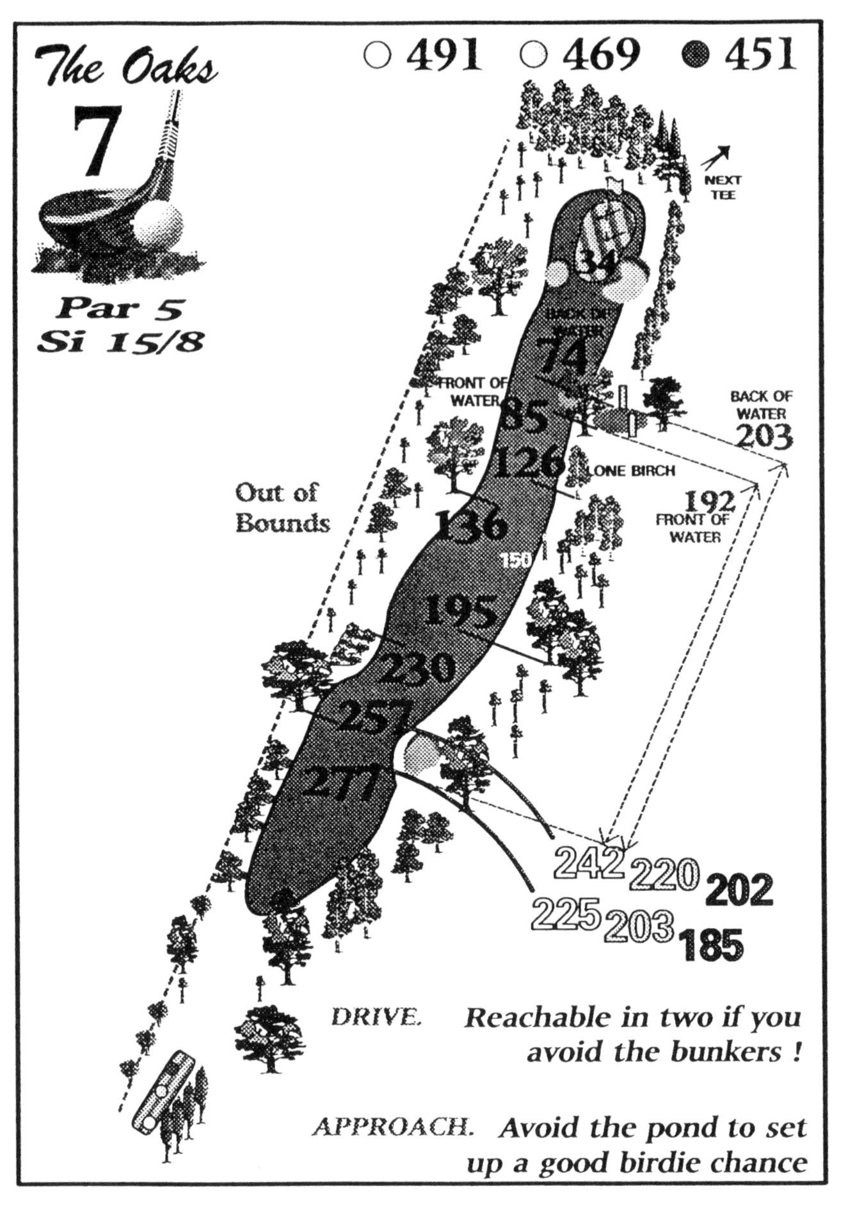
The Oaks
7
Par 5
Si 15/8
491
469
451
NEXT TEE
34
BACK OF WATER
74
FRONT OF WATER
85
BACK OF WATER
203
126
LONE BIRCH
Out of Bounds
192
FRONT OF WATER
136
150
195
230
257
277
242
220
202
225
203
185
DRIVE. Reachable in two if you avoid the bunkers !
APPROACH. Avoid the pond to set up a good birdie chance

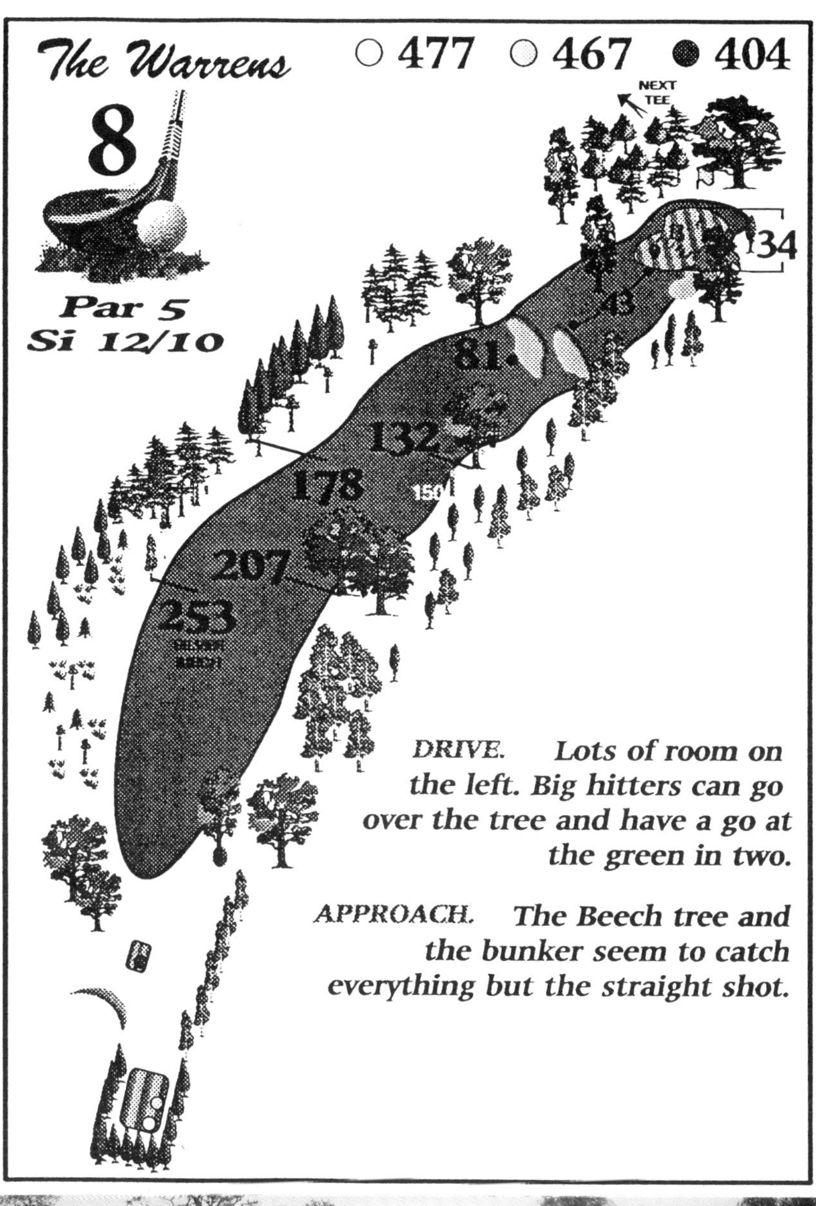

DRIVE. ***Lots of room on the left. Big hitters can go over the tree and have a go at the green in two.***

APPROACH. ***The Beech tree and the bunker seem to catch everything but the straight shot.***

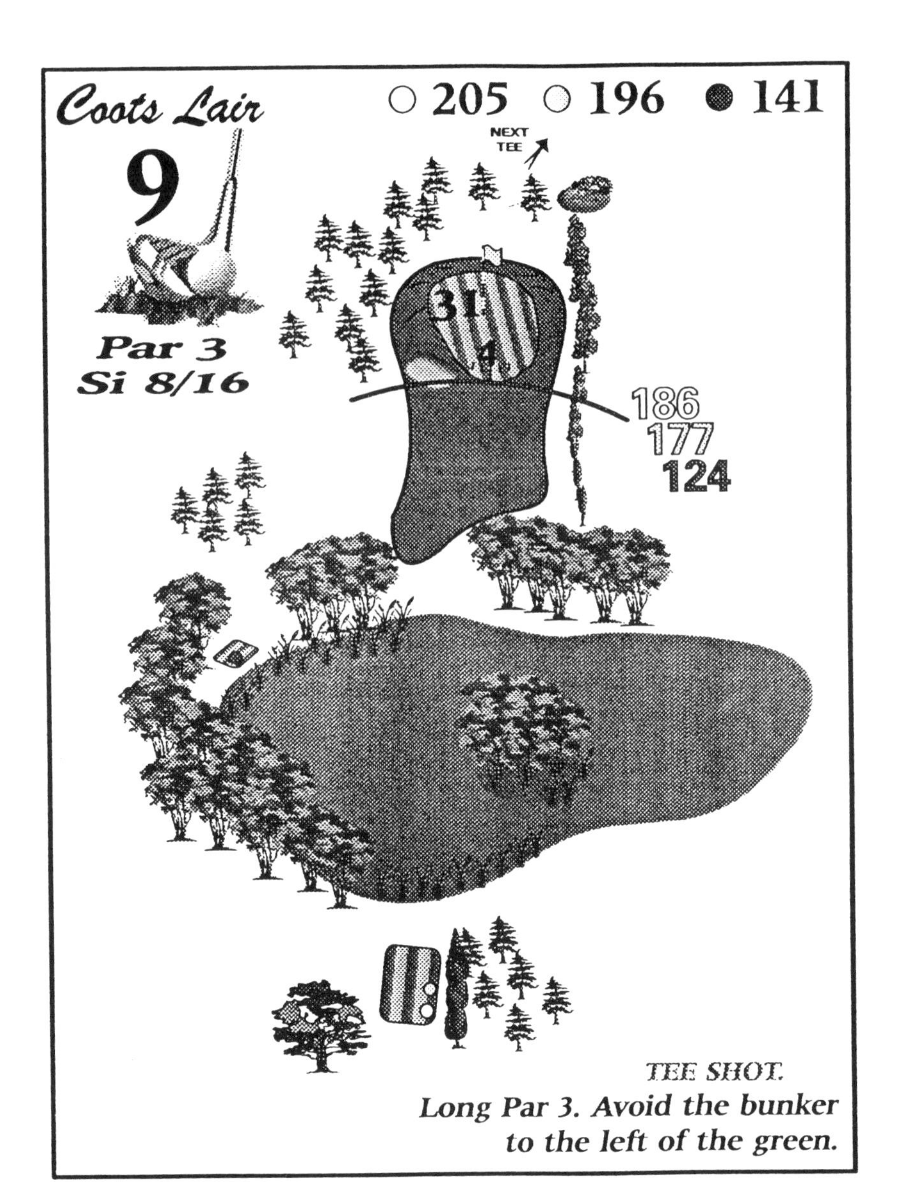
Coots Lair
○ 205 ○ 196 ● 141
9
NEXT TEE
Par 3
Si 8/16
186
177
124
TEE SHOT.
Long Par 3. Avoid the bunker to the left of the green.

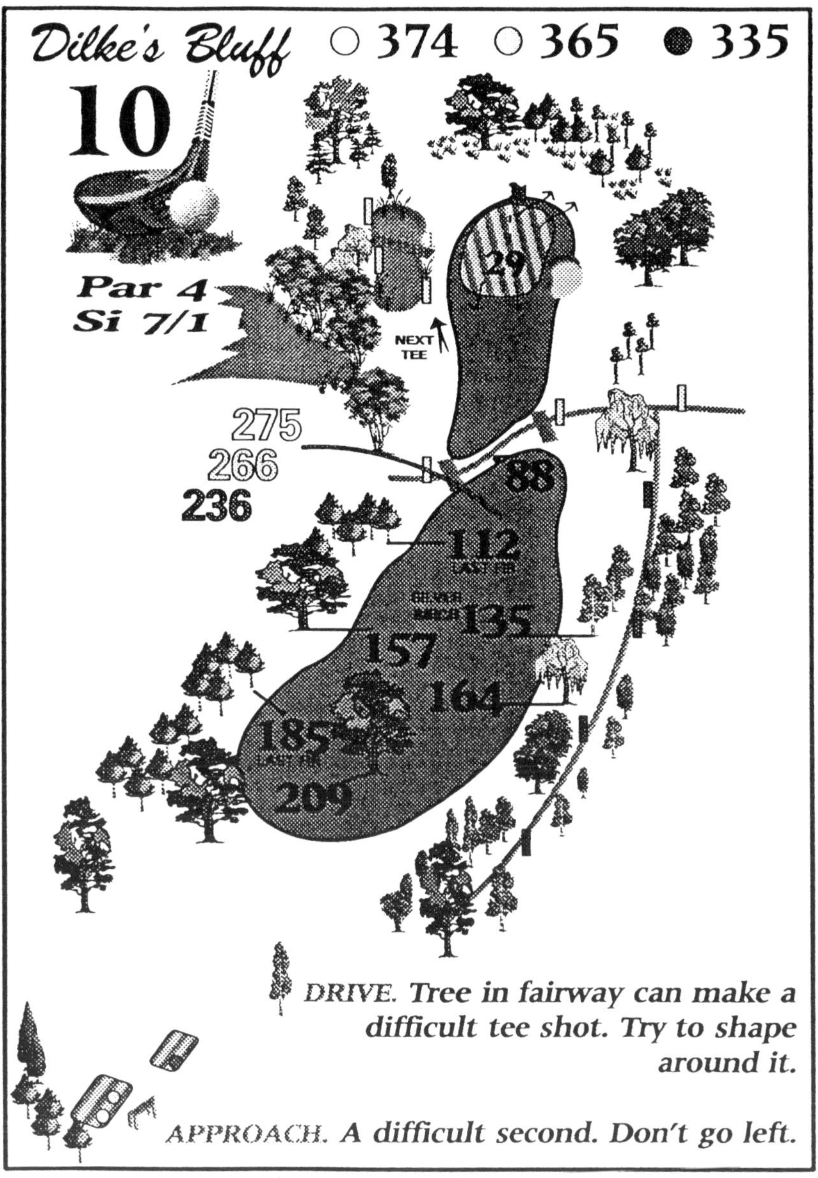

DRIVE. Tree in fairway can make a difficult tee shot. Try to shape around it.

APPROACH. A difficult second. Don't go left.

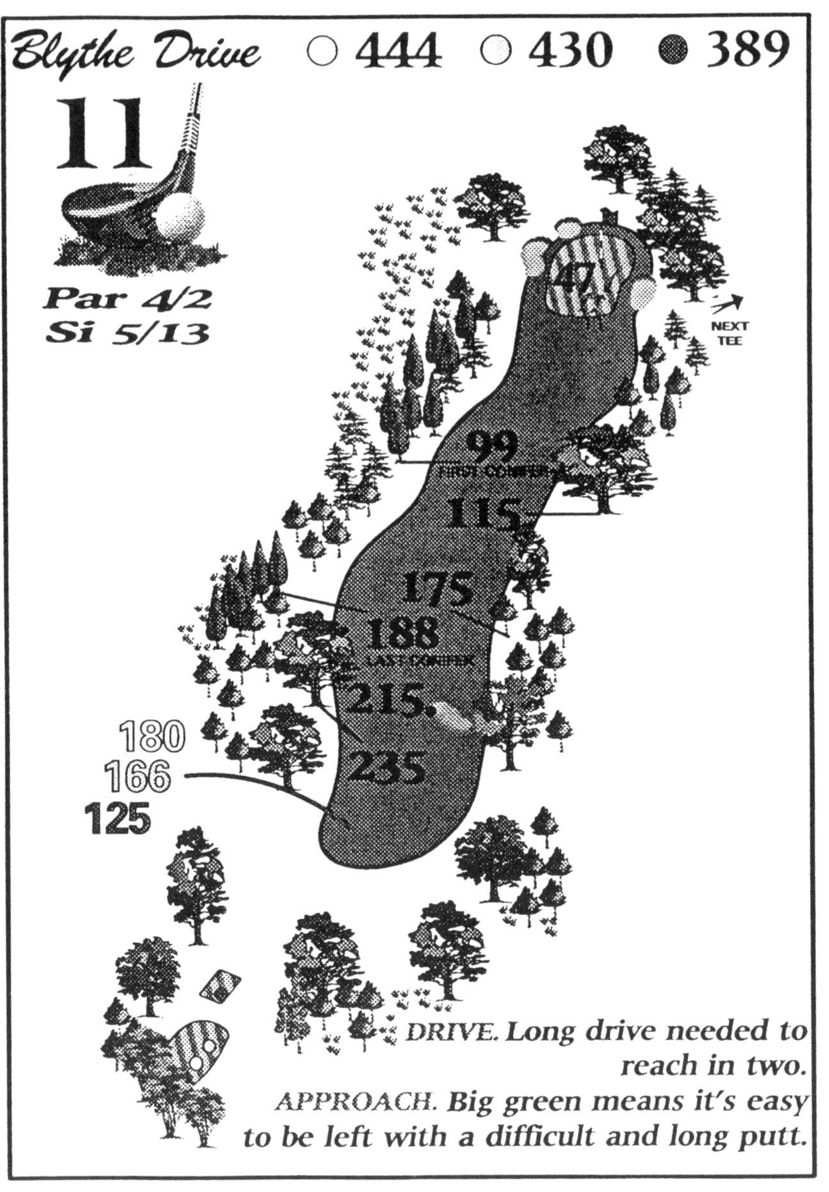
Blythe Drive
444
430
389
11
Par 4/2
Si 5/13
47
NEXT TEE
99
115
175
188
LAST CONIFER
215
235
180
166
125
DRIVE. Long drive needed to reach in two.
APPROACH. Big green means it's easy to be left with a difficult and long putt.

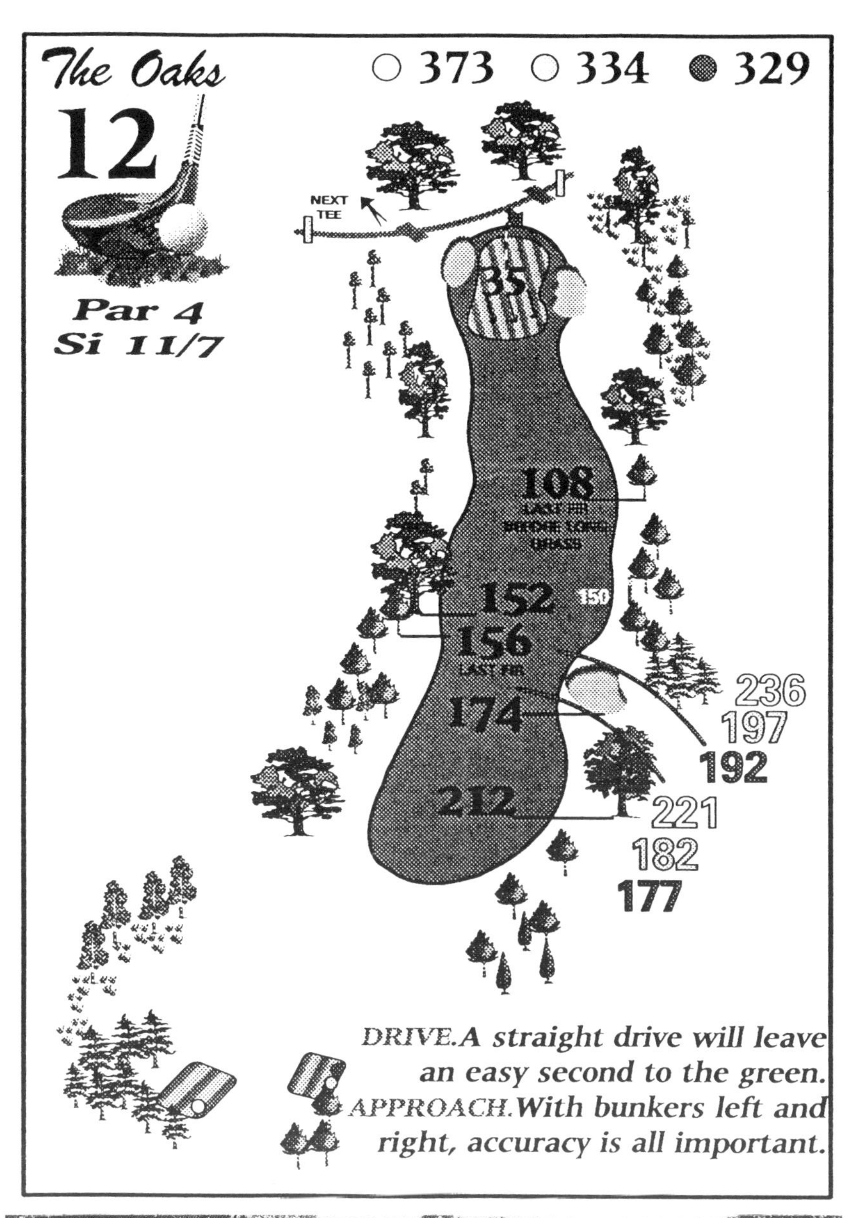

DRIVE. **A straight drive will leave an easy second to the green.**
APPROACH. **With bunkers left and right, accuracy is all important.**

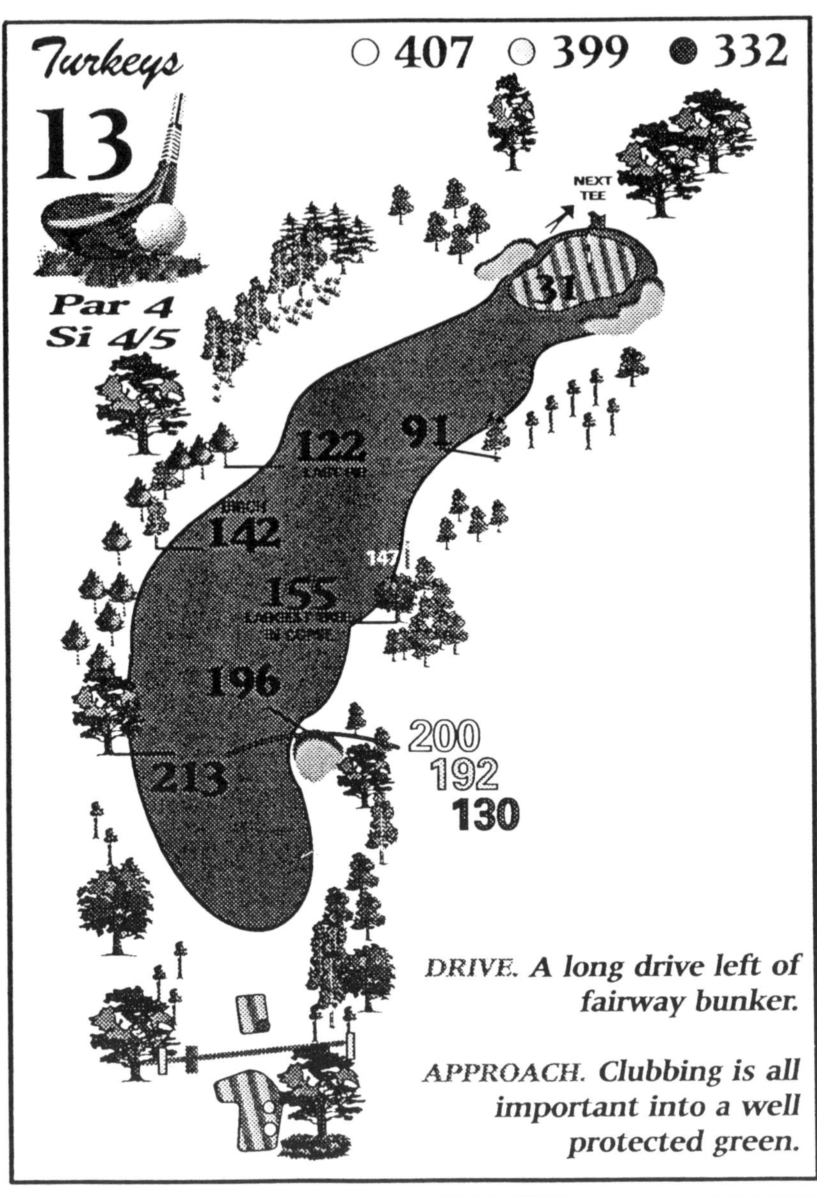

DRIVE. **A long drive left of fairway bunker.**

APPROACH. **Clubbing is all important into a well protected green.**

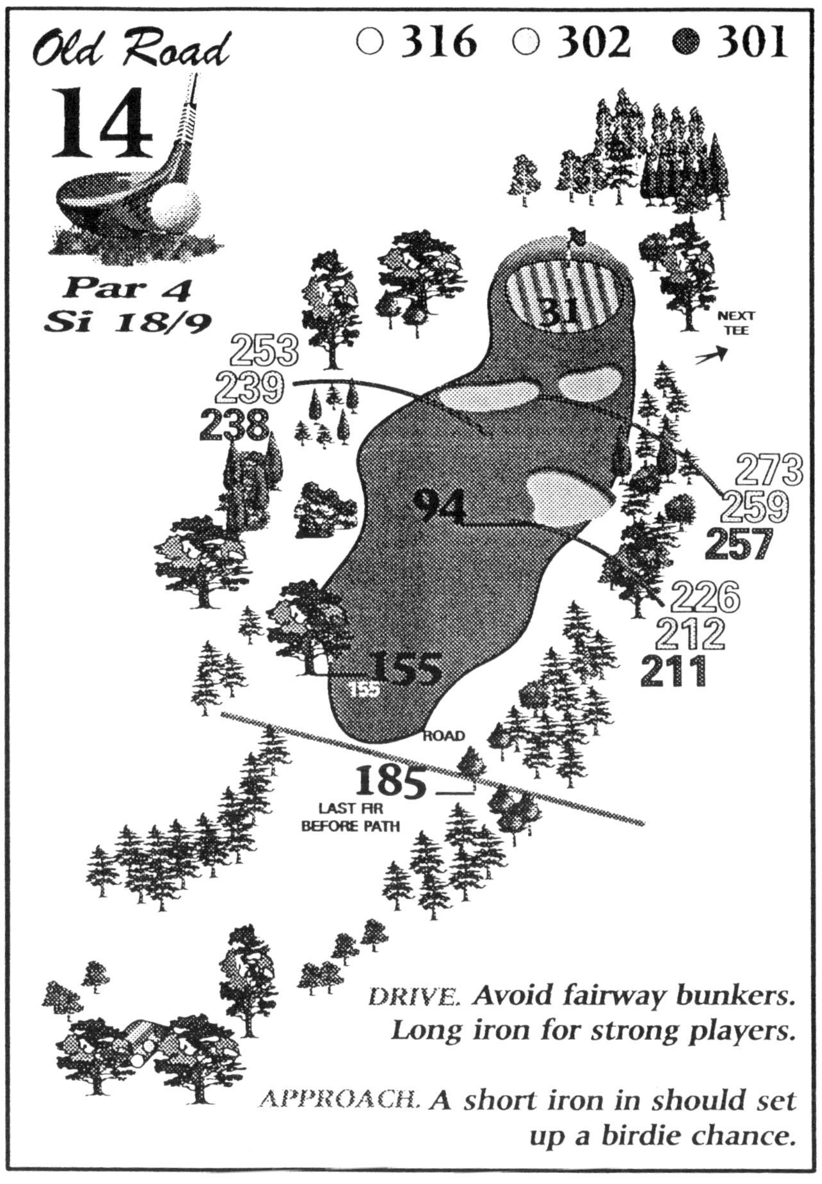
Old Road
○ 316 ○ 302 ● 301
14
Par 4
Si 18/9
31
NEXT TEE
253
239
238
273
259
257
94
226
212
211
155
155
ROAD
185
LAST FIR BEFORE PATH
DRIVE. Avoid fairway bunkers. Long iron for strong players.
APPROACH. A short iron in should set up a birdie chance.

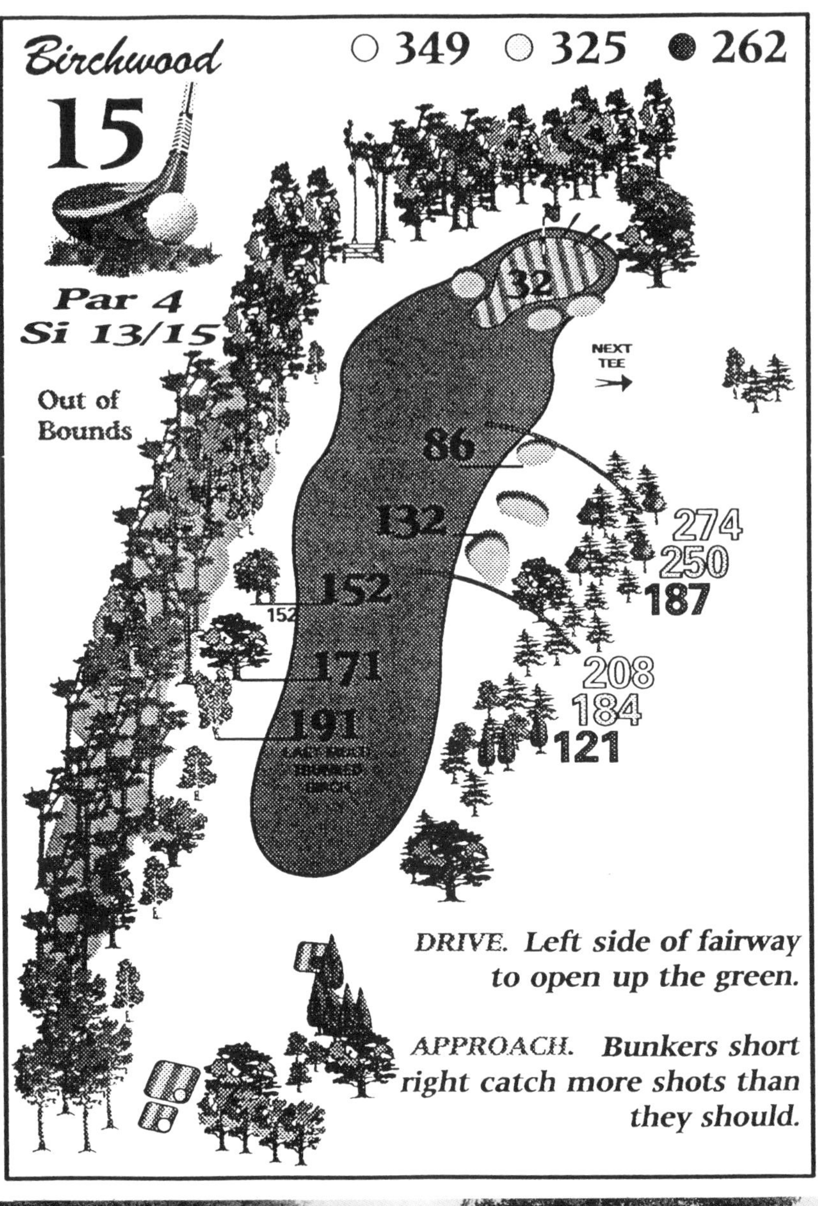
Birchwood
349
325
262
15
Par 4
Si 13/15
Out of Bounds
32
NEXT TEE
86
132
152
152
171
191
274
250
187
208
184
121
DRIVE. Left side of fairway to open up the green.
APPROACH. Bunkers short right catch more shots than they should.

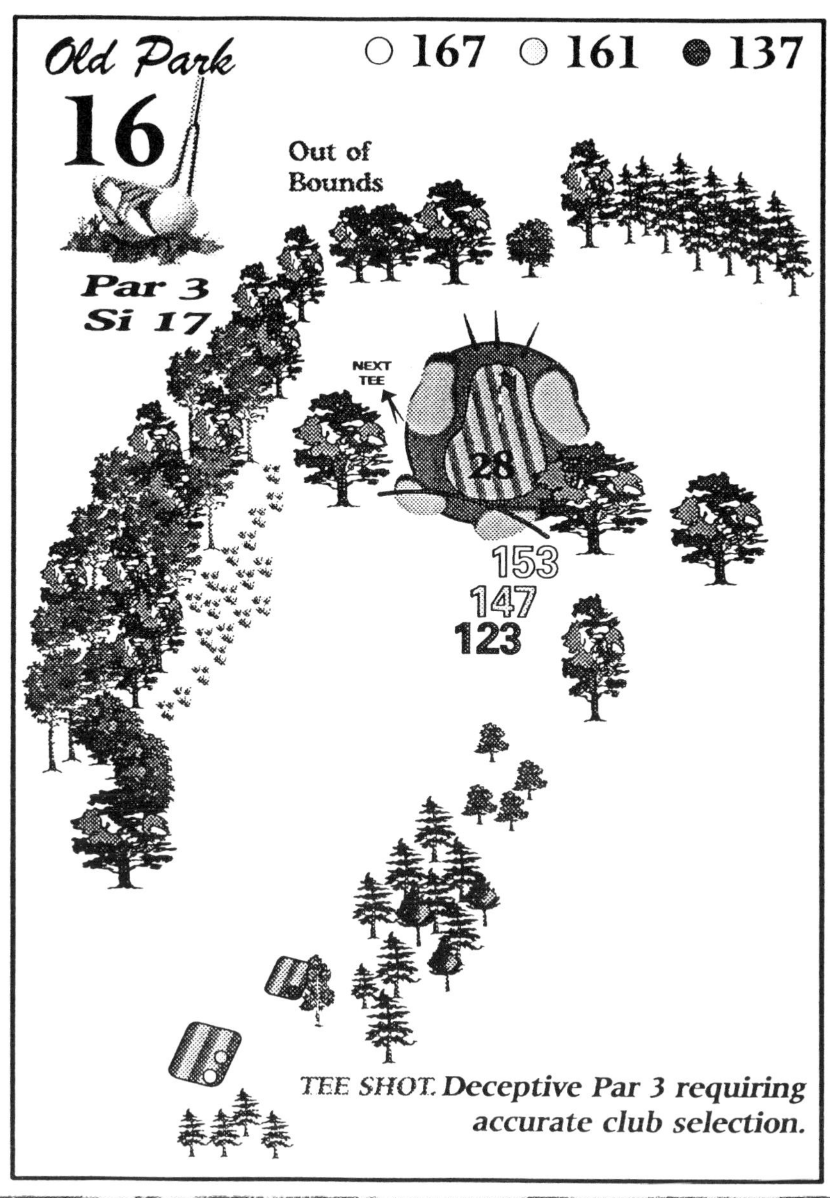
Old Park
○ 167 ○ 161 ● 137
16
Out of Bounds
Par 3
Si 17
NEXT TEE
28
153
147
123
TEE SHOT. Deceptive Par 3 requiring accurate club selection.

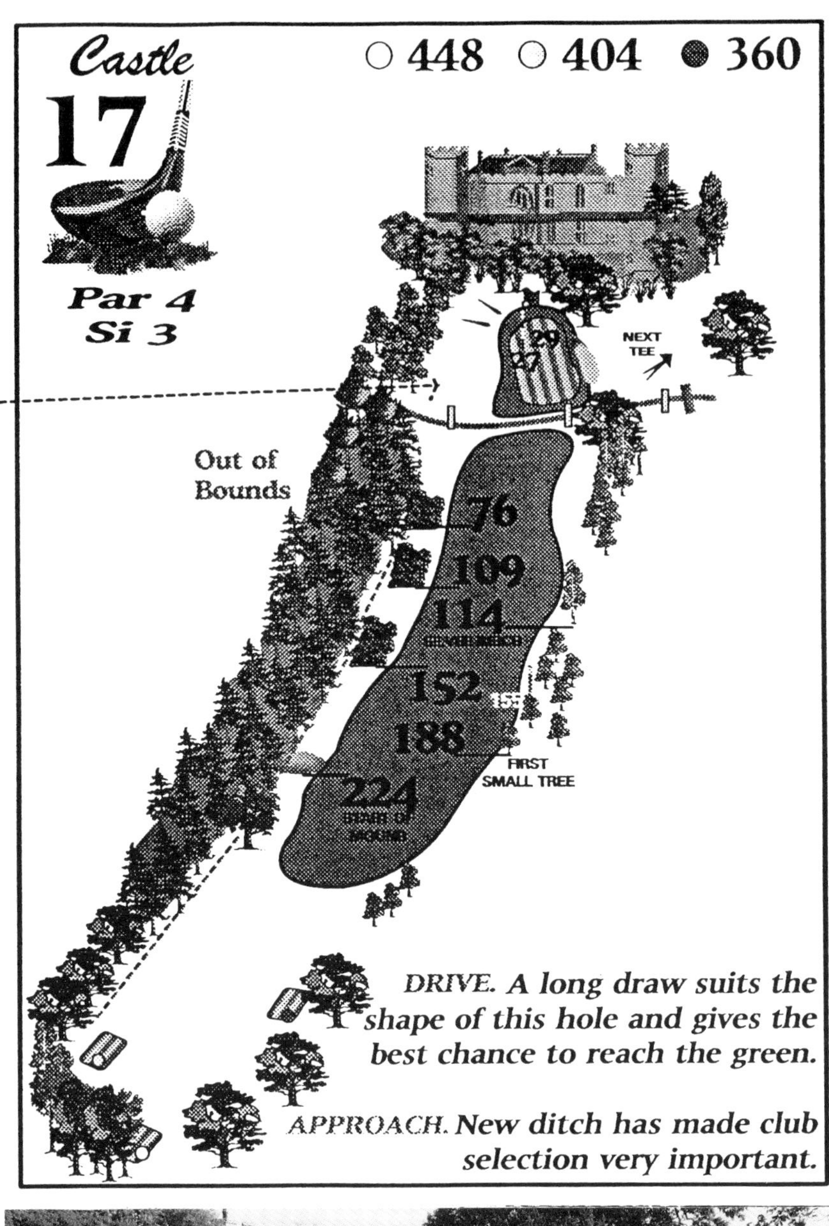

DRIVE. ***A long draw suits the shape of this hole and gives the best chance to reach the green.***

APPROACH. ***New ditch has made club selection very important.***

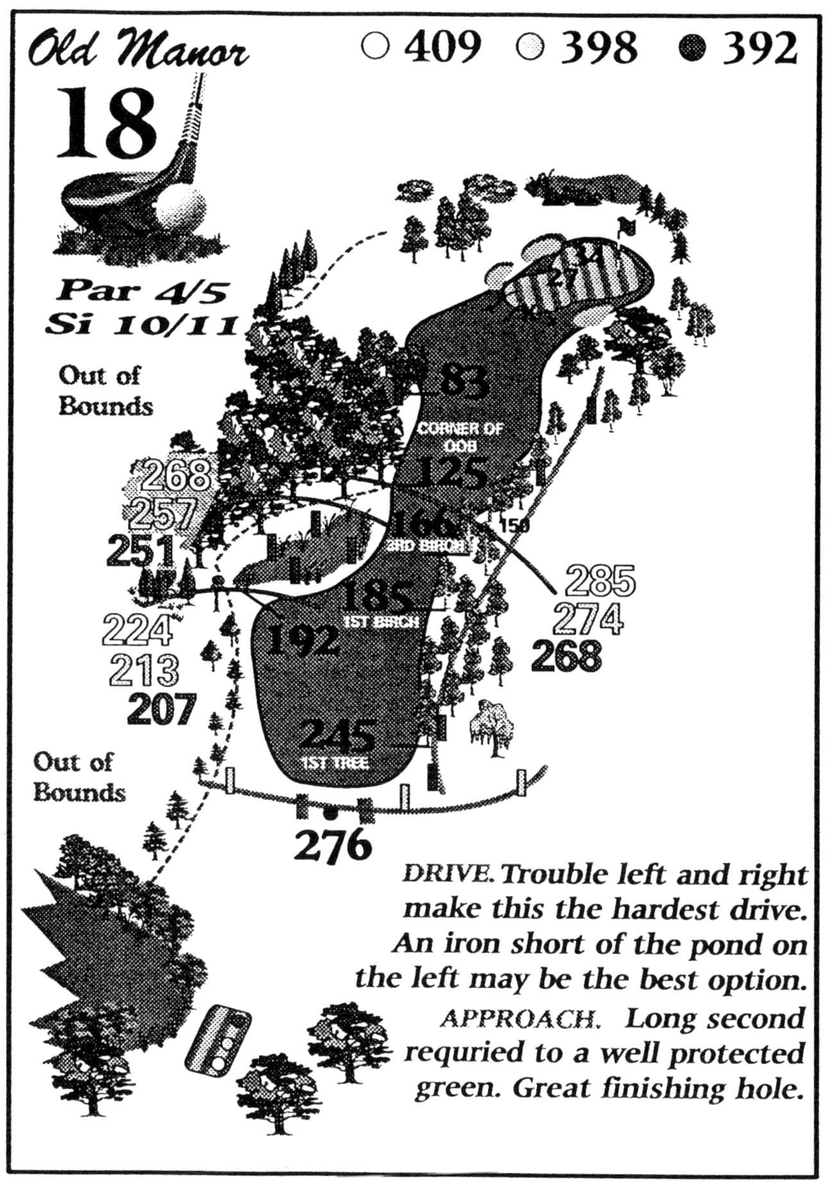

DRIVE. **Trouble left and right make this the hardest drive. An iron short of the pond on the left may be the best option.**

APPROACH. **Long second requried to a well protected green. Great finishing hole.**

THE PRESIDENTS

It is really quite remarkable that for a Club just about to celebrate its Centenary, that in all of those 100 years, only six gentlemen have served the Club in the capacity of President. Apart for a short period totalling some ten years, the Presidents have in fact been the Club's Landlords. Lord Bradford for fifty years at Castle Bromwich, and three members of the Fetherston-Dilke family at Maxstoke for almost the same period of time.

COLONEL ASH

President 1898–1904.
The first President of the Club (Ward End Golf Club) is quoted as Colonel Ash. There is no indication of who he was, whether he was in fact a member of the Club or merely a local gentleman who having a military rank was deemed appropriate to serve as President. He presumably remained as President until the Club moved to the new course off Bromford Road in October 1906.

Quite coincidentally, there is a remote possibility that Colonel Ash may have been related to the then owners of Packwood House, who bought the estate from the Dilke family in 1860. The purchaser was a Graham Baron Ash who lived there at the turn of the century and restored the house before passing it to the National Trust in 1941.

LORD BRADFORD

President 1904–1945.

Viscount Newport, who later became Lord Bradford on the death of his father in 1915, officially opened the new Castle Bromwich Golf Club, as President on October 24th 1906. The family had lived at Castle Bromwich Hall since the 16th century, they were one of the richest landowners in Warwickshire and in 1792 they were created Barons of Bradford. A marriage in the family brought the Newport estate (Weston Park) into their possession. Today descendants of the family still reside at Weston Park.

Lord Bradford, actually named Orlando Bridgeman Bradford, (Bridgeman being the family name) was born in 1873, and on succeeding his father in 1915 became the 5th Earl of Bradford. He was a Justice of the Peace and Deputy Lieutenant of the County of Warwickshire, he served in the 3rd Battalion of the Royal Scots and reached the rank of Lieutenant Colonel. He married Margaret Cecilia Bruce (eldest daughter of Baron Aberdare in 1904, and they had one son and two daughters.

He was Private Secretary to the Prime Minister Rt. Hon. A. J. Balfour from 1902 until 1905 and a Lord in Waiting to King George V from 1919 to 1924.

He remained President of Castle Bromwich Golf Club until the move was made to Maxstoke Park in 1946 and he died on March 21st 1957 at the grand old age of 84.

DR BEAUMONT A. FETHERSTON-DILKE

President 1946–1968.

Dr Fetherston-Dilke was the first member of the Fetherston-Dilke family to serve as President of Maxstoke Park Golf Club. He spent many years in the Colonial Medical Service in Trinidad, Gibraltar and Nigeria before inheriting Maxstoke Castle from his uncle in 1918. He retired from the Colonial Medical Service in 1928 and served as a Justice of the Peace – and later as Chairman of the Coleshill Bench.

When the family moved to Leamington Spa in 1934, he was elected to the town council of which he was Mayor in 1945/46 and 1950/51. He was a member of the Warwickshire County Council of which he became an Alderman. He was much in demant to serve on committees dealing with education and mental health.

He was instrumental, through his agents, in agreeing the terms on which the Golf Club first took a lease of the deer park at Maxstoke to create the course after the Second World War. He always believed that clearance of the bracken would be a major problem but he lived to see the course fully established before he died aged 92 in 1968.

CAPTAIN CHARLES B. FETHERSTON-DILKE, RN

President 1968–1990.

Captain Fetherston-Dilke served in the Royal Navy from 1935 until 1968. He spent most of the Second World War in destroyers in the Mediterranean and the Battle of the Atlantic. He also served in the Korean War and then successively as an adviser to the Royal Danish Navy in South Africa and in Paris. He then commanded HMS St. Vincent, a large training establishment for new entry sailors in Gosport and three submarine support ships.

He married in 1943 and has a daughter and a son Michael, five grand children and a great grandson.

In 1987, he handed over the Castle to his son Michael, and two years later moved into 'Keeper's Cottage' from which he can see the Castle and the golf course. He has served as High Sheriff of Warwickshire, as a Justice of the Peace, Chairman of the County Council and was until 1996 Vice Lord Lieutenant of the County.

WILLIAM N. DUDLEY EVANS

President 1991–1996.

William Dudley-Evans was by profession a Chartered Accountant and became a partner in the Birmingham practice of Bowker Stevens and Co. He joined Castle Bromwich at the age of 11 as a Junior and remained a playing member virtually up to his death in 1996. His services to the Club and to Warwickshire County Golf are legendary. He was Hon. Secretary of the Club from 1945 until 1956, he was Club Chairman from 1963 until 1976 and Club Captain in 1945. When Captain Fetherston-Dilke stood down in 1990 Bill was an obvious successor.

MICHAEL C. FETHERSTON-DILKE

President: 1996–

The son of Captain Charles Fetherston-Dilke, Michael was educated at Abberley Hill in Worcestershire, and Rugby School. He has a degree in Politics and Economics from the University of Bristol.

After qualifying with a large firm of accountants in London, he spent a number of years working in London, principally for BET a large industrial group, before moving to the Castle in 1989. He now has a range of business interests in Midlands industry, and lives at the Castle with his wife Rosemary, and three young children. His two young sons have a growing interest in golf, and he finds to his chagrin that their prospects of becoming good golfers are a great deal better than his own.

Michael's election as President coincided with the 50th Anniversary of the arrival of the Club at Maxstoke Park.

CLUB CAPTAINS

AT CASTLE BROMWICH

1898	Dr P. Campbell
1899	Dr P. Campbell
1900	Dr P. Campbell
1901	Dr P. Campbell
1902	Dr P. Campbell
1903	Dr P. Campbell
1904	Dr P. Campbell
1905	Dr H. W. Pooler
1906	Dr H. W. Pooler
1907	Dr J. Cochrane
1908	Dr J. Cochrane
1909	H. I. Hobbiss
1910	H. T. Perry
1911	W. Bentley
1912	C. K. Black
1913	W. G. Oxley
1914	J. R. Woodward
1915	J. R. Woodward
1916	Arthur Fleet
1917	W. H. Abbott
1918	C. T. Holder
1919	H. T Perry
1920	F. Parkes
1921	A. Armishaw
1922	G. H. Tyler
1923	A. Abbott
1924	H. C. Wright
1925	John Hall
1926	E. H. Maddocks
1927	F. Fletcher-Mills
1928	A. S. Langley
1929	W. J. Maryan
1930	R. Roden
1931	G. J. Withington
1922	G. H. Tyler
1923	A. Abbott
1924	H. C. Wright
1925	John Hall
1926	E. H. Maddocks
1927	F. Fletcher-Mills
1928	A. S. Langley
1929	W. J. Maryan
1930	R. Roden
1931	G. J. Whithington
1932	George Allman
1933	DR. J. Sangster
1934	M. MacDonagh
1935	J. Broughton
1936	Harry Hall
1937	A. Dudley-Evans
1938	C. H. Alger
1939	E. G. Lawrence
1940	L. E. Greenwwod
1941	George Stubbings
1942	T. A. Neale
1943	Harry Crump
1944	H. T. Perry
1945	W. N. Dudley-Evans

AT MAXSTOKE

1946	A. E. Shaw
1947	A. E. Shaw
1948	J. P. Nicholson
1949	A. G. Jordan
1950	V. W. Wilder
1951	J. Ralston
1952	A. D. Marston
1953	W. Thompson
1954	F. T. Blakey
1955	P. Srivens
1956	E. W. Smith
1957	J. S. Luke
1958	F. A. Walker
1959	F. A. Walker
1960	W. J. Martin
1961	S. E. Davis
1962	A. G. Moseley
1963	C. B. Hatton
1964	A. Blundell
1965	G. Brennan
1966	A. J. Wenham
1967	G. W. Dowse
1968	P. G. F. Whitehouse
1969	A. A. Trippas
1970	T. H. Marks
1971	J. R. Edwards
1972	B. C. Jolley
1973	R. G. Trippas
1974	N. E. Taylor
1975	N. C. Littleford
1976	H. Field
1977	Jim King
1978	H. Poynton
1979	P. J. Colgan
1980	V. Johnson
1981	C. C. Turner
1982	H. W. A. Evans
1983	A. G. Reading
1984	E. W. Murphy
1985	E. W. Bodger
1986	S. S. P. Marklew
1987	E. M. Wyatt
1988	H. J. Cooper
1989	S. Howell
1990	F. H. Smith
1991	D. Haywood
1992	R. D. Clarke
1993	W. Rendall
1994	Dr K. M. Rehmany
1995	D. R. Walker
1996	R. L. P. King
1997	G. E. Crawford

THE CAPTAINS AT MAXSTOKE PARK

A. E. Shaw
1946–1947

J. P. Nicholson
1948

A. G. Jordan
1949

V. W. Wilder
1950

J. Ralston
1951

A. D. Marston
1952

W. Thompson
1953

F. T. Blakey
1954

P. Scrivens
1955

E. W. Smith
1956

J. S. Luke
1957

F. A. Walker
1958–1959

W. J. Martin
1960

S. E. Davis
1961

A. G. Moseley
1962

C. B. Hatton
1963

A. Blundell
1964

G. Brennan
1965

A. J. Wenman
1966

G. W. Dowse
1967

P. G. F. Whitehouse
1968

A. A. Trippas
1969

T. H. Marks
1970

J. R. Edwards
1971

B. C. Jolley
1972

R. G. Trippas
1973

N. E. Taylor
1974

Club Captains

N. C. Littleford
1975

H. Field
1976

J. King
1977

H. W. Poynton
1978

P. J. Colgan
1979

V. Johnson
1980

C. C. Turner
1981

H. W. A. Evans
1982

A. G. Reading
1983

E. W. Murphy
1984

E. W. Bodger
1985

S. S. P. Marklew
1986

E. M. Wyatt
1987

H. J. Cooper
1988

S. Howell
1989

F. H. Smith
1990

D. Haywood
1991

R. D. Clarke
1992

W. Rendall
1993

Dr K. M. Rehmany
1994

D. R. Walker
1995

R. L. P. King
1996

G. E. Crawford
1997

Both ***Vernon Wilder*** and ***John Ralston*** had much to do with the laying out of the course in the early days at Maxstoke.

Vernon Wilder, 1950 was a Director of the family firm who were at that time one of the largest manufacturers of fireworks. He served the Club in a number of roles on the Committee including Chairman for some time, but more importantly, as Green's Chairman when the original 9 hole course was laid out. He was Chairman in 1953 when the Club nearly folded, but the Club survived thanks to generous hand outs made by the members.

J. Ralston, 1951. John Ralston, according to surviving colleagues from that time was a tremendously energetic and enthusiastic member of the Committee. Whilst he was Green's Chairman he organised and took part in working parties that spent weeks literally hand picking stones from the areas which had previously been under the plough.

A. D. Marston, 1952. Douglas Marston was one of the longest serving members of the Club. Doug joined Castle Bromwich Golf Club in 1927 as a young man, and was elected to the Club Committee for the first time in 1943.

He lived at Handsworth – travelling to the course must have been difficult in those days. Doug was a low handicap player for many years and for a long period was an enthusiastic member of the Green's Committee but when arthritis took over he took over as Competition and Handicap Secretary.

F. T. Blakey, 1954. Frank Blakey one of the members who played at Castle Bromwich and Maxstoke. Scratch golfer for many years, He played County Golf for both Warwickshire and Durham. He was Club Champion six times and had lengthy spells as Green's Chairman.

W. J. Martin, 1960. Wilf Martin was born in Small Heath in 1909 and moved with his parents to Marston Green in the early '20s when the Digby Estate was broken up and the village being developed. He became very active in the local community playing soccer, rugby and apparently a reasonable standard of tennis of which he the Club Secretary for a number of years.

He was a prominent member of the local dramatics society and made many appearances on stage in various presentations. He also held office as Secretary and Chairman of the Village Club. Was a staunch supporter of the local Free Church and was a founder of the 1960 Boy Scout movement in Marston Green.

When he joined Maxstoke, he soon became involved in Committee activities and was Hon. Secretary for a number of years. For a short time he served as Green's Chairman. For his endeavours over the years with the Club he was honoured by being awarded a Life Membership of the Club. His wife Marjorie who he married in 1940, was Lady Captain in 1961 following Wilf's Captaincy year, and she also was awarded a Life Membership.

During his entire working life Wilf worked for 'Simms Motor Units' in Coventry and rose to the position of General Manager. Wilf was a long serving Free Mason and was instrumental in forming the Marston Green Lodge and received provincial honours from both Warwickshire and Worcestershire. Wilf died in 1992, and his wife Marjorie in 1997.

Stan Davis, 1961. Stan Davis had a six year spell as Hon. Treasurer in the late '50s.

A. G. Moseley, 1962. Was Green's Chairman in the early '60s.

G. W. Dowse, 1967. George Dowse born in 1917, was one of the longest serving members of the Club having joined in 1951. In 1962 elected to the Green's Committee. His main contribution was as Handicap Secretary, older members will recall his encyclopaedic knowledge of the Rules of Golf. George was very much involved with the first computer programme introduced in 1983. Met his wife Madeline in 1938, and they had two sons. Madeline was Lady Captain in 1965. George played most sports in his youth and won many trophies in cycle racing. His working life was spent at 'Alfred Herberts'. George always carried his clubs more or less right up to the time of his passing in June 1997.

P. G. F. Whitehouse, 1968. 'Pip' Whitehouse as he was always known joined the Club in 1950 as a 'novice' but soon was down to single figures. Served on Committee in the early days, and was last Captain at the Castle. Won Club Championship seven times and many other trophies at Maxstoke. 'Pip' was a teacher by profession and in his youth played many sports and amongst his other leisure activities he cites mountain climbing and bridge. At bridge he has won many Warwickshire and Inter County Pairs and Team Events and has been a County Representative Player for 47 years.

A. A. Trippas, 1969. Arthur Trippas joined the Club at the end of the '50s and from conversation from older members who were involved at that time, he was very active in ensuring that the Club remained solvent in a very troublesome period when the Club was desperately short of money and indeed members.

Arthur joined the Committee in the early '60s and was one of a 'gang of four' mentioned in Bert Jolley's earlier 'History of Maxstoke Park Golf Club' that held 21 meetings in twelve months at Arthur's Princip Street office in an attempt to sort out the apparent shambles of the Club's Membership Records and finances.

Arthur Trippas had a spell as Chairman and was much involved in researching the members to ascertain their requirements for the new Clubhouse, and also in the planning negotiations. When Wilf Martin stood down as Hon. Secretary, Arthur took over for a couple of years in 1971/72 and then moved to Green's Chairman in 1973/74.

Arthur resigned from Committee activities after an Extraordinary General Meeting held in 1974. In 1984 in due recognition of his long service as a member of Committee, he was appointed as Vice President of the Club but sadly died within a few weeks of the appointment.

T. H. Marks, 1970. Tom Marks has more or less been associated with the Club from the day that he was born, as his father Roland (Harry as he was known) Marks was Head Green Keeper at Castle Bromwich. The family home was in Bromford Road right opposite to the course at Castle Bromwich, and Tom played as a Junior from the age of 17 years.

When the move to Maxstoke was made, Tom was probably more involved than anyone is setting out the course. He had three lengthy spells as Green's Chairman in the early days when the original holes were laid, and then later when the present layout of holes came into play.

Tom was a low handicap golfer for a number of years and continued playing well into his 80s. Tom was made a Vice President of the Club some years ago in recognition of his services to the Club. Tom passed away in August 1997.

B. C. Jolley, 1972. Bert Jolley was born in Bordesley Green and went to school at Saltley Grammar School, and his Maths teacher, Hugh Cooke was a long time member of the Club. Bert served through the war years, was commissioned in 1940 and served with the Field Artillery in North Africa, until he was wounded at Tobruk in 1942. When recovered he landed at Normandy with the Royal Artillery and went through Europe finishing at Hamburg when the war ended. Going into the teaching profession Bert served at several schools finishing as Headmaster at Cockshut Hill Comprehensive from 1960 until 1976 when he retired.

Bert's association with the Club began in the late '50s and he soon went on the Committee. He was an active member of the Membership Sub Committee which was set up to sort out the problem of establishing how many authorised members there were, who had paid subs, and who not. He was House Chairman in 1967 and 1968, back in the Castle days, and had a lengthy spell as Club Chairman from 1977 until 1981 following Bill Dudley-Evans.

Bert Jolley has been honoured being awarded an Honorary Life Membership of the Club as well as a Vice Presidency. Bert claims that he was also given the title of the 'Wettest Captain' the Club has ever had due to the fact that his Captain's Day in 1972 was washed out. He still plays golf two or three times a week, not bad for an octogenarian, but insists that he is now a 'fair weather golfer'.

R. G. Trippas, 1973. Ron Trippas was another of the four gentlemen who joined the Club in the late'50s and later formed the Sub Committee who sorted out the membership anomalies that existed at the time.

He served on the Committee for a number of years but in his Captaincy year, several unpopular decisions which did not meet the approval of the members caused a mass resignation of the Committee including himself as Club Captain. Rather sadly, shortly after, Ron died on the course.

N. E. Taylor, 1974. Norman Taylor joined the Club in 1957 on April Fool's Day and was one of the four members who sorted the mockery of the Club's Mebership Filing System. Norman remained on the Committee for 19 years from 1964 unti 1983, which included 6 years as Hon. Secretary. He won the 'B' Team Cup in his year of Captaincy, and has also won the 'Stableford Foursomes' with Walter Mason as partner in 1968, the 'Maxstoke Plate' with Colin Bailey in 1988 and this year 1997, the 'Hewlett Memorial Shield' partnered by Warren McDivitt. Norman is Birmingham born, in his younger days he played Rugby for Old Centrals. His working life was spent with 'Harmo Industries' and 'Walker U. K. Ltd' totalling 41 years service. In recognition of his service to the Club he was made an Honorary Life Member and is also a Vice President.

N. C. Littleford, 1975. Norman Littleford was Hon. Secretary for three years from 1974 until 1976 with his Captain's year coming at the same time in 1975. Norman was involved with local government and served for many years as a Magistrate.

H. Field, 1976. Harry Field joined Maxstoke in 1967 and like many other members 'migrated' from the old Marston Green Municipal course. He served on the Club Committee for a lengthy period extending back to 1973, which included two spells as Hon. Treasurer 1974–1980 and 1986–1991, both periods which were extremely fraught as far as the Club's finances were concerned. Much credit is due to Harry that after each of his Treasurer's terms, the accountancy and control of the finances were in good shape. In 1973 he inaugurated the 'Invitation Open' followed by the 'Open Mixed Foursomes' in 1978. He ran this competition for several years, then handed over to his wife Lena. Harry donated the 'Jubilee Cup' for the best nett score in this competition. Golfing achievements include winning the 'Perkins Putter' and the Veteran's Cup. In his youth Harry was a prominent competitive time trials cyclist, and his wartime service 1943–1947 was spent in Coastal Command. Harry's services were much appreciated and he is honoured as a Club's Vice President.

J. King, 1977. Jim King born in Acocks Green in 1912 is one of the 'octagenarians' who regularly play the course some two or three times each week. Having been hospitalised a couple of times in recent years he has made a splendid recovery and joins the 'Maxies' in their activities. Jim joined the Club in 1963 back in the Castle days. Jim joined the old 'Bakelite Company' in 1926 when there were 48 employees and rose to the position of Distribution Manager, and there were then 13,000 employed. Jim retired in 1971 and took up farming. Jim listed his youthful sporting activities as cricket, football and swimming but modestly states only for fun. A rare and unusual occurrence following his own Captaincy in 1977, was completing the Captaincy of his successor, who resigned in mid-term.

H. W. Poynton, 1978. Harry Poynton was born in Coventry in 1918, and joined the Club in 1964 and has been an active member over the years. In his Captain's Year he entertained a party of golfers from Sweden who came to Maxstoke and were invited to join in a Bank Holiday Foursomes Competition. They were so pleased with the hospitality extended to them that they donated the 'Forsbacka Cup' which is now played for each year. Harry went through the war years 1939–1946 in the Army, played cricket and football in his younger days, lists gardening as his main leisure activity. Harry has three sons, ten grandchildren and five great grand-children.

P. J. Colgan, 1979. Pat Colgan was another member who came to Maxstoke after many years at Marston Green Municipal Golf Course. Pat was a low handicap golfer, very competitive, and like several other golfers from across the Irish Sea, he used a two handed grip which gave his drives a low trajectory but a considerable run on the ball after it landed. Pat was a very successful Captain of the 'Scratch League Team' for a number of years in the '70s. In appreciation of his enthusiasm and obvious leadership qualities, Pat was awarded an Honorary Life Membership of the Club in 1983 but unfortunately he did not have much opportunity to enjoy this achievement as he died suddenly in 1984.

V. Johnson, 1980. Victor Johnson joined the Club in 1963 and was elected to the Committee in 1971. He took over as House Chairman and continued in this role for 12 years, almost certainly longer than anyone else. His achievements include winning the 'Winter League' with Ray Carter in 1968 and the 'Stableford Cup' with David Brayley in 1984. Memories from his Captain's year were presenting the prizes at the 'Dunhill' Professional Golf Clinic and at the 'Warwickshire Seniors Championship, both played at Maxstoke Park. Vic is married to Catherine an active golfer with the Ladies Section, they have two daughters and four grandchildren. Vic served in the Royal Electrical and Mechanical Engineers during the war from 1940–1946. Vic and his wife are Honorary Life Members of the Club.

H. W. A. Evans, 1982. Harold Evans is I believe the longest serving member of the Club, and I would add, one of the most popular, having joined way back in 1956. Harold was born in Birmingham and has a twin brother who is also a keen golfer. He was employed as a springmaker by 'Smiths Production Works Ltd' for all of his working life. Harold played at Marston Green for some years before moving to Walmley, and then to Maxstoke, His golfing successes at Maxstoke include winning the 'Ward End Cup' (our oldest trophy) with George Lea in 1960 and the 'Captain's Shield' in 1979.

In his younger days Harold was a keen table tennis player and won many league titles and cups. On Committee he was House Chairman from 1982 until 1985 and also the Hon. Secretary from 1984 until 1987. His services to the Club were recognised when he was made a Vice President. Harold being in a reserved occupation during the war but did the next best thing by being a member of 'Dad's Army'

A. G. Reading, 1983. Tony Reading was born in Coleshill, is married and has two sons, a daughter and three grand-children. He has his own building contracting business and is now semi-retired. Tony joined Maxstoke in 1971 and has won the 'Hewlett Cup' partnered by Adrian Harrison and the 'Stableford Cup' with Les Patterson. In his yeat of Captaincy Tony presented the Club with the splendid 'Trophy Cabinet' which is located in the Lounge. He also donated the 'Pat Colgan Cup' which is played for annually between the Club and 'Walmley Golf Club'.

Tony managed the 'Warwickshire Junior and Youth Teams for 5 years and it is worthy of note that he gave Steve Webster his first County game. Has been on the County Executive Committee for over 10 years and at the present time is Manager of the Warwickshire Union of Golf Clubs County Membership Scheme. Apart from his golfing, activities Tony is a keen 'Rotarian'.

E. W. Murphy, 1984. 'Eddie' as he is generally known born in 1917 is a well loved 'Dubliner' and has all the blarney associated with traditional Irishmen. He came to the Midlands and spent his entire working life in the motor industry with 'Rover'/'British Leyland'.

He joined Maxstoke in 1966 and has won the 'Perkins Putter'. These days, Eddie can be found on the first tee for all major competitions, Club 'Opens', 'Invitation Opens', AM/AMs etc. He takes great pleasure in explaining the complexities of our local rules and those of the particular Competition to all of the visitors playing at Maxstoke. He has a reserve of well aired homilies and stories, which are narrated to his captive audience with great enthusiasm and amusement. These are intended to calm down those with 'big match nerves' but giggles on the tee are not always the best approach to a good drive.

During his youth Eddie was a semi-professional footballer and was an enthusiastic member of a choral society. Eddie is married, has two children and four grandchildren, and during the war served in the Merchant Navy from 1942 until 1946.

E. W. Bodger, 1985. Eric Bodger was born in Birmingham and spent his working life as Metallurgical Chemist and Laboratory Manager with the Aeroplane and Motor Aluminium Castings Company. He is married to Gladys, a past Lady Captain at Maxstoke and they have a son and a daughter and three grand children. Eric joined Maxstoke in 1968 and remembers that the Subscription was £22. 00. Eric won the 'Invitation Open' in 1982 partnered by Ron Wright from Sutton Coldfield and the 'Strawberry Tea' in 1985 with Edna Clare. Eric recalled that because the 'Ladies versus Gents' was so 'one sided' he introduced the 'Bisques' which was appreciated by the Ladies but not so the Gents. Eric's leisure activities include water colour painting, photography and contract bridge. He also flies radio controlled model aircraft.

S. S. P. Marklew, 1986. Peter Marklew was born in Birmingham in 1923 and was employed by Telecommunication Engineering where he became General Manager of the Coventry area. Peter has married twice, firstly to Margaret (who died in 1973) with whom he had seven children (six surviving) and eleven grand children, and to Teresa who has just finished her year as Lady Captain.

Peter joined Maxstoke in 1973 and won the 'President's Trophy in 1984 with his wife's half set of clubs, under the impression he was playing in a monthly medal. Won a Championship at Brand Hall in 1970 with a nett score of 63. Played at Marston Green when it was 9 hole, and was Chairman for a few years whilst a member.

Items of note from his Captain's Year, Tony Allen scored a record 63 around the course, and Neil Connolly became Warwickshire Junior and the Warwickshire Schools Champion – 2 Championships in 5 days – he won the School's Championship by 12 clear shots.

E. M. Wyatt, 1987. Ernie Wyatt a very popular member of the Club ran with his brother a small toolroom and Garage business in Tile Cross. In his younger days Ernie played soccer and cricket with the local clubs at Marston Green. He was a big man and as centre half was usually capable of dominating the penalty area. As Benny Hill would say ' not many got the better of Ernie'.

Ernie lived life to the full, he loved his golf, and despite failing eyesight he carried on playing until further ill health prevented it.

H. J. Cooper, 1988. Jack Cooper, a Londoner, born in Hackney he spent his whole working life more or less equally divided between the Royal Navy and Barclay's Bank. Jack is married and has 2 daughters and two grandchildren.

In his younger days Jack was Schools Rifle Champion in 1935, and he also excelled in 100 yards and 220 yards sprints.

Jack joined the Navy in 1936, served throughout the war years, was mentioned in dispatches 1942, and remained 'afloat' until 1962. The following year Jack joined Maxstoke, and in his year of Captaincy admits to introducing 'Burns Night' to the social calendar.

S. Howell, 1989. Stan Howell born and bred in Birmingham, has his own business of Haulage Contractor, warehouse and garage owner. His three children all work in family business.

Stan joined Maxstoke in 1972 and has won the 'Winter League' and the 'Hewlett Trophy' both times partnered by his son Martin.

Stan recalls that in his year of Captaincy he was also 'B' Team Captain. He served for a couple of years on Committee and was involved in the refurbishment of the Clubhouse, Dining Room, Kitchen and the building of the 19th hole Bar. Stan also presented both of the Starter's Huts (the first one came to grief, upside down in the pond). Stan spends his leisure time Horse and Carriage driving and showing 'horses in hand'.

F. H. Smith, 1990. Frank Smith was born in Liverpool but has spent his adult years in the Midlands. He is married with one daughter. He is now retired and shared his working years with Coventry Gauge and Tool, Brico Engineering and Jaguar Cars. Frank completed a stint of National Service from 1953 until 1956 spent in Korea. Egypt and Hong Kong.

Frank joined Maxstoke Park in 1968, and has been an enthusiastic member of the Club since then. He recalls that in his year of Captaincy, he presided over the Celebration Evening arranged to commemorate Bill Dudley-Evans 70th year with the Club. Frank lists his leisure activities as rambling, gardening and giant vegetable growing. Has any other Captain achieved an entry in the 'Guinness Book of Records' – Frank did with his giant pumpkin. He also lists wine making and for those fortunate enough to have had the pleasure of a sample tasting – Frank is pretty good at that too.

D. Haywood, 1991. Doug Haywood born and bred in Corley, was educated at King Henry VIII School in Coventry. He was self-employed with his own Wholesale and Retail Company. He is married and has two daughters. Doug did his spell of National Service in the R. A. F. as a Physical Training Instructor.

Doug played football and cricket for Corley and is a Life Member of both clubs. Doug joined Maxstoke in 1972 and won the 'Ward End Cup' in 1994. He was 'B' Team Captain in 1986 and was a Committee Member 1987–1991 and has been Club Secretary since 1993.

Memories from his Captaincy include first Prize Presentation Evening, bringing along the Fillongley Choral Singers for a Christmas Carol Evening, introduction of Vice-Captain to run with Captain in office, and of course the now renowned opening of 5th green. Also arranging Celebration Evening for Bill Dudley-Evans. Not so memorable, food poisoning of some members participating in Mixed Match at Fulford Heath.

Apart from sporting activities Doug was a member of the Fillongley Parish Council for 17 years which included 14 years as Chairman.

R. D. Clarke, 1992. Roy Clarke was born in Coventry, but was educated at the old Coleshill Grammar School. Has been an Agricultural Merchant throughout his working life running his own business. Roy is married, has three daughters and six grandchildren.

He joined Maxstoke in 1971 and amongst his successes are winning the 'Invitation Open', the 'Captain's Cup' in 1986 with D. L. Patrick as partner and the 'Hewlett Memorial Trophy'. In the years before golf, Roy remembers with pride winning the School 5 mile Cross Country Championship in 1945. He was also a long serving and very active member of Coleshill Cricket Club up to 1970.

Amongst his other leisure activities Roy lists Parish Council and other local public work, involvement in fund raising for local charities and watching football at Highfield Road.

Roy presented the Captain's Bell to the Club during his year in office.

W. Rendall, 1993. William Rendall was born in 1930 in Edinburgh and is married to Charlotte, a Lady Captain in 1994, and they were in office together for some six months. Bill and Charlotte had three sons and have two grandchildren. Bill has been employed in the pattern and model making business with his own company.

Bill joined Maxstoke in 1971 and was the inaugural Captain for the now keenly contested 'Celts versus English' match.

In his younger days, Bill played football and has 7 or 8 medals in his trophy cabinet to prove it. In his leisure activities Bill simply lists 'golf'.

His National Service 1948 to 1950 was spent in the Royal Electrical and Mechanical Engineers.

Dr K. M. Rehmany, 1994. 'Doc' as he is more often called by most Club members was born in Pakistan. Doc is married and has three daughters.

He is a General Medical Practitioner, and is one of the partners in the local doctors surgery at Marston Green.

Doc joined Maxstoke Park in 1967 having previously been a member at Harborne Golf Club. He has always been a very competitive golfer with a single figure handicap and difficult to beat in match play.

He presented the 'Rehmany Shield' which is presented to the player with the best nett score in the Club Championship.

Excellent player of table tennis in his youth and represented Pakistan internationally at that level.

D. R. Walker, 1995. Dennis R. Walker was born in Shustoke and was educated at the old Coleshill Grammar School. Dennis married to Gisela and they have two children and two grandchildren.

In his younger days Dennis played soccer and cricket. At cricket he had a long association with Coleshill Cricket Club, including several years as Club Captain.

Dennis is an Insurance Consultant running his own well established family business in Coleshill, in which both Gisela and their son Andrew participate.

Dennis joined Maxstoke in 1973, and in recent years has been an active Committee Member. Fond memories from his Captaincy include not losing a mixed match with Lady Captain, Chris Glynn and playing with Bill Dudley-Evans at Handsworth in their Centenary Celebrations.

Dennis presented a ceremonial 'gavel and stand' for the Captain's use at meetings and functions.

Dennis is a keen rotarian.

R. L. P. King, 1996. Les King was born in Lincolnshire, went to boarding school to the age of 15 years, then attended Nautical College and joined Merchant Navy. He travelled world wide in the next four years, then left and joined Birmingham City Police in 1937, but was released for RAF duties 1943–1945 as Navigator/Wireless Operator on 'Mosquito' bombers.

Rejoined Police and rose to rank of Inspector before leaving after 30 years. Was then appointed as Property Manager for 'Hales Properties' where he remained until final retirement.

During his police days, Les represented them at table tennis, cricket, golf and lawn tennis. Les married in 1938 Les and his wife had two daughters, since then three granchildren and six great grandchildren. Sadly his wife died in 1987 after many years as an invalid.

Sad memories from his Captaincy – ten funerals, scattering ashes of one member and unveiling wall clock in memory of another.

G. E. Crawford, 1997. Graham Crawford was born in Small Heath in 1926 but parents moved to Marston Green shortly after. Educated at old Coleshill Grammar School, when it was a single sex boy's school. Joined Royal Navy early 1945 and spent 3 years in Far East. Played soccer, cricket, hockey plus Rules Football in Australia. Outstanding memory being selected as hockey goalkeeper for Royal Navy representative team which played against four Australian Universities.

Married wife Joan in 1955, they have three daughters and four grand daughters. Working life employed in engineering with Metro-Cammell, Hawker Siddeley and Land Rover.

In younger days played soccer and cricket for local teams, Long association with Marston Green Cricket Club, Captain for many years in '50s and '60s and was Club Secretary for 33 years. Honoured by Midlands Club Cricket Conference in 1973 and 1992 as 'Secretary of the Year' and current holder of the 'Norman Sharpe Trophy' for services to cricket.

Joined Maxstoke in 1972, after playing earlier at Marston Green 1949 until 1960. Turned out for both 'A' and 'B' teams over the years and was 'Maxies' Captain in 1995 and 1996.

Member of Bickenhill Parish Council for some years including term as Chairman.

OFFICERS OF THE CLUB

There is a considerable difference when the appointment of an officer of the Club is made today compared with the old Castle Bromwich days. In days gone by the principal officers retained their positions for lengthy periods of time. It seems that the members were quite happy for them to remain in office and indeed they seemed quite happy to do so, until old age or illness caused them to stand down.

There were not so many other leisure activities in those days, people did not have such long holidays, certainly there was no television, then being a member of a golf club was probably a most satisfactory way of spending one's spare time. Not many people had cars in those days so the golf club was the place where you relaxed, you took exercise there, you met your colleagues and friends there and it became your centre for most of your social activities.

Today times are much different. There is so much choice and so many ways to spend your leisure hours. Unless a person is utterly dedicated to one activity, it is not often that you have anyone prepared to take on officer status for long periods. There are exceptions – Bill Dudley-Evans for instance, who did more or less devote a considerable part of his leisure time to golf.

Today it is not often that you get continuity with committee members and officers of the Club. We are therefore grateful when members are prepared to take on these roles, and accept the fact that they will stand down after two or three years in office.

The administration of Maxstoke Park Golf Club has not changed much over the years. We have a President, Club Captain and Vice Captain who are appointed each year. We have Hon. Secretary, Hon. Treasurer, House Chairman and Green's Chairman who are augmented by nine elected members who then form a General Committee. Each year three of these officers retire in rotation and stand for re-election.

The Officers of the Club in 1997 were:

President	Michael C. Fetherston-Dilke
Club Captain	Graham E. Crawford
Hon. Secretary	Douglas Haywood
Hon. Treasurer	John Hannon
House Chairman	Thomas Sutcliffe
Green's Chairman	Raymond Barratt
House Committee	Robert Cooper, Roger Davies, Neil Mutter and John Truman.

Maxstoke Park Golf Club

Green's Committee	Adrian Harrison, Peter Kirby, James McCulloch, David Newman and Dennis Walker.
Vice-Captain	Frank Williams.

Neil Mutter acted as Chairman of the General Committee.

OFFICERS AT MAXSTOKE

	SECRETARY	*TREASURER*	*CHAIRMAN*
1946	W. N. Dudley-Evans	M. MacDonagh	J. P. Nicholson
1947	W. N. Dudley-Evans	F. A. Walker	J. P. Nicholson
1948	W. N. Dudley-Evans	F. A. Walker	J. P. Nicholson
1949	W. N. Dudley-Evans	F. A. Walker	J. Ralston
1950	W. N. Dudley-Evans	F. A. Walker	J. Ralston
1951	W. N. Dudley-Evans	F. A. Walker	V. W. Wilder
1952	W. N. Dudley-Evans	F. A. Walker	V. W. Wilder
1953	W. N. Dudley-Evans	F. A. Walker	V. W. Wilder
1954	W. N. Dudley-Evans	F. A. Walker	J. P. Nicholson
1955	W. N. Dudley-Evans	S. E. Davis	J. P. Nicholson
1956	W. N. Dudley-Evans	S. E. Davis	J. S. Luke
1957	F. Shutt	S. E. Davis	J. S. Luke
1958	F. Shutt	S. E. Davis	J. S. Luke
1959	A. Dempsey	S. E. Davis	J. S. Luke
1960	A. Dempsey	S. E. Davis	J. S. Luke
1961	A. Dempsey	F. A. Walker	A. J. Burton
1962	W. J. Martin	F. A. Walker	A. J. Burton
1963	W. J. Martin	F. A. Walker	W. N. Dudley-Evans
1964	W. J. Martin	F. A. Walker	W. N. Dudley-Evans
1965	W. J. Martin	F. A. Walker	W. N. Dudley-Evans
1966	W. J. Martin	F. A. Walker	W. N. Dudley-Evans
1967	W. J. Martin	F. A. Walker	W. N. Dudley-Evans
1968	W. J. Martin	B. R. Pulley	W. N. Dudley-Evans
1969	W. J. Martin	B. R. Pulley	W. N. Dudley-Evans
1970	W. J. Martin	L. C. R. Hemmings	W. N. Dudley-Evans
1971	A. A. Trippas	L. C. R. Hemmings	W. N. Dudley-Evans
1972	A. A. Trippas	L. C. R. Hemmings	W. N. Dudley-Evans
1973	L. C. R. Hemmings	L. C. R. Hemmings	W. N. Dudley-Evans
1974	N. C. Littleford	H. Field	W. N. Dudley-Evans
1975	N. C. Littleford	H. Field	W. N. Dudley-Evans
1976	N. C. Littleford	H. Field	W. N. Dudley-Evans
1977	N. E. Taylor	H. Field	B. C. Jolley
1978	N. E. Taylor	H. Field	B. C. Jolley

1979	N. E. Taylor	H. Field	B. C. Jolley
1980	N. E. Taylor	H. Field	B. C. Jolley
1981	N. E. Taylor	M. V. N. Finerty	B. C. Jolley
1982	N. E. Taylor	M. V. N. Finerty	H. W. A. Evans
1983	N. E. Taylor	M. V. N. Finerty	H. W. A. Evans
1984	H. W. A. Evans	M. V. N. Finerty	H. W. A. Evans
1985	H. W. A. Evans	M. V. N. Finerty	H. W. A. Evans
1986	H. W. A. Evans	H. Field	S. S. P. Marklew
1987	H. W. A. Evans	H. Field	E. M. Wyatt
1988	J. C. Evans	H. Field	various
1989	J. C. Evans	H. Field	S. Howell
1990	J. C. Evans	H. Field	R. D. Clarke
1991	J. C. Evans	H. Field	D. Haywood
1992	J. C. Evans	R. H. Beckett	R. D. Clarke
1993	D. Haywood	R. H. Beckett	N. Mutter
1994	D. Haywood	B. R. Morton	N. Mutter
1995	D. Haywood	R. H. Beckett	N. Mutter
1996	D. Haywood	R. W. Somerville	N. Mutter
1997	D. Haywood	J. Hannon	N. Mutter

Managers

L. R. C. Hemmings	1974/76
L. Hatton	1977/82

GREEN'S CHAIRMAN		*HOUSE CHAIRMAN*
1946	H. T. Perry	
1947	J. P. Nicholson	
1948	V. W. Wilder	
1949	V. W. Wilder	
1950	J. Ralston	
1951	J. Ralston	
1952	F. T. Blakey	
1953	F. T. Blakey	
1954	F. T. Blakey	
1955	F. T. Blakey	
1956	F. T. Blakey	
1957	T. H. Marks	
1958	T. H. Marks	
1959	C. W. Mann	
1960	A. G. Moseley	
1961	A. G. Moseley	
1962	F. B. Cartwright	
1963	F. B. Cartwright	S. E. Davis
1964	A. D. Marston	N. E. Taylor

During the period from 1946 until 1962, the appointment of a House Chairman did not appear seperately on the Agenda for AGMs. The Club Chairman of the General apparently took the Chair at House Meetings, or the Club Captain in his absence.

Maxstoke Park Golf Club

1965	A. D. Marston	G. Brennan
1966	A. D. Marston	G. Brennan
1967	T. H. Marks	B. C. Jolley
1968	T. H. Marks	B. C. Jolley
1969	T. H. Marks	L. C. R. Hemmings
1970	P. Deebank	L. C. R. Hemmings
1971	W. J. Martin	E. W. Hemmings
1972	W. J. Martin	J. R. Edwards
1973	A. A. Trippas	V. Johnson
1974	A. A. Trippas	V. Johnson
1975	T. H. Marks	V. Johnson
1976	T. H. Marks	V. Johnson
1977	T. H. Marks	V. Johnson
1978	T. H. Marks	V. Johnson
1979	T. H. Marks	V. Johnson
1980	T. H. Marks	V. Johnson
1981	T. H. Marks	V. Johnson
1982	T. H. Marks	V. Johnson
1983	A. C. Cartwrigh	V. Johnson
1984	A. C. Cartwright	V. Johnson
1985	A. C. Cartwright	H. J. Cooper
1986	A. C. Cartwright	M. J. Carroll
1987	A. C. Cartwright	J. McCulloch
1988	A. C. Cartwright	H. W. A. Evans
1989	T. A. Maddox	H. W. A. Evans
1990	T. A. Maddox	H. W. A. Evans
1991	T. A. Maddox	H. W. A. Evans
1992	T. A. Maddox	T. Sutcliffe
1993	R. P. Barratt	T. Sutcliffe
1994	R. P. Barratt	A. Hines
1995	R. P. Barratt	J. Hannon
1996	R. P. Barratt	J. Hannon
1997	R. P. Barratt	T. Sutcliffe

PERSONAL PROFILES

DOUGLAS HAYWOOD – HON. SECRETARY.

For the past four years I have been privileged to be involved with my fellow Club Officers, Committee members and Staff in the management of Maxstoke Park Golf Club. During that time many changes have taken place. Following the decision of Captain Charles B. Fetherston-Dilke to stand down as President after some 30 years in the position, we have had two more Presidents – Bill Dudley-Evans for a short five year period followed by Michael C. Fetherston-Dilke.

Michael, our present President has already shown considerable enthusiasm and has expressed a desire and is keen to improve the standards of our golf course. He is also very pleased with the substantial areas of the course which have been allowed to grow naturally thereby improving the environmental benefits to plant and wild life.

The major effluent problems that we have experienced for many years have now been resolved by the sustantial investment and continual maintenance of the filtration plant.

Senior staff including Steward, Professional and Head Greenkeeper have all departed, and their Hon. Secretary appointed successors have proved to be most competent.

On the financial side, the repayment of brewery loans, more prudent purchasing, improved cash controls and stricter budget accounting has enabled the Management Committee to repay VAT refunds to members, (some Clubs kept them) and subscriptions to be frozen for the years 1994 and 1997.

The Tom Curry inheritance has enabled the very attractive Club entrance to be constructed and is invested such that other improvements can be made when appropriate.

The adverse press comments on the occasion of the 'County Open Championship' in 1991, when the texture of our greens were described as 'Ryvita' seem hard to believe, when you consider the many accolades of praise that we have received this year.

After the County match 'Warwickshire versus Worcestershire' played at Maxstoke, both Captains expressed their appreciation of the course and Bill Nicholson, the Warwickshire Captain later took the time to write and point out that in his opinion *'he considers Maxstoke Park Golf Club as a premier venue, if not the best in Warwickshire'*. We are indebted to everyone concerned in the first class condition of the course.

On the playing side, the honour of having a member who has represented England, and is the current County Champion, with Maxstoke winning the County Team Championship and another of our younger players being honoured as the Warwickshire County Youth Captain, all augurs well for the future, and is a splendid tribute and testimonial to the experise of our Professional Staff.

The friendliness and *'esprit de corps'* of all of our members, a first class Ladies Section and Staff that project a Club ambience and atmosphere second to none. This is reflected by the fact that over three hundred application interviews have taken place during the past four years, most of whom have become very grateful, worthy Maxstoke members.

Finally, I would personally thank the Centenary Committee for their support, and hope that everyone participates and enjoys the Club's 1998 Centenary Year.

JOHN HANNON – HON. TREASURER.

Being the Hon. Treasurer of Maxstoke Castle Golf Club during the past twelve months has been a challenging task, but one which I have enjoyed nonetheless. It was essential that we programmed a budgetary control plan to ensure that we have up to date information over the day to day income and expenditure. Long term we have also needed to make contingency plans in order that revenue is always available for major purchases of equipment when required, and to plan for the next phase of Clubhouse improvements.

I have been a member of Maxstoke Park Golf Club since 1982, and have always enjoyed the friendly atmosphere that prevails with the members. I have served on the Committee previously to my appointment as Hon. Treasurer and during 1995 and 1996 I undertook the duties of House Chairman.

In 1996 I acted as Social Organiser and we had many well supported events, including a Cabaret Evening, a May Ball, a Summer Disco, a Casino Night Social and a Black Country Night in addition to the regular traditional functions.

As well as being Hon. Treasurer I am a member of the Buildings Committee which at the present time is involved with preliminary discussions with the Architect regarding the next stage of Clubhouse improvements. I am also a member of the Finance Committee, and acting as Treasurer for the Centenary Committee which has its own budget.

Another activity with which I am involved is the 'Investment Fund' set up to maximise the splendid legacy Hon. Treasurer left to the Club by past member Tom Curry. I am one of the trustees who are responsible for monitoring the investments made from this fund and which may be used from time to time.

I am employed as Business Adviser Manager with 'Business Link – Birmingham' and I hold the qualification of Master of Business Administration. This is of considerable help to me in establishing a satisfactory system for the control and budgeting of the Club's finances. My desires for the Club is to establish world class facilities for the members, and would like more involvement from younger members, i. e. under 50.

ANCILLIARIES:

A golf club of the size of Maxstoke Park in reality comes into the category of a small business. With the membership numbers running at the 650 level it is a considerable task to monitor control of the different classes of membership, subscription levels and the ongoing problem of members leaving and new members arriving.

Some years ago, the Committee of the day in their wisdom decided that a Full Time Manager was neccesary to be able to cope with the administration requirements of the Club. It was an experiment that in hind sight, was not succesful and in the opinion of most members, a venture that the Club could not afford.

In 1995 the Club Committee were fully conscious of the enormous work load that was imposed upon the Hon. Secretary and the Hon. Treasurer of the Club. After some deliberation it was decided that there was little alternative but to take on additional staff in the office to tackle the task of setting up computer programmes that would monitor all aspects of financial control, membership classes and many other activities.

David Goodman was therefore engaged on a part time basis as Office Administrator, and since then has established and laid down programmes that at the touch of a keyboard will give full details of membership records, their subscription levels, their golfing status, their handicaps, the Club's expenditure on a daily basis, budget requirements and monthly analysis. This gives both the Hon. Secretary and Hon. Treasurer a complete picture available at any time, of the exact status of the Club's activities.

At the same time Brenda Hindle was taken on as Assistant to David Goodman, and she takes on all the secretarial activities, clerical work, correspondence and mailing of all club literature both to members and at inter club and county levels.

Brenda Hindle

NEIL MUTTER – CHAIRMAN

I first played golf way back in 1952 and have been a regular player and member of a golf club since 1955. I joined Maxstoke Park Golf Club in 1988 when I move from Oxfordshire to the Midlands. I have found the course to be very pleasant and an excellent test of golf with some outstanding features (how many course have a Castle and a Moat)

The Club members and staff are very friendly, and visitors and guests to the Club are assured of a warm welcome at all times. During my membership I have served on the committee for the last six years and acted as Committee Chairman for 5 of those years. During my term of office I have seen many changes in committee management and administration that should take the Club into the next century in a very strong position.

A golf club is now very big business, and Maxstoke Park is no exception with an annual turnover in excess of £500,000 per annum. A budgetary control system has been introduced to ensure that both revenue and capital expenditure is available when required to maintain the Course and Clubhouse to a high standard and to replace equipment when required.

The Clubhouse has been re-furbished and a building fund has been in operation for three years to allow the changing rooms and office accomodation to be upgraded in the near future. A course development and improvement plan has been put in place on a rolling three year cycle.

The Tom Curry bequest has been invested on a low risk strategy basis and is showing a very steady improvement. The fund, with other controls in place should ensure the financial stability of the Club in the years ahead.

I am pleased to report that the Club is in a very sound position approaching the end of our first 100 years, and will remain as eminent as it is now, and provide much enjoyment for members in the future.

N J Mutter

TOM SUTCLIFFE – HOUSE CHAIRMAN

I was born in Birmingham in 1941 and after leaving school went straight into the police force at 16 years of age. I married Sheila in 1962 and we have two daughters Amanda and Leanne and two grandchildren, Thomas and Maria.

In my school years I played representative rugby, and became the first secondary modern schoolboy to Captain the Greater Birmingham Schools Under 16 Team.

Went on to Captain the North Midlands and Midlands Youth XVs. Had trials for England at school and youth level but never gained elusive cap.

In the police force I transferred to CID in 1968 and remained with that force until I retired in 1985, aged 44. From 1985 have been employed by TSB as Fraud Investigator and retired for the second time in 1996.

I represented the Police at rugby, soccer, cricket, boxing and golf. I was awarded the Queen's Commendation for bravery in 1979.

I first played at Maxstoke Park with the Police Block Membership scheme in 1974 and became a full member in 1985.

I was elected to the Committee in 1989 and House Chairman was 'A' Team Captain in 1991.

In 1992 and 1993 I was House Chairman but had to resign before the second year was out, due to work commitments. This year I have been able to take on the duties again and have been involved in the preliminary arrangements for the Centenary Year programme of events.

JAMES MULLEN McCULLOCH

James M. McCulloch or simply Jim as he is usually addressed was born in Motherwell in the year of the General Strike – 1926.

He spent his entire working life as a Technical Officer with British Telecommunications apart from the period 1943 to 1945 when in the Second World War he served with the Gordon Highlanders. Jim married his wife Irene in 1948, and they have had 5 children, three girls – Sandra, Angela and Barbara, and two boys Steven and Jamie. They have 5 grand children and it is obvious that there is a liking for golf in the family and the Maxstoke contingent numbers now numbers 8. Angela married Tony Allen and daughter Lisa is a Junior in the Ladies Section. Barbara married Bob Woolley and son Neil is a Junior in the Men's Section. Jamie is also a good golfer although he is no longer at Maxstoke.

Jim joined Maxstoke Park in 1972 and went on to the Committee in 1984. He had a spell as House Chairman in 1988 but then took over as Competition and Handicap Secretary in 1990.

Since taking over in this important role, Jim (like George Dowse before him) has become an expert on the Rules of Golf, and the complexities of the handicap system, and he has gained himself a reputation as a 'computer wizard'. He organises all the Competitions, including numerous 'Open' Competitions, and makes arrangements for the Annual Prize Presentation when something in the order of 75 trophies and awards are given out.

Not content with this normal programmed activity there is also the Wednesday and Friday 'fiddle' which is named after him and which always gets well supported. Jim in his younger days was a keen amateur soccer player.

Jim McCulloch

COURSE MANAGEMENT

Almost certainly the one job on the Management Committee that attracts most criticism is that of Green's Chairman. It is certain that whatever improvements that he introduces, he will not please everybody. The greens are too slow or are uneven, the rough is too long, the bunkers want more sand or have too little, the fairways need cutting, are frequent cries often heard in the Clubhouse when a disgruntled member has had a poor round. We all do it – it is never our fault that we played way over our handicap allowance.

Yet remarkably, if you look at the former holders of the position, you will find that most of them have stood the criticism for lengthy periods of time. Over the past twenty four years we have had just four Green's Chairmen. Tom Marks, (who has actually been Green's Chairman on 13 occasions), Alan Cartwright, Trevor Maddox and for the past five years, Ray Barratt. Having talked to three of them however, they all have had a common desire about the course.

They have all been above average golfers, they have obviously fell foul of the problems that most of us use as excuses for bad scoring, but in their case, they have been in a position where they can attempt to bring about an improvement, to try and produce a course that is a fair test of golf and more importantly is in an acceptable condition.

Tom Marks excepted who was more involved with laying out the course in the first place, the other three have been involved when changes to the course have been carried out in order to improve the course.

Ray Barratt
Green's Chairman
1993–1997

In the past fifteen years there have been four new greens laid, several tees have been repositioned or enlarged, something in the order of twelve new bunkers introduced, four new water hazards opened up, thousands of trees planted and considerable additional drainage added.

The retiring Green's Chairman Ray Barratt has been in office for five years and has tackled the problems in an enthusiastic and reliable manner. He has devoted many hours of his spare time out on the course with the Green's staff and has earned the respect of most of the members who are fully aware of the problems that he has faced from time to time.

Three hot summers, with dry winters did little to help the fairways, but now after large investment in specialised equipment, even the most critical can see evidence of improvement with less bare patches and signs of renewed grass growth.

The present Green's Staff are led by Andy Ross the Head Greenkeeper. Andy took over in 1993 from Trafford Stonebridge who had been Head Greenkeeper since 1972 and obviously had been involved in most of the changes that had occurred in recent years. The 1997 Green's staff number five in total, they are all reasonably young and work well as a team. They do not have specific duties but each one of them is capable of operating the different items of machinery now used on the course.

At the time of writing, the Green's Committee have identified some twenty items of areas around the course where improvements can be made. These items have been prioritised and it is the intention to carry out these improvements as a matter of urgency, as and when the conditions are suitable.

As a contribution to the Centenary Year, it was agreed by the Club General Committee that it was appropriate to introduce new tee marker plates around the course. The existing arrangement comprised concrete back tee blocks and a mixture of aluminium and wooden boards for the Mens Forward Tees and the Ladies Tees.

The Green's Staff (left to right) Arthur Sproson, Nick Smith, Andy Ross, Clifford Lewis and Chris Clarkson.

Trevor Maddox
Green's Chairman
1989–1992

Trafford Stonebridge
Head Greenkeeper
1972–1993

The new back tee markers are from sand stone blocks with a cast iron metal plate having a diagram of the hole inlaid, complete with hole description and yardages. The forward tees and ladies tees will be smaller versions of the same design but minus the hole diagram.

Trevor Maddox the previous Green's Chairman is a long time member of the Club having joined way back in 1963. He has therefore seen the course progress from the original settling down period at the Castle up to the present high standard which compares favourably with any of our immediate neighbours.

Trevor has been, and still is a very fine golfer, and was in fact Club Champion back in 1968. He has won the Captain's Shield on two occasions, in 1968 and 1971 both times partnered by A. Orson. He also has his name on the Challenge Cup in 1969 and present day is turning out with the 'Maxies' and putting his name on their trophies.

With that track record Trevor was ideally suited to the role of Green's Chairman. He was Chairman in the four year period, 1989–1992, and followed another conscientious Chairman in Alan Cartwright, unfortunately no longer with us.

Trafford Stonebridge has certainly held the position of Head Greenkeeper longer than anyone else at Maxstoke Park. Only Reg Marks, father of Tom, has been likely to have exceeded Trafford's length of service and that was in prewar days at Castle Bromwich.

Trafford more than anyone else has been involved in the expansion of the course since the layout based upon the new Clubhouse was laid out. Coincidentally, his time as Head Greenkeeper has spanned the period of time of the four Green's Chairmen mentioned, Tom Marks, Alan Cartwright, Trevor Maddox and Ray Barratt.

It is worth pointing out that Trafford did not have the machinery that is available to the present green's staff. Pretty well all of the new greens were laid in his time, likewise new tees and considerable drainage problems were rectified in Trafford's time.

It is a fitting testament to the excellent service Trafford contributed over the years, that the Club Committee honoured him by awarding him an Honorary Life Social Membership of the Club on his retirement.

MAXSTOKE PARK MEMBERS – 1997

HONORARY LIFE MEMBERS

L. Brennan
Mrs B. Cartwright
Mrs E. M. Cooper
Mrs M. Dowse
Capt. C. B. Fetherston-Dilke
M. C. Fetherston-Dilke
P. Fleming
Mrs D. Hemmings
L. C. R. Hemmings
Mrs C. Johnson
V. Johnson
B. C. Jolley
C. Mann
E. W. Smith
Mrs L. J. Spooner
N. E. Taylor
Mrs E. Wenman

HONORARY LIFE SOCIAL MEMBERS

E. W. Bodger
C. Julian
T. M. Richardson
Mrs E. I. Smith
R. W. T. Stonebridge
Mrs E. Trippas
Mrs P. Trippas

MALE MEMBERS

Male Members
Abson M. V.
Allen A. M.
Allen L.
Allen P. J.
Allen R. J.
Allen S. J.
Allwood A. G.
Andrews M. G.
Armstrong P. T.
Arnatt P.
Arnold K. J.
Arnold R.
Arnott B. C.
Askey K.
Ataria P.
Atherley B. T.
Avery R. W.
Axcell I.

Bailey C. E.
Bailey N. J.
Baker P. R.
Bakewell F. E.
Bambridge P. R. Dr

Bancroft I.
Barker J.
Barnes R. A.
Barney R. P.
Barratt R. P.
Barrett A.
Barrett G. P.
Barritt R. J.
Bartlett R.
Barton F. C.
Battle R.
Bayley D.
Bayliss S. V.
Beckett R. H.
Beech A. J.
Bell N.
Birch C. J.
Birt F. R.
Blades A.
Blake E. J.
Blake M. I.
Boneham R. W.
Bott D.
Bowcott J. H.
Bowron T. J.
Bradley N. E.
Brandish D.
Brayley D. H.
Brennan D. W.
Brennan M. J.
Brennan V. C.
Breslin P. J.
Brickland D. W.
Brock L. H.
Brown A. J.
Brunn H.
Bryan M.
Buckland G.
Burrows B.
Busby F. W.
Butcher G. A.
Butler A. G.
Butler P. J.

Carter R. G.
Cash P. J.
Castallucci F.
Chambers C.
Clare F. J.
Clarke D. E.
Clarke R.
Clarke R. D.
Clayden I. C.
Clements B. S.
Clough G.
Clueit A. R.
Cole D. J.
Cole H. J. E.
Cole M. J.
Colgan J. C.
Colgan P. J.
Collett J. D.
Conroy M. J.
Cooke B.
Cooke J.
Cooke L. R.
Cookson L.
Cooper H. J.
Cooper R. B.
Cope H.
Corrigan M.
Cowell B.
Cowles N. S.
Cowley A.
Cox M.
Crawford G. E.
Craythorn J. T.
Cridge F. H.
Crofts G. J.
Crompton M.
Crook R. V.
Cruise P.
Cullen M. J.
Curzons P.
Curzons R. J.

Davies H.
Davies J. R.
Davies N.
Davies R. K.
Davies S. R.
Davies T. J.
Deakin F. J.
Deeprose D.
Dicken B.
Dixon A. P.
Dodd B. N.
Dowell R. H.
Dowell S. H.
Doyle M.
Dryton G. J.
Duckers S. J.
Dunkley K. R.
Dunn H.
Dunn P.
Dunnicliffe P.G.

Earl C. J.
Ebbutt R. J.
Edrop A.
Elson C. J.
Etheridge G.
Evans G.
Evans H. W. A.
Evans J. C.
Evans J. J.

Farmer B.
Farn G. O.
Farrell B. P.
Featherstone A. J.
Field H.
Fisher R.
Flannagan A.
Foley J.
Fordyce S. R.
Fordyce W.
Freeman D. G.
French B. A.

Frost E. E.
Frost G.
Frost R.

Garlick R. V.
Gascoigne A. D.
Gascoigne N.
Gibbs J. W.
Gibbs S. J.
Gillson R. G.
Glynn R. I.
Goode L.
Goodman D. L.
Gough R.
Grafton P. J.
Graham L. W.
Green A. M.
Gregory A. E.
Griffiths D. A.
Griffiths F. J.
Griffin S. J.
Griggs W. E.
Gumbley P.
Gupwell R. M.

Hale R.
Hall A.
Hall B. E.
Hall D. R.
Hall W. L.
Hancock G. E.
Hannon J. J.
Hanson M.
Harris A. J.
Harris S. E.
Harris S. T.
Harris W. J.
Harrison A. C. J.
Harrison B. T. J.
Hartland D.
Hayes D. A.
Hayes G. E.
Haynes D. G.
Haynes S. J.
Haywood D.
Hazle W. S.
Hearn R. G.
Heatherington E.
Hewson I. W.
Hickinbotham N.
Hill A. M.
Hill P. S.
Hindle C.
Hines A. H.
Hinks D.
Hiorns B. M.
Hobday J. J.
Hobson D. E.
Hobson G. E.
Holbrook R.
Holliday A.
Holwill C. O.
Hooper D. N.
Hopkins R. D.
Howe C. F.
Howe F. B.
Howell M. J.
Howell S.
Hubble F. J.
Hudson A. B.
Hughes F. C.
Hunt A. E.
Hunt N. L.
Husbands H. G.
Hyde C. J.

Ingleston W. J.

Jackson G.
Jackson J.
Jackson P. B.
James B.
Jesson G.
Johnston S.
Jones D. M.
Jones G.
Jones H.
Jones J.
Joynson A.

Kelly T. G.
Kennea D. O.
Kettrick G.
King D.
King H. J.
King J.
King P.
King R. L. P.
Kirby P.
Kitchen C.

Lane K.
Lawrence C.
Lawson K. M.
Lazurus H.
Lea R. A.
Leonard N. F.
Lewis R.
Lewis T. L.
Lindsay K. B.
Lisle P. O.
Lock T.
Longstaf B. W.
Longstaff K. R.
Longworth A. J.
Lord A. M.
Lowe C. P.
Ludoski M.
Lynth D. A.
Lyon T. H.
Lyttle K. L.

Mackintosh G. G. W.
Macleish S. T.
Maddox T. A.
Malone M. T.
Manders K.
Marin E.
Marklew S. S. P.

Marsh R. W.
Mason W. P. F.
Maycock C.
McCloskey T.
McCulloch J. J.
McDivitt W. H.
McFerran M. D.
McGovern M.
McGrath D. P.
McGrath K. J.
McGrath M. E.
McGrath W. J.
McNeill J. M.
McPhillips J.
Meakin D. L.
Merricks F. N.
Metcalfe D.
Micklewright C.
Milledge D. T. Dr
Mills D.
Mitchell D.
Mitchell J.
Mobley A. J.
Mooney F.
Moore K.
Moore L.
Morris J. F.
Morris R. E.
Morton B. R.
Moulton S. R.
Mountford G. K.
Munday J.
Munday L.
Munday A. T.
Murphy E. W.
Murray D.
Mutter D. J.

Nagle S. C.
Nagle W. P.
Nash A.
Newman D. J.
Nicholls W. S.
Norman I.
Nortcliffe A.
Northam R. A.
Nugent P. J.
Nugent S.

O'Connor T. J.
O'Donnell N.
O'Kane D. J.
O'Neill P. J.
O'Rourke J. P.

Padfield R. G.
Palmer M.
Parkes R. J.
Parry G. A.
Partington L.
Patrick D. J.
Patterson G. P.
Payne F.
Peakman F. W. C.
Pearson G. T.
Pegg A. C.
Pendry T. J.
Penrice D.
Pickman R. G.
Pitt K.
Pittaway F. E.
Platts H. J.
Plows M. J.
Portman E. J.
Poulton A. G.
Powell A. S.
Powell M. J.
Power P. J.
Poynton H. W.
Price A. A.
Price A. J.
Price D. G.
Prince R. J.
Pritchard F. C.

Quaid C. A.
Quinn D.

Rackham J. R.
Rai E.
Reading A. G.
Reading J. N.
Rehmany K. M. Dr
Rendall S. R.
Rendall W.
Rennie A.
Rex H.
Reynard D. T. D.
Reynolds W. S.
Richards E. B.
Richardson G.
Ricketts A. R.
Roberts A. R.
Robinson E.
Robinson F.
Robinson R. J.
Rolfe G. R.
Ryan C. J. A.

Sammons M. R.
Sanders R.
Sanders R. D.
Saul A. C.
Scott K.
Scrivens B. K.
Seymour E.
Sharman M. J.
Sharman S. J.
Shaw D.
Shaw W. C.
Sheehan P. J. A.
Sheppard D. W. F.
Sherratt G. J. T.
Shipley P.
Shipley S. J.
Shirley J.
Skidmore J. T.
Slowley R. V.
Small D. M.

Smallwood G. K.
Smart C. G.
Smedley G.
Smith A. G. R.
Smith F. H.
Smith M. A.
Smith N. E.
Smith P. J. R.
Smith R. A.
Smith S. H.
Somerville R. W.
Souster P.
Souster R.
Sparrow G. A.
Stafford R. A.
Stanley D. R.
Stevens R. C.
Stevens W. D.
Stokes P.
Styles G. J.
Summers A. W.
Sutcliffe A. J.
Sutcliffe T.

Taverner K.
Taylor G. L.
Taylor P.
Teeling J. G. J.
Thomas B. C.
Thomas D. J.
Thompson P. R.
Thompson R.
Thornhill D. T.
Trout G. J.
Truman J. W. E.
Twigg J.
Tyler J. F.

Vaisey A. J.
Vuckovic P.

Walden M. K.
Walker A. M.
Walker D. F.
Walker D. R.
Walker G. C.
Wall M. A.
Walsh R. V.
Ward C.
Ward R. V.
Ward T. J.
Wathens S. J.
Wedge S.
West A.R.
West M. W.
Wheeler K. G.
Whitehouse C. J.
Whitehead D. J.
Williams F.
Williams K. A.
Wilson A. R.
Wilson A. L.
Wilson M. C.
Winnett D. R.
Winters W.
Wood D.
Wood H.
Woodhead C. J.
Woodhead R. G.
Woodward B.
Woodward N. R.
Wright C. D.
Wright G.
Wright R. F.

Young G. A.

Male Juniors
Ash D. G.
Birch P.
Bincow M.
Brennan P. J.
Brookes R.

Cartwright R.
Cruise I.

Davies

Ebbutt D.

Foley M.

Harrison J. A. G.
Hearn T. C.
Hopkins N.

Kendall R. M.

Lawrence L.
Lyon A.
Lyon D. T.
Lyttle S. G.

McGrath D.
Mundy I.
Murphy S. H.

Newman M.

Pearson J. G.
Poulton G.

Senior B. E.
Sheehan M. J.
Stafford B. A.
Summers M. A.

Teeling S. J.
Thomas N.
Thornhill I. A. G.

Walker S. J.
Walker S. M.
Whitehouse T.
Winnett S. D.
Woolley N. J.

THE PROFESSIONALS

In the early days of golf at Ward End it was stated that a Professional was appointed, but he was not named. There was no indication of how long he stayed and until the move to Castle Bromwich there was no mention of any other. The first mention of a Professional being appointed at Castle Bromwich was a gentleman simply referred to as Reid and he was appointed in 1908 shortly after the Castle Bromwich course at Bromford Road was opened.

In 1913 he was followed by Charles H.Wingate who remained with the Club until 1947 when he retired at the age of 70. Wingate originally came from Halifax and joined his brother as assistant at Harborne Golf Club. After some time he was appointed as the first Professional at Handsworth Golf Club.

At that time the Professional, in addition to the duties nowadays associated with the position, also had the task of looking after the course at Handsworth.

Sadly after eighteen months, he was given a months notice to leave, due, as the minutes of Handsworth Golf Club state 'to the unsatisfactory state of the course, and the manner in which he had carried out his duties'.

He then moved to Olton Golf Club where he remained for sixteen years, proving very popular with the members.

In 1913 he moved again, this time to the re-constructed course at Castle Bromwich. He remained until the Club moved to Maxstoke. There is no record that he ever moved to Maxstoke so presumably he remained at Castle Bromwich simply to assist with the closure of the course.

C. H. Wingate

The first mention of a Professional at Maxstoke was

around 1950 when the original 9 holes were laid out. His name was Grenville Lovatt and it appears that he too was expected to carry out work on the course in additional to his professional duties. He was followed by Reg Garrad and he in turn by Warren Green.

There is little information about any of these gentlemen, there are comments in the minutes from meetings when dissatisfaction is recorded about 'the poor performance of the Professional' from time to time. I don't believe any of them stayed for any length of time, and there were obviously times when there was no Professional at the Club. Other minutes refer to 'the lack of Professional and when can the members expect a replacement to be appointed'.

The three Professionals mentioned served a total of roughly ten years between them. From 1960 onwards to the present day the Club have been fortunate in appointing three Professionals that in different ways have served the Club reasonably satisfactorily.

In 1960, Don Knight came to Maxstoke, he was a young Assistant to Jack Cawsey at Pype Hayes. He was actually 'loaned' for a trial period but very quickly was offered the position of Professional and he remained with the Club from the old Castle days right through to the move to the new Clubhouse and the present course layout.

He resigned in 1973 and moved to Newbold Comyn near Leamington Spa. There is no indication as to why he resigned, presumably he felt that he would have more responsibility there, it being a Municipal Course. Don had been very popular with the members and he went with the best wishes of the Committee of the day.

In 1974 Roy Young, a Londoner was appointed, and he too had a lengthy spell as Club Professional. Roy was a cheerful character, and generally got on well with the members. Later on he had a couple of spells when ill health affected his attitude and he seemed to get rather despondent. A couple of burglaries at the shop did not help and his relationship with the Committee deteriorated and Roy left in 1993 after 19 years with the Club.

The same year, our present Professional Neil McEwan was appointed to take over. The Committee were impressed with his credentials, as Neil had certification indicating that he was fully qualified, having completed comprehensive coaching programmes in Europe and America.

Neil settled in very quickly, and within a very short time was able to take advantage of our practice area by offering coaching sessions with video back up, which to disbelieving golfers made a considerable difference when Neil was able to show the faults that he had already verbally pointed out to them.

Now in his third year with the Club, Neil's reputation with his coaching expertise has spread around. Members from Maxstoke of all age groups are often seen on the practice area with Neil; golfers from other clubs and

Lee Lawrence, Neill McEwan and Anthony Gascoigne together, with the eighteenth fairway and Maxstoke Castle as an ideal background.

indeed from other areas, come to Maxstoke to benefit from the tuition that he is able to offer.

During the summer months, it is almost certain that Neil will be found out on the practice area, and it is well known that Neil takes a particular pleasure in being able to give guidance to the many fine young golfers that we have at Maxstoke at the present time.

Another aspect of the Professional's role that Neil has taken under his wing is control of the tee on competition days. This had been a problem for some years, and there have been frequent occasions in recent years when late arrivals on the tee have caused delays which have caused annoyance and indeed anger to those following.This should not have happened, and unfortunately the person responsible for the problem invariably got away with it. Nowadays Neil ensures that a 'starter' is available and usually this role is taken by one of his assistants, Anthony Gascoigne or Lee Lawrence.

The other long standing problem with competition days was of course the starting sheet. This has also been taken over and now there is control over allocation of times, entrance fee payments and someone to contact in the case of cry offs.

The atmosphere in the Professional's Shop is a credit to Neil. He has built up a good relationship with the members, and one always gets a friendly welcome from Neil and his assistants. The shop is well stocked, advice is always freely given, and from experience I know that I am speaking for members and visitors alike, when I say that we appreciate the service extended to us.

Both assistants Lee Lawrence and Anthony Gascoigne have benefitted from the tuition and experience obtained from Neil, both are very promising young golfers and are capable of obtaining PGA acceptance in due course.

PERSONAL PROFILE – NEIL McEWAN

My first round of golf was played at Marston Green Municipal Golf Course in 1977 at the tender age of 13 years. I joined the Club as a Junior and then at the age of 16, I was asked by the Professional Trevor Short if I would like to become his assistant.

I accepted, and worked at Marston Green for twelve months until the closure of the course due to the ongoing demands for runway extensions at Birmingham International Airport.

The next eighteen months were spent working at Olton Golf Club. Then in 1982 I moved to Boldmere Golf Club where for nine years I completed my training to become a member of the PGA.

In 1990 I won the Warwickshire PGA Stroke Play Championship and on inspection of the trophy, I noticed that previous events had been played at Castle Bromwich Golf Club. Until then I had never realised that there had ever been a course at Castle Bromwich. On questioning older members at Boldmere, several of them recalled what a good course it had been. Even then, at that stage, nobody indicated that Maxstoke Park Golf Club had evolved from the old course at Castle Bromwich.

From 1991 until 1994 I worked at Lea Marston driving range. In an effort to develop my teaching skills I attended various coaching conferences in both Europe and America during this period.

Neil McEwan

I applied and was then offered the position of Professional at Maxstoke Park in March 1994. I was thrilled to have been offered such a position, not only because of the good reputation of the Club, but also for the excellent practice ground area it offered to enable me to work with some of the most exciting junior prospects in the country.

Summing up my relatively short time here, my opinion is that the members of Maxstoke Park Golf Club show on a daily basis their love for both the

Club and the game of golf. As Professional, I would like to take this opportunity to say that I have had a very enjoyable time at Maxstoke, and would like to add my congratulations to the Club on their Centenary Year, and look forward very much to serving you all in the future.

THE CATERING STAFF

The appointment of a Steward or Stewardess to a golf club is always a risk. So much has to taken on trust, and even when good references are produced, there is still a problem if the person appointed does not get the confidence of the members.

Maxstoke Park Golf Club Committee and the members are fully aware that Sheila Cardwell is probably the most popular and proficient Stewardess in the local golfing fraternity. Her personality and ability to cope with all aspects of her involvement stand her in good stead with members and visitors alike.

Over the fifty odd years that the Club have been at Maxstoke there have been a considerable number of Stewards and Stewardesses. It is difficult to pinpoint a reason for an apparent inability to retain their services of a Steward for any length of time. The living accommodation at the Castle was quite reasonable as the Steward and his wife were housed in the 'Coachman's House' which was halfway up the driveway to the Castle.

However the Clubhouse housed in the Stables was not exactly comfortable in those days, and the kitchen area was very small and did not really have the capacity to provide much in the way of catering. Having said that, referring to Minute Books of the day, it is apparent that many of the Stewards employed in those days, were way short of experience and were obviously not suitable.

When the move to our present Clubhouse was made, the Steward's quarters were an integral part of the building. It was basic having a bedroom, a small lounge and a bathroom. Several Stewards were very good and did stay for reasonable periods of time, but were not retained for a variety of reasons.

When the Clubhouse was extended the new bungalow was built and this obviously improved the amenities and comfort offered to the Steward. Throughout these years however, there was one complaint which has been emphasised time and time again in the Minute Books – the standard of catering which was not always up to the standard expected. The Stewards in this category were eventually asked to move on, other Stewards were dismissed for dubious activities, and probably the longest serving Steward at that time Les Buonvino resigned.

Almost overnight there was an instant improvement when Bob and

Sheila Cardwell arrived from 'Purley Chase' in 1987 and soon established an excellent rapport with the members of the Club. Bob looked after the licensing side of the stewardship and Sheila took over the catering. The catering improved beyond all expectations and members started using the dining room on a more frequent basis.

About the same time, there was an enthusiastic Social Committee and many very successful social events were organised. These were well supported by the members who appreciated the fact that were going to get an excellent meal at these functions which obviously went a long way towards making an enjoyable evening out.Then rather sadly in 1992, Bob Cardwell resigned as Steward, and left Maxstoke suddenly, leaving Sheila behind.

To Sheila's credit however, she made an approach to the Club Committee requesting that she be given the chance to take over as Stewardess, to be responsible for the Bar activities as well as the catering. She was granted a three month trial period, and in that time, she efficiently not only made the point that she was capable, but significantly brought a new atmosphere to the Club. The members were very sympathetic to her, very supportive of her, and she responded with considerable cheerfulness under the circumstances.

Since then Sheila, has gone from strength to strength, she has gained experience, and the standards that she has set are a credit to her and her

The catering staff taken on Captain's Day – 1997
Mandy Williams, Kerry Bond, Sheila Cardwell, Sadie Middleton, Melanie Daniels, June Cooper, Louise Parker, Tim Day and Avril Wilkins.

staff. Sheila and her staff have built up a wonderful reputation throughout local golfing circles for the high standard of menu available for our own members and visitors to the Club.

The high standard of catering is masterminded by Sadie Middleton who has worked under Sheila's guidance since she arrived 10 years ago. She too has gained experience since taking over the responsibilty for preparation and cooking of the varied meals which are now available.

The table waiting team, often including young students as 'casuals', motivated by Mandy Williams have a wonderful rapport with the members and have worked happily together for the past few years.The bar staff ladies, June Cooper, Melanie Daniels and Tim Day always provide a pleasant and welcome reception to all seeking sustanance and sympathy (after a bad round). June having been with the Club for 18 years, says that she now feels part of the furniture.

Visiting societies and golfers from other Clubs invariably made complimentary remarks at the high standard of the meals supplied. Indeed many actually take the trouble to write expressing their appreciation of the friendliness, the enthusiasm and efficiency of the catering and bar staff.

Sheila's team are a happy bunch, they get on well together and when big functions are on, such as Captain's Day, Burn's Night, (when a traditional Haggis is piped into the Lounge), St.Patrick's Night and New Year's Eve when as many as 130 people have to be looked after, they work as a team and they provide excellent service.

Not forgetting of course that most days, dining room service is usually available, and every day a variety of bar snacks can be supplied in the 19th hole Bar.

The ladies all have earned, and certainly have the respect of the members, and there is no doubt that the members of Maxstoke Park Golf Club are fully appreciative of the efforts and cheerfulness of Sheila and her ever smiling team of young ladies.

It should also be pointed out that apart from all her obvious capabilities, Sheila is no mean golfer herself. She plays off a very creditable 10 handicap, has taken the odd pound or two off several members from time to time, and is often a winner in competitions organised by the Steward's Association, Licensing Trade and other Societies in which she is invited to play.

Sheila, now our longest serving employee in the position of Stewardess to date, was happy to state how much she has enjoyed the last ten years. She is pleased to congratulate the Club on reaching it's Centenary Year which she is certain will be a wonderful success, and she looks forward to many more happy years at Maxstoke Park.

THE LADIES SECTION

According to the 'Birmingham Gazette' on January 16th 1902, an article reported that a Ladies Section had been formed at the Ward End Golf Club. The Honorary Secretary of the Ladies was quoted as a Mrs Wilmot and on the Committee were Mrs Hawkins and Mrs Hall.

What happened over the next few years is not certain but according to the Lady Captain's Board the first Lady Captain was in 1909 when a Miss James is noted as being the Lady Captain.

She in fact retained the Captaincy for some 5 years until 1913. Golf was obviously played during the first World War as Lady Captains were appointed during these years. In 1935 there is no mention of Lady Golfers in the Club's Yearly Handbook or even the name of the Lady Captain. It does state however that both the Ladies Entrance Fee and the Annual Subscription for Ladies was 3 guineas (£3.15).

In 1939 the Handbook has a full list of members playing at Castle Bromwich, but again no mention of lady members or even a mention of the name of the Lady Captain of the day. However in the fixtures quoted it does specify that Wednesday 28th June was Ladies Day.

Assuming therefore that the 'Birmingham Gazette' article is correct, and there is no reason to doubt the authenticity, then in theory, our Ladies are due for their own Centenary in 2002.

LADY CAPTAINS AT CASTLE BROMWICH 1909–1939

1909 Miss James
1910 Miss James
1911 Miss James
1912 Miss James
1913 Miss James
1914 Mrs Lancaster
1915 Mrs Tabling
1916 Mrs Shephard
1917 Mrs Shephard
1918 Miss Salt
1919 Miss E. M. Ryley
1920 Miss E. M. Ryley
1921 Mrs Day
1922 Miss T. Jeyes
1923 Miss T. Jeyes
1924 Miss T. Jeyes
1925 Miss T. Jeyes
1926 Mrs Silvester
1927 Mrs Silvester
1928 Mrs Silvester
1929 Mrs Silvester
1930 Mrs Silvester
1931 Mrs Chick
1932 Mrs Silvester
1933 Mrs Nicholson
1934 Mrs Nicholson
1935 Mrs Jenkins
1936 Mrs Jenkins
1937 Miss N. Field
1938 Mrs Hepworth
1939 Mrs C. Baker

During the war years there were no Lady Captains appointed and one must assume that the ladies were almost certainly otherwise occupied during those troublesome years, and that as their numbers were small, the section probably disbanded for the duration.

In 1946 the Club moved to Maxstoke Park, and again there does seem to be some confusion. In the Club's Annual Report in March 1949 it was stated that the full nmmbership of the Club was 168 members, and of this figure it quoted 20 lady members and 1 junior.

There was a Lady Captain named in 1950 when Mrs C. Baker was again re-appointed. The Ladies Entrance Fee and Annual Subscription were both quoted as 4 guineas (£4.20) which was again half of the figure quoted for men. Maimmee Cooper, a Past Captain of the Ladies Section, recalled that she joined Castle Bromwich Golf Club when it moved to Maxstoke Park in 1946. She was 'sponsored' by Mr L. E. Greenwood who had been Club Captain in 1940, and his wife and she quoted them as being two members who had kept the Club going during the war years.

At that time the Ladies had no Changing Rooms at Maxstoke, the Stables had not then been converted to Clubhouse status and there was no Professional's Shop.

At the time of her joining the Club she was a beginner and had to learn how to play. She gave thanks to the few ladies who came from Castle Bromwich who were very helpful to her in her novice days, and pointed out that in the absence of not being able to receive a 'lift' in a car, she had to travel to Coleshill by bus and then walk along the right of way from Coleshill Church.

She remembered that she began to 'swing a club' reasonably well about 1950, had lessons from the first Professional Grenville Lovatt, and played in 'competitions' by 1952.

Yet during this period of time there is no mention in Minute Books of any activities within the Ladies Section, and there was a gap between Mrs Baker's Captaincy of 1950, and the next appointment in 1953 when Mrs W. Robbins was appointed as Captain.

Maimmee must have had tremendous enthusiasm. For anyone learning to play golf in the circumstance she described, to travel the distance she travelled without transport to a course which at that time left much to be desired was really quite remarkable. It does appear that she recorded every game in which she played, as she quoted from her diary of March 5th 1952, that she played with Doreen Lovatt, the wife of the Professional in that months medal. Doreen Lovatt was apparently one of the best lady golfers at that time.

From the diary again, Maimmee quoted that the last Ladies Christmas Party held at the old Clubhouse (The Comet) was on December 9th 1953.

In 1966 Maimmee became Captain of the Ladies Section, and Teresa Marklew, the present Ladies Captain has researched the Lady Captain's Book, and from Maimmee's year has found several interesting items which are worth recording.

Following the Christmas Party of that year, the gratuity paid to the Catering Staff from the entire section was £2.00. To put that amount into perspective with today's values, a good week's salary at that time was probably about £20.00 so the amount given would roughly equate to about ten per cent of a good salary. Ten per cent of a reasonable present day salary would probably be £20.00 to £25.00.

In that year the Ladies were asked to do the catering on June 11th for Captain's Day. After a long day, preparing the meal, serving at table and then cleaning up after which finished at 9.30 pm, they were then allowed to join the men in the evening's festivities. How times have changed. Today there are no problems with catering, ladies are allowed to participate in the morning competitions, but in the afternoon – men only. After leaving home at 8.00 am on my Captain's Day, I did not see my wife Joan again until 11.00 pm and that was at home.

The wife of Club Captain A. J. Wenman on June 12th the very next day, had a 'hole in one'.

The Ladies Charity Open raised £18.7.0. (£18.35) and results of Ladies Competitions regularly appeared in the Coventry, Coleshill and Birmingham press reports.

In 1967 Maxstoke Park hosted the Warwickshire Ladies Match for the first time. The Lady Captain, Catherine Black presented a Cup for the Lady Captain's Day Competition and was invited with Past Captain Maimmee Cooper to attend an Extraordinary Meeting of the Club to discuss and comment on plans for the proposed new Clubhouse.

Quite unprecedented events took place the next year on the day of the Ladies Invitation Open, when the Lady Captain Mrs Hughan had to clear the course of men golfers so that the event could proceed. Apparently there was a national engineering strike taking place that day and the male members of the Club turned up in force to play. Obviously the Shop Stewards of the day were completely out of touch.

The new Clubhouse was opened in 1969 and Lady Captain Bess Cartwright was one of the speakers at the opening function. Thirty two played in the 'Strawberry Tea' and in a DIY exercise some 14lbs of strawberries were picked.

Joan Carter was Lady Captain in 1970 followed by Hazel Stevens in 1971. On December 12th the Ladies ran a Children's Party when 65 children between the ages of 2½ and 12 years turned up. Margaret Dyche holed in one on the old 5th hole.

1972 the Lady Captain was Joan Spooner, followed by Catherine Johnson and Margaret Dyche in 1974. She presented the Margaret Dyche Trophy for the Best Nett Maxstoke Lady in the Ladies Invitation Open.

The 'Strawberry Tea' became a Ladies Invitation instead of drawing for partners.

Maimmee Cooper became Lady Captain for the 2nd time in 1977 and in 1978 Lady Captain Christine Timms and former Club Captain J. R. Edwards presented trophies for the 'Strawberry Tea'.

Lady Club member Marilyn Fielding won the 'Evening Mail Golfer of the Year Award' at the Belfry.

Carole Patterson became Lady Captain in 1979 and the Club hosted the 'Charles Healey Finals'. Marilyn Fielding won the Best Gross award with 74 which apparently was the course record for a Maxstoke Lady equalling the course record set earlier by Mrs A. Wells of Northampton. Marilyn also won the Best Gross at the Belfry in the 'Midland Golfer of the Year Competition.

Carole Patterson nominated Cancer Research for her charity and a cheque for £2000 went to this worthy cause.

During the year the Club entertained 10 couples from Sweden at the Easter Foursomes and the match was followed by a meal and a pleasant evening 'socialising'. Following their return to Sweden, the visitors forwarded a trophy to be competed for at our Easter Foursomes. This has been played for ever since and is known as the 'Forsbacka Trophy' which is name of the club from which the Swedish visitors originated.

An interesting adjunct to this episode is that in 1995 Peter Marklew and his wife Teresa, visited Sweden on a caravan holiday, and made a point of visiting the Forsbacka Golf Club. To their astonishment they found that the present Club Officials had never heard of Maxstoke Park and were quite unaware of the pleasant events of some 15 years earlier.

In 1980 during Lena Field's Captaincy, the Ladies Section were awarded

Lady Captain Edna Clinton and the ladies who took part in her Captain's Day on 23 September 1981

Edna Clinton on the right with Lena Field, Joan Old, Bess Cartwright, Betty Hubble, Iris Handy, Muriel Robinson and Joan Carter

the Silver Candelabra' – one of the Men's trophies, in recognition of their creditable performance in raising £2000 for Cancer Research.

Angela Allen (nee McCulloch) won her Warwickshire County Colours in 1981, which were presented to her by Lady Captain Edna Clinton at the 'Charity Open' held in October. Angela came 3rd in the Birmingham City

The proceeds from the 'Charity Open' were donated by Edna to the old 'Chelmsley Hospital' who purchased four 'sag bags' (bean bags) for the children at the hospital. The 'sag bags'are used to aid children who are recovering from epileptic fits.

The captaincies of Muriel Robinson 1982, and Joan Old 1983 passed peacefully but Betty McLaughlin ran into problems on the day of the 'Ladies Charity Open'.

When she arrived bright and early in good time to ensure that everything got off to a good start, she was dismayed to find that the 'Boys in Blue' were out in force. There had been a break in during the night and the Police had taken over the Lounge and Bar area. Details were being recorded of the means of entry, what had been stolen and the whole area was being checked for finger prints.

With the Clubhouse virtually out of bounds for the day, the Ladies were restricted to their own Changing Rooms, and with some 100 competitors it is apparent that they were a little cramped. Betty recalled that everyone was very understanding, put up with the inconvenience, and at least enjoyed a good days golf.

In 1985 Lady Captain Edna Clare requested that 'working ladies' be allowed to play their medal rounds on Saturday or Sunday during the winter months – it is not recorded as to what the reply was. Edna and Club Captain Eric Bodger won the 'Strawberry Tea'. Time sheets for L. G. U. medal competitions were introduced in 1986 during the Captaincy of Gladys Bodger.

Pat Clarke was Lady Captain in 1987 but the following year there was sadness at the sudden death of Captain Kit Mitchell shortly before the AGM and Vice Captain Irene McCulloch took over for the remainder of her term of office. In 1989 her own year of office, the Ladies Section presented the Club at their Christmas Lunch with the Flag that is displayed on the flagpole each day.

Joan Old was Lady Captain in 1990 followed by Sylvia Hobday and in her year of office, it is recorded that the Ladies Subscriptions were waived for the first time ever.

What did seem to be an attempt to achieve a better understanding between the Club Committee and the Ladies Section occurred during the Captaincy of Mary Clarke in 1992. The Ladies Officers were invited to meet the Club Committee for the first time on April 4th, and this consultative meeting is now an annual event.

In 1983 Barbara Wooley became Lady Captain and Lena Field was elected to the Warwickshire County Committee. Charlotte Rendall was Lady Captain in 1984, and the unusual point of this appointment was that it does seem to have been only the second occasion that husband and wife have held office at the same time with Bill Rendall being Club Captain. 1985 /86 was the first time with Gladys and Eric Bodger.

Chris Glynn must have done quite a lot of congratulatory handshaking during her year of office in 1995 for the following reasons.

- Margaret French holed in one on April 4th on the 6th hole and again on May 25th on the 16th hole.
- Barbara Woolley holed in one on June 7th on the 6th hole.
- Marie Swindells holed in one on June 29th on the 6th hole.

Maxstoke Park hosted the 'Goodyear Cup' on August 7th for the triangular match between Warwickshire, Leicestershire and Northamptonshire Ladies.

Jackie Shirley became Lady Captain in 1996 and organised a very succesful 'Celebrity AM/AM which realised a magnificent profit of £3206 which she donated to the Breast Cancer Unit at the George Eliot Hospital.

Maxstoke Ladies won their Division in the Warwickshire County

League and met Edgbaston in the semi final at Coventry but unfortunately lost by the narrow margin of 3 matches to 4. Edgbaston went on to win in the final.

Colette Brennan and Marie Swindells won the Midlands Final of the Famous Grouse Competition organised by the LGU Teresa Marklew succeeded Lena Field as League Organiser for the Warwickshire Ladies.

To round off her year of office, Jackie held the first Lady Captain's Formal Dinner Dance. 1997 with Teresa Marklew as Lady Captain, the Maxstoke Ladies again won their Division in the Warwickshire League, but again went down in the semi final, this time to Ladbrook Park with the match being played at Edgbaston.

In November Teresa became Handicap Advisor for the County.

At the Ladies AGM the new Lady Captain Kay Williams took over for her term of office and will represent the Ladies Section throughout the Club's Centenary Year.

LADY CAPTAINS AT MAXSTOKE PARK 1950–1997

1950 Mrs C. Baker	1966 Mrs E. M. Cooper	1982 Mrs M. Robinson
1951 –	1967 Mrs C. Black	1983 Mrs J. Old
1952 –	1968 Mrs M. O. Hughan	1984 Mrs E. McLaughlin
1953 Mrs W. Robbins	1969 Mrs B. Cartwright	1985 Mrs E. Clare
1954 Mrs W. Robbins	1970 Mrs J. Carter	1986 Mrs G. Bodger
1955 Mrs W. Robbins	1971 Mrs H. Stevens	1987 Mrs P. Clarke
1956 Mrs E. Burrows	1972 Mrs J. Spooner	1988 Mrs L. Mitchell
1957 Mrs E. Burrows	1973 Mrs C. Johnson	1989 Mrs I. McCulloch
1958 Mrs E. W. Smith	1974 Mrs M. Dyche	1990 Mrs J. Old
1959 Mrs C. B. Hatton	1975 Mrs I. Handy	1991 Mrs S. Hobday
1960 Mrs C. B. Hatton	1976 Mrs D. Hemmings	1992 Mrs M. Clarke
1961 Mrs M. Martin	1977 Mrs E. M. Cooper	1993 Mrs B. Woolley
1962 Mrs Moseley	1978 Mrs C. Timms	1994 Mrs C. Rendall
1963 Mrs P. Scrivens	1979 Mrs C. Patterson	1995 Mrs C. Glynn
1964 Mrs E. M. Wenman	1980 Mrs L. Field	1996 Mrs J. Shirley
1965 Mrs M. M. Dowse	1981 Mrs E. Clinton	1997 Mrs T. Marklew

A memorable picture taken on Lady Captain's Day of Teresa Marklew in September 1997 with twenty one past Captains and a Captain-to-be. Back Row: Catherine Johnson, Hazel Stevens, Pat Clarke, Gladys Bodger, Edna Clinton, Carol Patterson, Edna Clare, Betty McLaughlin, Lena Field, Chris Glynn, Joan Old, Rene McCulloch and Muriel Robinson. Front Row: Mary Clarke, Joan Spooner, Maimmee Cooper, Bess Cartwright, Jackie Shirley, Teresa Marklew, Kay Williams (Incoming Lady Captain), Charlotte Rendall, Joan Carter and Sylvia Hobday.

MAXSTOKE PARK LADIES – 1997

Lady Members:
Mrs B. J. Abell
Mrs P. Adams
Mrs A. J. Allen
Mrs M. Andrews
Mrs C. E. Archer
Mrs A. Arnold

Mrs C. Bancroft
Mrs B. Bethell
Mrs E. M. Blake
Mrs G. L. Bodger
Mrs E. Boneham
Mrs A. C. Brennan

Mrs R. G. Carter
Mrs B. Cartwright
Mrs E. M. Clare
Mrs P. E. Clarke
Mrs R. M. Clarke
Mrs E. M. Clinton
Mrs A. J. Curzons

Mrs L. P. Davies
Mrs Y. Davies
Mrs J. Davis
Mrs H. T. Dickerson
Mrs M. Dowse

Mrs B. T. Ensor
Mrs P. D. Evans

Mrs L. Field
Mrs M. French
Mrs E. Frost

Mrs J. A. Gascoigne
Mrs C. Glynn
Mrs J. Griffiths

Mrs E. A. Hall
Mrs J. M. Hall
Mrs J. Harris
Mrs C. Hiorns
Mrs S. M. Hobday
Mrs E. Hubble

Mrs C. Johnson

Mrs C. Lester
Mrs L. Lewis
Miss A. C. Louden
Mrs P. Louden

Mrs T. A. Maddox
Mrs T. H. Marklew
Mrs I. McCulloch
Mrs P. A. McGrath
Mrs P. F. McGrath
Mrs P. E. McLaughlin
Mrs M. Moffatt

Mrs B. M. Nicholls
Mrs R. E. Northam

Mrs C. M. J. Old

Mrs R. Parry
Mrs C. Patterson
Mrs J. A. Payne
Mrs S. A. Plows
Miss L. J. Power

Mrs C. M. Rendall
Mrs C. Rennie
Mrs S. L. Reynard
Mrs D. Robinson
Mrs W. M. Robinson

Mrs M. H. Scott
Mrs J. Shirley
Mrs R. Slowley
Miss K. Smith
Mrs P. Smith
Mrs P. M. Somerville
Mrs R. Souster
Mrs H. J. Stevens
Mrs S. M. Swindells

Mrs L. W. Taylor

Mrs D. Walsh
Mrs J. Ward
Mrs S. Whitehouse
Mrs K. Williams
Mrs B. E. Wooley

Miss R. C. Yates

Junior Members – girls
Miss L. M. Allen
Miss E. L. Frost
Miss G. L. Hall
Miss R. Kirby
Miss S. Longstaff
Miss J. Taylor

'MAXIES' HISTORY:

Way back in 1975 an enthusiastic group of elderly gentlemen golfers at Maxstoke who had all retired, believed that there was more to golf than playing friendly four balls two or three times a week. After discussion on the concept of competitive seniors golf with the social aspects as a predominate consideration, it was decided to seek approval for this proposal from the Maxstoke Club Committee.

The Club Committee sanctioned the concept of senior's golf and the 'Old Maxies' were formed. The Club Committee of the day allowed the courtesy of the course for them to play on Tuesday and Thursday mornings, and permission was also given for them to play 'home' matches against other clubs on these days.

A small committee was then elected woth Charlie Turner as Chairman, Les Green as Treasurer and Les Jones as the first Captain. A handicap sub committee was also formed comprising Les Jones and Arthur Blades and later Tom Boland was co-opted to this sub committee.

Charlie Turner the Chairman, in his inaugural year of office, made a positive contribution towards giving the 'Old Maxies' an identity, by presenting every member with an 'original' Maxies Tie on his birthday. There were 13 original members way back in 1975, and in addition to those already mentioned there were Jim Burnett, Cyril Julian, Jim King, Stan Lester. Bob Old, Reg Randle, Dick Rose, Cyril Toy and Ray Watkins. Early in 1976, three others, Jack Edwards, George Jackson and Les Mountford joined the section.

From that intrepid band of early pioneers, Les Mountford who is believed to be close to 90 years of age, is the oldest survivor, whilst Arthur Blades, George Jackson and Jim King still participate with the present day 'Maxies'

Social functions were soon introduced. A 'Christmas Lunch' was held, an autumn 'Social Evening' with wives and friends in attendance was arranged, and an annual visit to the 'Castle' followed by tea was a much enjoyed outing.

Matches were soon arranged against 'Seniors' from other clubs and some of those early contacts have survived and remain within the present day 'Maxies' fixture list. The original list of opponents comprised North Warwickshire, North Worcester, Pype Hayes Municipal, Boldmere Municipal, Kenilworth, Leamington and County, Coventry – Finham, Great Barr and Moor Hall.

Les Jones, the original Captain remained in office until 1980 when he stood down due to failing health, and he was honoured by being presented with an inscribed candelabra at the Club's AGM as an appreciation of his Captaincy. Charlie Turner handed over as Chairman and Arthur Blades

The most recent 'Maxies' Captains – Bob Cooper, Graham Crawford, Alan Ricketts and Ted Robinson

took over. Les Green then took over the Captaincy and remained in Office until 1984, when he handed over to to Ted Hunt.

Ted became the longest serving Captain of the 'Old Maxies' holding the position for seven years until 1990. Since that time Alan Ricketts held office from 1991 until 1993, Bob Cooper 1994, Graham Crawford in 1995 and 1996 whilst Ted Robinson is the the current Captain of the present day 'Maxies'.

The Committee of 1997 comprised Bob Cooper as Chairman, Peter Marklew as Secretary and Alan Cowley as Treasurer. Peter has been in Office since 1983 and Alan since 1989. Amongst the active members are 5 former Club Captains, Harry Field, Peter Marklew, Doug Haywood, Jim King and Les King whilst Graham Crawford is completing his year of office as Club Captain for 1997 and Ted Robinson will be Vice Captain to Frank Williams in the Centenary Year. Other ex 'Maxies' who have received the honour of Club Captain were Jack Edwards, George Dowse, Charlie Turner and Eric Bodger.

The present fixture list comprises matches against 10 clubs on a home and away basis. The Clubs are: Coventry – Finham, Drayton Park, Gay Hill, Kenilworth, Leamington and County, Moor Hall, North Warwickshire, Nuneaton, Olton and Shirley. Matches are also played against Maxstoke 'B' Team and Maxstoke 'Ladies'.

Several trophies have been presented over the years and the competitions for which these have been donated are keenly contested each year by the present members which number around 50. The annual autumn 'Social Evening' is still the main social event of the year and is always well supported. In recent years the Club Captain and Club Secretary have been invited as 'Guests of Honour' The 'Christmas Lunch' is also very popular and at this function the Club Professional and Head Greenkeeper are invited. Presentation of the trophies to the seasonal prize winners are made at this function. According to William Shakespeare's 'As You Like It' in the seven ages of man:

The sixth age shifts
Into the lean and slippered pantaloon
With spectacles on nose and pouch on side,
His youthful hose well saved, a world too wide
For his shrunk shank, and his big manly voice
Burning again towards childish pipes
And whistles in his sound.
Last scene of all
That ends this strange eventful history
Is second childishness and mere oblivion,
Sans teeth, sans eyes, sans taste
Sans everything.

Try telling that to the present day 'Maxies' and you are likely to receive replies which would not be appropriate to be printed here. The 'Maxies' are a hardy bunch, many of them into their '80s, and they play all year round golf in weathers 'fair and foul'

The criteria for admittance to the 'Maxies' are simple enough in that 'one must be over 60 years of age and fully retired, or over 65'. Many approaches are made by prospective 'new' members approaching this point in their life, anxious that they will be allowed to join this envied group of senior golfers. They too will then experience the enjoyment of playing regular competitive golf both at Maxstoke and on other courses invariably against friendly opponents of similar age, and who, all agree "that it is far better than working".

'MAXIES' TROPHY WINNERS

L. V. GREEN Singles K. O.	A. BLADES 4 Best Medal	C. C. TURNER Pairs K. O.
1976 S. W. Lester	–	J. King
1977 S. W. Lester	–	S. G. Watts
1978 J. King	–	J. King
1979 J. King	–	S. W. Lester
1980 L. A. Jones	–	C. Arnott
1981 G. W. Dowse	–	G. W. Dowse
1982 G. W. Dowse	G. A. J. Sable	J. King
1983 L. V. Green	R. E. Moore	R. E. Moore
1984 C. Chambers	C. Chambers	H. R. Watkins
1985 C. Chambers	T. Boland	–
1986 G. W. Dowse	E. Hunt	–
1987 H. Field	T. S. Robinson	R. Crook/E. Reay
1988 D. R. Hall	G. Padfield	S. S. P. Marklew/H. Platts
1989 R. L. P. King	T. S. Robinson	G. E. Crawford/R. Davies
1990 K. Walsh	S. S. P. Marklew	E. Reay/K. Walsh
1981 A. Ricketts	D. R. Hall	P. Taylor/G. Padfield
1982 F. Pittaway	S. S. P. Marklew	E. Robinson/T. Lewis
1983 A. Ricketts	R. Davies	F. Pittaway/E. Robinson
1984 R. Davies	K. Wheeler	A. Ricketts/S. S. P. Marklew
1985 R. Curzons	E. Robinson	
1986 E. Robinson	R. Cooper	E. Robinson/L. Munday
1997 W. Griggs	T. Maddox	R. Woodhead/S. Reynolds

L. A. JONES
2/3 Stableford

1976 G. Jackson/S. W. Lester
1977 L. A. Jones/Humphries
1978 J. Burnett/L. V. Green
1979 F. Clarke/S. W. Lester
1980 Humphries/S. W. Lester
1981 H. W. Rose/L. A. Jones
1982 A. Blades/L. V. Green
1983 A. Blades/L. V. Green
1984 E. Hunt/A. Nansen
1985 G. W. Dowse
1986 A. Ricketts
1987 C. C. Chambers
1988 G. Padfield
1989 R. V. Crook
1990 D. R. Hall
1991 L. Matthews
1992 F. Pittaway
1993 K. Williams / F. Pittaway
1994 S. S. P. Marklew
1995 P. Taylor/M. Wilson
1996 R. Cooper
1997 F. Smith

R. V. CROOK
Winter Shield

Year	R. V. CROOK Winter Shield	W. HAWLEY TROPHY
1988	H. Cope	
1989	R. V. Crook	
1990	A. Cowley	
1991	G. E. Crawford	
1992	A. Ricketts	
1993	K. Walsh	
1994	W. Griggs	
1995	E. Robinson	K. Wheeler
1996	R. Cooper	R. Cooper
1997	E. Robinson	F. Pittaway

COTTOM TROPHY

Highest placed 'Maxie' in Senior's Open	COTTOM 9 HOLE	ECLECTIC 3 short holes
1996 G. Padfield	B. French/S. Reynolds	
1997 S. S. P. Marklew	J. McCulloch	K. Wheeler

Over the years, for reasons not always known, the specific competition for which a particular trophy was presented may have changed. The current (1997) status was as shown above.

COMPETITIONS AND TROPHIES

CHALLENGE CUP: The oldest trophy originating from Castle Bromwich days.

Singles match play knock out competition played over 18 holes
Handicap limit 18.
Played off 3/4 difference of handicaps
Final played over 36 holes.

YEAR	*WINNER*
1945	A. D. Marston
1946	J. McDowell
1947	V. W. Wilder
1948	V. W. Wilder
1949	T. J. Murphy
1950	F. T. Blakey
1951	F. T. Blakey
1952	J. P. Nicholson
1953	A. D. Marston
1954	W. H. Haden
1955	F. T. Blakey
1956	L. H. Maidment
1957	P. G. F. Whitehouse
1958	D. Proctor
1959	A. Colin Moseley
1960	H. K. Cooke
1961	K. C. MacDonagh
1962	A. G. Moseley
1963	A. G. Moseley
1964	H. K. Cooke
1965	K. C. MacDonagh
1985	C. Breslin
1966	W. N. Dudley-Evans
1967	A. F. Cartwright
1968	A. F. Cartwright
1969	T. A. Maddox
1970	A. F. Cartwright
1971	G. Hitchman
1972	A. F. Cartwright
1973	J. M. Buxton
1974	J. J. Evans
1975	A. C. J. Harrison
1976	W. F. Hearnshaw
1977	W. J. H. Baker
1978	D. Deeprose
1979	S. Johnson
1980	C. C. Wykes
1981	A. F. Cartwright
1982	C. Breslin
1983	K. M. Rehmany
1984	D. Greenfield
1985	C. Breslin
1986	M. R. Adams
1987	A. C. J. Harrison
1988	D. J. Newman
1989	A. C. J. Harrison
1990	N. Cowles
1991	A. C. Saul
1992	P. Cruise
1993	A. C. J. Harrison
1994	C. Hydes
1995	E. W. Worwood
1996	B. James
1997	D. Mills

THE WARD END CUP: Originating from the early days of the Club.

Medal competition played over 18 holes.
Handicap limit 18.
Played in conjunction with September Medal.

YEAR	*WINNER*
1945	W. Thorne
1946	K. G. MacDonagh
1947	
1948	
1949	
1950	C. J. Wall
1951	J. R. Thompson
1952	T. H. Marks
1953	J. T. Gough
1954	S. E. Davis
1955	D. W. Haden
1956	A. J. Burton
1957	T. W. Harman
1958	D. O. Keeffe
1959	G. Hitchman
1960	H. W. A. Evans
1961	T. H. Marks
1962	K. C. MacDonagh
1963	A. G. Moseley
1964	G. Brennan
1965	E. A. Stych
1966	W. Robinson
1967	K. A. Williams
1968	K. M. Rehmany
1969	R. G. Carter
1970	A. Millar
1971	G. Lowery
1972	F. S. Rennie
1973	P. Markland
1974	D. W. Brennan
1975	N. C. Taylor
1976	R. G. Carter
1977	J. M. Buxton
1978	E. W. Dodd
1979	L. V. Patterson
1980	J. Groutage
1981	P. Stokes
1982	K. M. Rehmany
1983	R. A. Northam
1984	G. Prokes
1985	P. J. Breslin
1986	B. E. Hall
1987	N. E. Bradley
1988	G. E. Hancock
1989	J. Twigg
1990	L. Matthews
1991	R. G. Carter
1992	S. J. Macleigh
1993	A. A. Price
1994	D. Haywood
1995	T. G. Kelly
1996	T. Sutcliffe
1997	P. Stokes

THE NEWPORT CUP: Another trophy originating from Castle Bromwich days.

Final Bogey Competition:
12 members from each division, with the best three cards from the previous year's May to October competitions to qualify for 36 hole final.

Div. 1: 0 to 12. Div. 2: 13 to 17.
Div. 3: 18 to 28.
Full handicap, draw for partners in Final.

YEAR	*WINNER*
1946	H. F. Trentham
1947	
1948	
1949	
1950	F. T. Blakey
1951	K. C. MacDonagh
1952	D. S. Prust
1953	F. T. Blakey
1953	F. T. Blakey
1954	P. G. F. Whitehouse
1955	J. S. Luke
1956	F. T. Blakey
1957	P. G. F. Whitehouse
1958	W. N. Dudley-Evans
1959	D. W. Haden
1960	W. N. Dudley-Evans
1961	C. Hartland
1962	G,Brennan
1963	A. F. Cartwright
1964	W. N. Dudley-Evans
1965	L. Goode
1966	P. G. F. Whitehouse
1967	A. G. Bridges
1968	G. Hitchman
1969	P. G. F. Whitehouse
1970	W. N. Dudley-Evans
1971	A. F. Cartwright
1972	F. S. Rennie
1973	A. L. Brock
1974	J. Gough
1975	P. G. F. Whitehouse
1976	J. M. Buxton
1977	A. M. Allen
1978	A. L. Brock
1979	A. L. Brock
1980	A. F. Cartwright
1981	A. C. J. Harrison
1982	A. F. Cartwright
1983	C. Brook
1984	R. A. Northam
1985	G. P. Hathaway
1986	N. Connolly
1987	A. Barr
1988	A. C. Saul
1989	K. M. Rehmany
1990	C. J. Hyde
1991	D. P. McGrath
1992	M. J. Foley
1993	F. M. Merricks
1994	S. M. Walsh
1995	A. D. Gascoigne
1996	M. A. Smith

GOLD MEDAL: Originated from Castle Bromwich

12 members from each division with the best four cards from the previous year's March to November competitions to qualify for 36 hole Final.

Div 1: 0 to 12. Div 2: 13 to 17. Div 3: 18 to 28.

Full handicap, draw for partners in Final.

YEAR	*WINNER*
1945	H. Scrimshaw
1946	
1947	
1948	
1949	P. Scrivens
1950	P. Scrivens
1951	W. N. Dudley-Evans
1952	J. S. Luke
1953	A. J. Wenman
1954	W. N. Dudley-Evans
1955	L. H. Maidment
1956	S. E. Davis
1957	A. J. Burton
1958	P. G. F. Whitehouse
1959	A. G. Moseley
1960	P. G. F. Whitehouse
1961	P. G. F. Whitehouse
1962	A. F. Cartwright
1963	A. F. Cartwright
1964	P. G. F. Whitehouse
1965	W. P. F. Mason
1966	A. F. Cartwright
1967	P. J. Colgan
1968	R. Souster
1969	H. W. G. Locker-Marsh
1970	D. H. Brayley
1971	A. F. Cartwright
1972	A. L. Brock
1973	A. L. Brock
1974	N. C. Taylor
1975	J. M. Buxton
1976	A. F. Cartwright
1977	A. M. Allen
1978	K. M. Williams
1979	B. A. Robb
1980	J. Brown
1981	C. C. Wykes
1982	C. C. Wykes
1983	B. Robb
1984	R. P. Barratt
1985	N. Connolly
1986	D. Stanley
1987	R. A. Northam
1988	A. M. Allen
1989	A. F. Cartwright
1990	K. M. Rehmany
1991	A. Edrop
1992	R. D. Clarke
1993	R. Lewis
1994	P. Kirby
1995	D. Mills
1996	D. A. Griffiths
1997	D. M. Jones

CLUB CHAMPIONSHIP: Originating from Castle Bromwich days

36 hole stroke play competition played off scratch.

YEAR	*WINNER*
1949	J. H. Sangster
1950	J. H. Sangster
1951	F. T. Blakey
1952	J. H. Sangster
1953	F. T. Blakey
1954	F. T. Blakey
1955	F. T. Blakey
1956	F. T. Blakey
1957	P. G. F. Whitehouse
1958	F. T. Blakey
1959	P. G. F. Whitehouse
1960	P. G. F. Whitehouse
1961	P. G. F. Whitehouse
1962	C. Hartland
1963	P. G. F. Whitehouse
1964	P. G. F. Whitehouse
1965	P. G. F. Whitehouse
1966	A. F. Cartwright
1967	A. F. Cartwright
1968	T. A. Maddox
1969	W. P. F. Mason
1970	P. G. F. Whitehouse
1971	A. F. Cartwright
1972	A. F. Cartwright
1973	A. C. J. Harrison
1974	J. Gough
1975	A. M. Allen
1976	A. M. Allen
1977	A. M. Allen
1978	A. M. Allen
1979	A. M. Allen
1980	A. L. Brock
1981	A. M. Allen
1982	C. C. Wykes
1983	M. G. Wharton-Palmer
1984	A. M. Allen
1984	A. M. Allen
1985	D. Greenfield
1986	A. M. Allen
1987	N. Connolly
1988	A. C. J. Harrison
1989	A. M. Allen
1990	P. Stokes
1991	A. C. J. Harrison
1992	A. M. Allen
1993	A. M. Allen
1994	A. M. Allen
1995	N. Bell
1996	A. M. Allen
1997	B. E. Senior

WEDNESDAY CUP: Originated from Castle Bromwich

18 hole medal competition under handicap with Handicap limit 18.

Monthly qualifying competitions and minimum of three cards eligibility for Final.

One division only.

YEAR	*WINNER*
1946	A. G. Allman
1947	
1948	
1949	A. Kirk
1950	A. G. Jordan
1951	J. L. Towns
1952	A. Procter
1953	W. R. Jones
1954	P. A. Fisher
1955	D. W. Haden
1956	W. J. Martin
1957	F. T. Edgecox
1958	D. Procter
1959	H. K. Cooke
1960	D. W. Haden
1961	P. G. F. Whitehouse
1962	J. M. Simpson
1963	J. G. Cresswell
1964	H. K. Cooke
1965	H. R. Locker-Marsh
1966	I. M. Wright
1967	S. Hale
1968	N. Gibbons
1969	A. Millar
1970	S. A. Carter
1971	J. Wilson
1972	J. D. Barber
1973	J. M. Buxton
1974	L. J. Jones
1975	G. Hitchman
1976	T. J. O'Connor
1977	B. Cooke
1978	G. Frost
1979	P. Taylor
1980	A. M. Allen
1981	D. G. Freeman
1982	G. Etheridge
1983	F. Castallucci
1984	P. Stokes
1985	B. Cooke
1986	J. M. McCulloch
1987	C. J. Hyde
1988	G. Prokes
1989	D. W. Washbourne
1990	E. Heatherington
1991	R. J. Barratt
1992	R. Lewis
1993	D. W. Hooper
1994	J. C. Evans
1995	N. J. Roberts
1996	S. Rendall
1997	W. S. Hazle

VETERAN'S CUP: originated from Castle Bromwich

18 hole stroke play competition with handicap limit 18.

Members aged 60 years and over on the day of the competition eligible to play.

Played off yellow tees.

YEAR	*WINNER*
1945	J. Gray
1946	G. Allman
1947–1953	*NOT PLAYED*
1954	R. Higgs
1955	R. Higgs
1956	D. O'Keeffe
1957	D. O'Keeffe
1958	D. O'Keeffe
1959	D. O'Keeffe
1960	D. O'Keeffe
1961	A. Blundell
1962	C. B. Hatton
1963	D. O'Keeffe
1964	A. Blundell
1965	N. Powell
1966	H. G. Pulley
1967	C. Toy
1968	C. Toy
1969	J. F. Edwards
1970	P. Clarke
1971	W. J. Martin
1972	F. G. Stickley
1973	L. A. Jones
1974	C. R. Randle
1975	T. H. Marks
1976	L. V. Green
1977	W. N. Dudley-Evans
1978	A. B. Poole
1979	S. Buxton
1980	H. Field
1981	A. B. Poole
1982	T. R. Davies
1983	R. E. Moore
1984	F. Lowe
1985	G. Frost
1986	J. Mitchell
1987	T. A. Maddox
1988	H. W. A. Evans
1989	A. Hall
1990	W. N. Dudley-Evans
1991	C. E. Bailey
1992	P. T. Armstrong
1993	E. Robinson
1994	F. Williams
1995	H. Field
1996	G. E. Hancocks
1997	N. Mutter

PRESIDENT'S CUP

Presented by Captain Charles B. Fetherston-Dilke

18 hole stroke play – handicap limit 18

Played in conjunction with June Medal

YEAR	*WINNER*
1971	M. J. Guinan
1972	H. T. Eaves
1973	D. Tipping
1974	J. M. Buxton
1975	A. Orson
1976	P. T. Armstrong
1977	D. Dean
1978	D. B. Pace
1979	L. N. Abel
1980	W. Lorne
1981	M. McGovern
1982	G. F. Collins
1983	S. S. P. Marklew
1984	A. W. Summers
1985	W. Shaw
1986	P. B. Jackson
1987	D. D. Kennea
1988	G. Jesson
1989	W. Fordyce
1990	R. A. Barnes
1991	G. P. Barrett
1992	G. T. Pearson
1993	W. H. McDivitt
1994	R. G. Frost
1995	N. Cowell
1996	D. Mills
1997	P. Stokes

SMEVANS CUP

18 hole stroke play – handicap limit 18 to 28 only

Played in conjunction with July Medal

YEAR	*WINNER*
1951	K. M. Riley
1952	C. B. Hatton
1853	W. T. Simmonds
1954	G. W. Knight
1955	P. Blundell
1956	A. G. Moseley
1957	W. Isaacs
1958	F. H. Marks
1959	F. A. Walker
1960	A. T. M. Neale
1961	S. J. Wathen
1962	J. Tougher
1963	P. J. Wright
1964	W. G. Black
1965	P. C. Deebank
1966	A. L. Brock
1967	J. King
1968	J. M. Moseley
1969	E. L. Harvey
1970	A. L. Buonvino
1971	N. C. Taylor
1972	J. D. Neal
1973	R. G. Barry
1974	L. Pipe
1975	A. Jervis
1976	A. Heads
1977	J. D. Ripley
1978	T. S. Parrish
1979	M. J. Ellis
1980	P. Cruise
1981	G. H. Paul
1982	C. J. Elson
1983	F. M. Merricks
1984	W. S. Reynolds
1985	D. R. Winnett
1986	D. R. Winnett
1987	D. E. James
1988	M. J. Sharman
1989	K. J. McGrath
1990	D. J. Cole
1991	R. Clarke
1992	K. J. Cox
1993	J. A. G. Harrison
1994	K. H. Cox
1995	A. Lyon
1996	R. H. Prince
1997	N. J. Hopkins

TRIPPAS TROPHY

Presented by: Ron. G. Trippas

Par/Bogey stroke play competition over 18 holes in April.

One division – full handicap

YEAR	*WINNER*
1975	L. A. Jones
1976	F. S. Rennie
1977	B. A. Robb
1978	R. P. Barratt
1979	M. R. Edwards
1980	J. V. Fielding
1981	A. L. Brock
1982	N. Smith
1983	F. J. Griffiths
1984	P. S. Hill
1985	R. Yeomans
1986	N. J. Bailey
1987	G. L. Taylor
1988	G. E. Hobson
1989	A. F. Cartwright
1990	S. R. Rendall
1991	M. J. Sharman
1992	R. J. Curzons
1993	A. A. Price
1994	J. J. Hobday
1995	S. C. Nugent
1996	R. M. Gupwell
1997	G. J. Styles

GEORGE DOWSE TROPHY

Presented by: George W. Dowse.

18 holes Medal Competition played in conjunction with July Medal
Winner – best nett score of the three divisions

Div 1; 0 to 12, Div 2: 13 to 17,
Div 3: 18 to 28.

YEAR	*WINNER*
1990	T. L. Lewis
1991	D. R. Stanley
1992	P. J. A. Sheehan
1994	M. Cox
1995	A. Barrett
1996	M. J. Colgan
1997	J. C. Evans

PERKINS PUTTER

Presented by: Thomas Philip Perkins (1928 Amateur Open Champion)

18 hole stroke play – handicap limit 18. In conjunction with October Medal.
Winner: Best nett score.

Winners of earlier competitions not available.

YEAR	*WINNER*
1990	M. W. West
1991	A. M. Walker
1992	D. Quinn
1993	C. P. Lowe
1994	S. Howell
1995	J. M. Bethell
1996	G. E. Hayes
1997	A. G. R. Smith

'A' TEAM CUP

Presented by; Eric W. Bodger

18 hole medal competition – handicap limit 28

Open to members who have played in at least one 'A' Team match during the current year.

YEAR	*WINNER*
1985	G. Kettrick
1986	P. Stokes
1987	G. E. Hayes
1988	B. Cooke
1989	P. J. A. Sheehan
1990	E. W. Worwood
1991	C. J. Hyde
1992	K. R. Longstaff
1993	S. R. Davies
1994	C. J. Hyde
1995	B. E. Hall
1996	I. Norman
1997	D. Mills

DUDLEY-EVANS TROPHY

Presented by Willian (Bill) N. Dudley-Evans

18 hole Medal played in conjunction with the June Medal

YEAR	*WINNER*
1991	J. C. Evans
1992	C. Kitchen
1993	C. Kitchen
1994	L. Lawrence
1995	S. J. Walker
1996	J. N. Reading
1997	G. K. Mountford

'B' TEAM CUP

Presented by Percy Scrivens

18 hole medal competition – handicap limit 28

Open to members who have played in at least one 'B' Team match in current year.

YEAR	*WINNER*
1961	G. W. Dowse
1962	A. F. Cartwright
1963	K. A. Williams
1964	C. W. Hawley
1965	L. Flynn
1966	A. A. Trippas
1967	W. G. Black
1968	P. C. Deebank
1969	J. Foley
1970	A. Markland
1971	M. J. Cole
1972	R. G. Carter
1973	N. C. Taylor
1974	N. E. Taylor
1975	A. Mitchell
1976	C. W. Hawley
1977	M. T. Brown
1978	S. G. Munro
1979	K. A. Williams
1980	G. R. Loveless
1981	M. Abson
1982	T. Poynton
1983	E. C. Fealey
1984	J. M. McCulloch
1985	P. T. Armstrong
1986	P. J. A. Sheehan
1987	R. G. Pickman
1988	M. J. Howell
1989	A. J. Beech
1990	F. Williams
1991	P. Cruise
1992	D. J. Whitehead
1993	A. E. Powell
1994	F. N. Merricks
1995	R. A. Smith
1996	W. Nagle
1997	A. R. Wilson

THE CAPTAIN'S SHIELD

Two ball Foursomes knock out competition over 18 holes – limit 24. Handicap allowances 3/8 of difference of combined handicaps.

YEAR	*WINNERS*
1961	T. H. Marks and P. G. F. Whitehouse
1962	B. C. Jolley and R. G. Trippas
1963	T. H. Marks and P. G. F. Whitehouse
1964	T. H. Marks and P. G. F. Whitehouse
1965	R. T. Hatton and R. W. Williams
1966	T. H. Marks and P. G. F. Whitehouse
1967	T. H. Marks and P. G. F. Whitehouse
1968	T. A. Maddox and A. Orson
1969	J. Stevens and A. M. Simmonds
1970	C. T. Card and E. C. Fealey
1971	T. A. Maddox and A. Orson
1972	F. S. Rennie and M. C. Vaughan
1973	W. F. Taylor and L. Goode
1974	J. W. Higgins and K. A. Williams
1975	P. J. A. Sheehan and E. J. Cates
1976	K. M. Rehmany and E. C. Fealey
1977	A. M. Allen and A. L. Brock
1978	D. W. Brennan and L. H. Brock
1979	H. W. A. Evans and G. T. Lea
1980	M. R. Edwards and A. G. Reading
1981	S. Johnston and N. Smith
1982	M. R. Edwards and N. C. Taylor
1983	R. E. Lea and C. Hutchings
1984	R. A. Northam and A. M. Walker
1985	M. V. Abson and S. Whittingham
1986	A. M. Allen and A. L. Brock
1987	A. M. Walker and R. A. Northam
1988	A. C. Saul and A. G. T. Saul
1989	B. W. Longstaff and F. W. Busby
1990	N. S. Cowles and R. A. Barnes
1991	N. S. Cowles and R. A. Barnes
1992	D. W. Brennan and L. H. Brock
1993	A. C. Saul and L. R. Cooke
1994	A. M. Walker and R. A. Northam
1995	I. C. Clayden and P. J. R. Smith
1996	G. Kettrick and B. C. Thomas
1997	C. J. Hyde and R. D. Hopkins

THE CAPTAIN'S CUP

PRESENTED BY: A. J. Wenman – Club Captain 1966.

18 hole stroke play under handicap (limit 28) played for on Captain's Day. Captain of the day to decide format of competition and draw will be made for partners.

YEAR	*WINNERS*
1966	P. Blundell and H. R. Locker-Marsh
1967	R. J. Parkes and T. H. Upton
1968	H. Poynton and V. Gray
1969	F. Clarke and E. A. Skip
1970	H. R. Locker-Marsh and H. Stanworth
1971	R. G. Carter and E. W. Hemmings
1972	J. B. Smith and D. Metcalfe
1973	W. N. Dudley-Evans and T. S. Parrish
1974	H. Louden and C. Raponi
1975	T. D. Smith and A. R. West
1976	J. M. Buxton and N. A. Lowe
1977	C. W. Chambers and K. B. Lindsay
1978	R. Dawson and R. E. Moore
1979	A. C. J. Harrison and A. J. Brown
1980	P. J. Colgan and V. Gray
1981	R. A. Lea and V. Weeks
1982	B. Robb and V. Weeks
1983	G. W. Dowse and J. J. Hobday
1984	G. W. Dowse and E. J. Cates
1985	N. A. Moore and M. Rollason
1986	R. D. Clarke and D. L. Patrick
1987	S. C. Nagle and M. K. Walden
1988	K. B. Lindsay and G. K. Mountford
1989	J. C. Evans and K. L. O'Rourke
1990	R. K. Davies and T. J. Davies
1991	J. J. Hobday and F. Pritchard
1992	I. C. Clayden and G. Wright
1993	F. N. Merricks and W. Winters
1994	K. G. Wheeler and A. D. Gascoigne
1995	R. L. P. King and J. C. Evans
1996	S. Nugent and F. E. Pittaway
1997	W. Winters and B. P. Farrell

'CHELPERS WINTER LEAGUE CUP'

18 hole 'Four ball – better ball' match play.

Played off yellow tees in winter months November to March

YEAR	*WINNERS*
1968	K. H. Booth and A. L. Brock
1969	V. Johnson and R. G. Carter
1970	W. A. Harrison and G. T. Card
1971	J. W. Higgins and K. A. Williams
1972	A. F. Cartwright and P. Colgan
1973	A. L. Buonvino and A. L. Brock
1974	E. W. Murphy and A. E. Scott
1975	J. W. Hayman and R. G. Frost
1976	R. A. Lea and C. Hutchings
1977	A. M. Allen and A. L. Brock
1978	A. G. R. Smith and S. Howell
1979	L. V. Patterson and B. J. Grinsell
1980	C. Brook and R. A. Northam
1981	A. Wall and D. Whitehouse
1982	W. E. Griggs and G. Hitchman
1983	D. Devitt and F. N. Merricks
1984	A. F. Cartwright and J. C. Colgan
1985	P. Cruise and G. R. Lea
1986	D. Freeman and P. B. Jackson
1987	A. F. Cartwright and R. P. Barratt
1988	B. W. Longstaff and F. W. Busby
1989	M. O'Donnell and M. S. Leeksma
1990	P. Cruise and A. G. R. Smith
1991	L. R. Cooke and A. C. Saul
1992	W. Fordyce and S. R. Fordyce
1993	K. Taverner and S. R. Rendall
1994	M. Plows and P. Taylor
1995	R. Sanders and N. V. Webster
1996	R. Cartwright and L. Lawrence
1997	C. J. Whitehouse and T. Whitehouse

STABLEFORD FOURSOMES CUP

18 hole 'Foursomes' stroke play competition – handicap limit 28 to be played off 7/16 of combined handicaps.
Played in July – no start sheet

YEAR	*WINNERS*
1962	S. K. Aves and C. Hartland
1963	H. Moulstone and R. Hitchman
1964	G. Bull and C. R. Randle
1965	K. Scott and A. A. Trippas
1966	R. T. Hatton and G. W. Lamb
1967	A. F. Cartwright and P. Colgan
1968	W. P. Mason and N. E. Taylor
1969	M. C. Vaughan and F. S. Rennie
1970	M. C. Vaughan and F. S. Rennie
1971	G. R. Loveless and D. Cadtmell
1972	A. F. Cartwright and P. Colgan
1973	A. R. West and G. Hitchman
1974	T. B. Curry and A. Brown
1975	L. V. Patterson and A. G. Reading
1976	C. A. Lawson and J. Settle
1977	A. L. Brock and J. Foley
1978	J. J. Evans and F. Hughes
1979	D. A. Jones and G. Lowery
1980	C. Breslin and B. R. Morton
1981	R. A. Lea and G. T. Lea
1982	R. Pickman and E. M. Wyatt
1983	D. Brayley and V. Johnson
1984	F. Hughes and S. Buxton
1985	R. D. Hopkins and C. J. Hyde
1986	C. Hutchins and D. Stanley
1987	F. E. Pittaway and K. G. Wheeler
1988	B. James and C. Hutchins
1989	J. C. Evans and R. W. Somerville
1990	R. H. Beckett and B. J. Grinsell
1991	E. Rai and R. G. Bacciochi
1992	E. W. Worwood and D. M. Jones
1993	K. Moore and K. R. Longstaffe
1994	T. Sutcliffe and K. Lane
1995	R. A. Smith and D. F. Walker
1996	P. J. O'Neill and K. O'Rourke
1997	S. R. Davies and P. Cruise

MAXSTOKE PLATE

Four ball better ball stroke play competition over 18 holes. Handicap limit 28 to play off 7/8 of handicap.

Usually played in May, select own partners – no start sheet

YEAR	*WINNERS*
1987	G. J. Crofts and B. Cooke
1988	C. E. Bailey and N. E. Taylor
1989	E. J. Rose and W. Ingleston
1990	G. Smallwood and F. Castallucci
1991	W. Winters and R. J. Barritt
1992	E. Worwood and D. M. Jones
1993	F. J. Griffiths and R. Davies
1994	R. K. Davies and B. Davies
1995	A. D. Gascoigne and J. A. G. Harrison
1996	A. D. Gascoigne and J. A. G. Harrison
1997	N. O'Donnell and R. Morris

GREENKEEPER'S CUP

18 hole 'Foursomes' stroke play competition, Handicap limit 28 to be played off 7/16 off combined handicaps.

No start sheet

YEAR	*WINNERS*
1994	S. C. Nagle and J. J. Hannon
1995	J. N. Reading and S. R. Davies
1996	N. S. Cowles and P. Butler
1887	S. Turley and N. Thomas